THE NOVELS OF ARUN JOSHI

A CRITICAL STUDY

THE NOVELS OF ARUN JOSHI

A CRITICAL STUDY

SHANKAR KUMAR

ATLANTIC
PUBLISHERS & DISTRIBUTORS

Published by
ATLANTIC PUBLISHERS AND DISTRIBUTORS
B-2, Vishal Enclave, Opp. Rajouri Garden, New Delhi-27
Phones : 5413460, 5429987, 5466842

Sales Office
4215/1, Ansari Road, Darya Ganj, New Delhi-110 002
Phones : 3273880, 3285873, 3280451
Fax : 91-11-3285873
web : www.atlanticbooks.com
e-mail : info@atlanticbooks.com

ISBN 81-269-0208-6

Typeset at
APD Computer Graphics, Delhi

Printed in India at
Nice Printing Press, Delhi

Foreword

Several years ago a young, smart boy came to me for a discussion on Arun Joshi's novels, and the way he conducted himself and placed his arguments before me, left me absolutely in no doubt that here was a research scholar who had read the whole of this author and who, in his own way, was committed to the self-evolved task of expanding his tentatively formed ideas into a full-length doctoral thesis. I gave him all possible encouragement as also my good wishes for his literary venture. I am happy to see that his work on Joshi, done so very meticulously and with patient toil under the able guidance of his supervisor, Dr. Amarnath Jha, Head of the Department of English, L.N. Mithila University, Darbhanga, Bihar, was not only accepted for the award to him of the Ph.D. Degree of this university, but is now also available to us in print for our careful perusal and necessary consideration.

Arun Joshi occupies a distinctive place in the post-colonial history of the Indo-English novel, and it is quite understandable that in respect of theme or spirit his novels are basically different from those of Mulk Raj Anand, R.K. Narayan, Bhabani Bhattacharya, or Khushwant Singh. He was not a prolific writer, and his novels, whether *The Foreigner* (1968), *The Strange Case of Billy Biswas* (1971), *The Apprentice* (1974), or *The Last Labyrinth* (1981), deal more, if not chiefly, with man's inner problems than with his outer problems, problems ostensibly social or political in nature. As a novelist, who is also a profound thinker, his concerns are different. He writes about the dilution or destruction of man's native innocence by experience, about his rootlessness, restlessness and existential dilemma, about the crisis of his identity in the present-day world. The rejection of traditional values by the modern ethos in India has created a climate of crisis in which man finds himself utterly bewildered and lost, without hardly any straw of hope or psychological succour to catch it. It is this very situation of anguish and agony that lies at the centre of Joshi's novels. In spite of physical comfort and material prosperity the sensitive minds of India and of the world are terribly at a loss to arrive at and understand the meaning of human existence. It is this meaninglessness of life, this futility of perceptible human endeavour that prompts Arun Joshi to wonder if the gospel of detachment, as enshrined in *The Gita,* could at all be able to bring about man's salvation in the contemporary world. Joshi's last novel, *The City and the River* (1990) considers a new theme, the theme of political oppression and is palpably an attack on the Emergency that Indira Gandhi clamped on India in the mid-seventies. Nevertheless, this novel too is a mixture of phantasy and allegory, of dream and fact, and works itself out as a parable of human life in its search for man's freedom of choice.

Arun Joshi's novels do also have, technically speaking, an experimental value of their own, for he keeps on patterning them on new and still newer models. In respect of both theme and technique these novels leave a lasting impression indeed.

Dr. Shankar Kumar's book on Arun Joshi considers all these thematic and formalistic aspects of Arun Joshi's novels with a kind of thoroughness and depth that is highly commendable. I have reasons to believe that it will receive the acclaim it so highly deserves.

DR. MOHAN JHA
Ex-Professor of English,
B.R.A. University, Muzaffarpur,
Bihar

Preface

The present book entitled *The Novels of Arun Joshi: A Critical Study* is a very modest attempt to analyse, explore and evaluate his novels, with a specific viewpoint to identify the nature of the characters present in them. Joshi has fascination for dealing with the theme of the crisis of identity affecting the lives of the fictional characters who are involved in the plots of the different works of fiction.

Arun Joshi is by now an established novelist of about twenty-five years standing. He has to his credit five works of longer fiction: *The Foreigner*, came out in 1968, though it had been written much earlier when he was a student at M.I.T., Boston, in the U.S.A. There are in it evidences of transformations of his American experiences at the M.I.T.. Coming back to India he took up an assignment with the D.C.M., and like the hero of his first novel, married the daughter of one of the proprietors of the corporate body. He could, however, find time in his busy corporate schedule to write novels which came out in trickles at regular intervals. *The Strange Case of Billy Biswas* (1971) was followed by *The Apprentice* (1976), *The Survivor*, a book of his short stories in 1975, *The Last Labyrinth* (1981), the Sahitya Akademi award winner for 1982, and finally *The City and the River* in 1990, which is unlike his previous novels, though not completely distanced from them in tone and temperament. Besides his fictional works, Arun Joshi has also written a kind of domestic tribute in *A Biography of Late Lala Sri Ram: A Study in Entrepreneurship in Industrial Management.*

Even during Arun Joshi's lifetime Indian critics and scholars commented upon Arun Joshi's novels in different periodicals and articles in books. The historians of English Literature, such as K.R. Srinivas Ayengar and M.K. Naik, among others, make passing references to the fictional works of Arun Joshi. Among books and journals printing articles on his different novels and short stories, mention may be made of R.K. Dhawan who has issued two books edited by him in which we find in-depth studies of Joshi's novels. The first one of his books *The Fictional World of Arun Joshi* came out in 1986. Besides a very short contribution by Joshi himself, it has a comprehensive introduction followed by investigations of "themes and techniques, insights and perspectives" in the novels, except *The City and the River*, which was not then published, and the short stories. The second book edited by him entitled *The Novels of Arun Joshi* came out in 1992 and deals with all the novels and short stories on the lines of the previous book. *Scholar Critic*, a journal published from Madurai, came out with a special number on the author: *Arun Joshi—A Study of His Fiction* edited by N. Radhakrishnan in 1994. Besides these books and journals, many articles on Arun Joshi have also appeared in other periodicals and as chapters in some of the books on Indian English fiction such as those by Ramesh K. Srivastava in *Six Indian Novelists in English* (Amritsar, 1987) and Dr. O.P. Mathur in *Modern Indian English Fiction* (New Delhi, 1993). Many other scholars as well have included chapters on Arun Joshi in the forms of collection of articles such as in *Five Indian Novelists* by V.V.N. Rajendra Prasad (New Delhi, 1990).

While there is no dearth of articles and periodicals and chapters on Arun Joshi in different books, not many scholars have perhaps published yet their individual works on Arun Joshi. Mention in this respect may be made of Dr. Hari Mohan Prasad's book, *Arun Joshi*, published in the Arnold-Heinemann Indian writers Series in 1985.

None of the above books on Arun Joshi or chapters in books or articles in journals and periodicals make any specific reference in detail to the problem discussed in the present book. Of the Indian scholars, perhaps Dr. O.P. Mathur and Prof. R.S. Pathak in several of their essays dwell upon this aspect. Their viewpoints have given the author fresh sights and insights to study Arun Joshi's fictions in the light of the specific aspect.

Most of the scholars in their articles or chapters on Arun Joshi in their books or articles in periodicals refer to the existential problems such as those of absurdity, alienation, meaninglessness, quest for survival and affirmation; but though their treatment of the subject may be multi-faceted, they do not deal in-depth with the problem of crisis of identity faced by the protagonists of Arun Joshi's novels.

I do not claim much originality in the modest academic pursuit that I have undertaken, but it would be no vanity on my part to posit that to the best of my knowledge and belief I have tried to bring out something sustained and composite on one major aspect of Arun Joshi, though this has been foregrounded in the background of the other facts of Arun Joshi's fictional world.

Chapter 1 is devoted to the study of "Crisis of Identity in Indian English Fiction and Arun Joshi." *Chapter 2* has been devoted to tracing the literary, philosophical and linguistic influences on the author. *Chapter 3* studies chronologically the first and the fourth novels together as they deal with the business world and the world of personal relationships together. *Chapter 4, 5 & 6* deal respectively with the problem under study in *The Strange Case of Billy Biswas, The Apprentice* and *The City and the River. Chapter 7* is devoted to the study of Joshi's fictional technique followed by Summing-up in *Chapter 8*. Bibliography lists the books and journals which I consulted while writing this book. Most of these have also been referred to, and quoted from, in the body of the book.

In the different phases of the writing of this book I have received co-operation and encouragement from several of my teachers and others associated with me. I express my sense of irredeemable debts which I owe to my *guru* Dr. Amarnath Jha under whose guidance I have written it. I am deeply indebted to my parents for their keen appreciation and constant encouragement which I have received from them in the course of my scholastic pursuit—a debt which is too deep and personal for formal acknowledgment. It is a matter of profound regret to me that my maternal grandfather, Late Dr. Sudhakar Jha 'Shastri,' Professor of Sanskrit and Maithili, Patna University, Patna, is no longer in the land of the living to see the result of my humble academic pursuit. Major portion of the book was written during my stay at Delhi, where I consulted the prestigious libraries such as those of the Sahitya Akademi, the University of Delhi and Jawaharlal Nehru University. I offer my thanks and indebtedness to the staff of the libraries concerned. I also express my deep sense of gratitude to Prof. Mohan Jha who has been the eternal source of information, knowledge and wisdom to me in course of my lucubration and scholastic pursuit. On my personal request he spontaneously consented to write a foreword to my book for which I have no words to acknowledge my profound indebtedness to him. I am sincerely grateful to Professor R.K. Dhawan, Bhagat Singh College, New Delhi who enlightened me with his comprehensive knowledge and expertise on Arun Joshi. Last, but not the least, is my deep sense of gratitude to Dr. K.R. Gupta, Managing Director, Atlantic Publishers and Distributors, who kindly consented to publish my book.

SHANKAR KUMAR

CONTENTS

Foreword *v*

Preface *vii*

PART-I
Introduction

1. Crisis of Identity in Indian English Fiction and Arun Joshi 1
2. Influences upon Arun Joshi: Literary, Philosophical and Linguistic 30

PART-II
Exposition

3. The World of Business and Personal Relationships in *The Foreigner* and *The Last Labyrinth* 60
4. The Primitive World *versus* the Civilized World in *The Strange Case of Billy Biswas* 95
5. The Innocence and Experience of the "Homespun" World of *The Apprentice* 113
6. People at Strife in *The City and the River* 132

PART-III
Conclusion

7. Fictional Technique of Arun Joshi 169
8. Summing-up 189

Bibliography 217

PART-I
Introduction

1

Crisis of Identity in Indian English Fiction and Arun Joshi

I

English literature in India is a product of the colonial rule over us. And even though this is a thing of the past, its hangover persists in the Indo-English literature which cannot ignore the native models. With the achievement of our national Independence we may be politically free but there is still an invasion of cultural colonisation from the West. Most of our Indo-English authors have been globe-trotters or educated in the West. They have not been able to shake themselves off either from their Oriental roots or from the Occidental influences. Their fictional creations as well grow out of their personalities and schism arising out of their predicaments in which the East and the West do not seem to meet.

It is with reference to this duality that K.R. Srinivas Iyengar has called the Indo-English writer "a confused wanderer between the two worlds."[1] The two worlds are those of India and Europe. The Indo-English novelists find it difficult to get out of Western influences. It is in this sense that in their effort to give an expression for individuality that "the Indian writers in English lose their sense of identity—both personal and national—and feel alienated in their own home making frantic efforts to seek, organise and affirm that identity."[2] In many cases, not only the novelists but also the characters in their novels face what psychologists call identity crisis.

Delivering his speech at the Australian Conference on National Identity in August 1968, Rodney Hall affirmed that "national identity is inescapable to anyone using his national tongue."[3] An affirmation of national identity takes the form of national glorification, an awareness of the historical sense. The loss of this also leads to the crisis of identity.

The problem of individual identity has a complexity in its different manifestations. Psychologists and philosophers have all discussed the predicament of modern life and man and found in both traits of deep-rooted anxiety, alienation and absurdity. Our international connections have rendered us rootless. One of the forms of rootlessness is self-alienation which in its turn is related to the loss of identity and its quest to get out of its crisis.

This theme has become commonplace not only in modern European fiction but also in Indo-English literature. Meenakshi Mukherjee has pointed out that alienation is "a very common theme in Indo-English novel."[4] R.S. Pathak has again written in this context:

> Indo-English novelist's reiterative treatment of alienation, his persistent delineation of rootless characters and awareness of his predicament seem to be symptomatic of his own uprootedness.[5]

The crisis of character, identity or consciousness or authenticity has grown out of man's looking before and after and pining for what he is not. It has become a very grave sociological problem which has resulted out of the international phenomenon of the shrinking of the world. The problem of the East-West encounter and North-South discrepancies has created a generation which has been influenced by cosmopolitan and international attitudes and connections. Countries of the world might geographically be islands but they are influenced by the mainland. In this, they are not isolated. As against this, men inhabiting these have become islands in the sense that some kind of inner crisis has made them alienated from themselves, their homes and surroundings and the community. R.S. Pathak catalogues a few of the modern man's fixations and obsessions growing out of some kind of alienation:

> Alienation is one of the greatest problems confronting modern man. Its corrosive impact can be seen in the form of generation gap, the anti-war movement, the hippie phenomenon, the credibility gap, the compartmentalization of our lives, the stunting of personal development, the conspicuous absence of a sense of meaningfulness of life, and so on.[6]

All these factors taken together have made this age not only the age of anxiety but also what Murchland calls "The Age of Alienation."[7]

Ever since India came in contact with the West, there has been a cross-fertilization of her life and literature. The impact of the West on Indian culture has penetrated deep into the Indian ethos. We have been influenced by our erstwhile rulers in the past and now by the cultural colonization of the nations that domineer over us. In this kind of situation, the cauldron of Indian civilization has amalgamated the outside influences to some extent but the dross settling in the bottom and the froth bubbling above have also caused upheavals in the Indian psyche. These amalgamated materials fail to make us identify ourselves either with one or with the other. Modern man poses to be cosmopolitan in nature; but he is neither purely cosmopolitan nor aware of his roots.

The alienated heroes of Indo-English fiction seem to live in a kind of an absurd world. This kind of absurdity has been defined by Ionesco as follows:

> Absurd is that which is devoid of purpose.... Cut off from his religious, metaphysical and transcendental roots man

> is lost; all his actions become senseless, absurd and useless.[8]

The hybridization of races and cultures is a feature not only of the East but also of the West. The history of India after the mediaeval ages is an example of it. The foreign invaders coming to India before the Middle Ages got "Indianized"[9] and did not ever endeavour to maintain their separate identity. But with the advent of Islam in the country, different communities became all the more conscious of their own identity and out of this clash results tension leading to crisis. A few of the Indian English novelists writing at the time of Partition have taken up this topic, but not so Bhabani Bhattacharya, who deliberately avoided referring to it, though *So Many Hungers* deals with situations in Bengal during the Quit-India Movement.

English language came to India in the early years of the seventeenth century, and though the language was popularised first by the Christian missionaries and later by the government agencies, the nineteenth century Indian renaissance witnessed few creative works especially in prose. It is because it took sometime for English to strike roots to become mature enough to produce literature in it. William Walsh writes the following in this respect:

> If literature is the most powerful, subtle and inclusive use of the language, then it is only when the language has been organically nourished that the life of art may be distilled from it. Shakespeare, as the philosopher Samuel Alexander averred, did not invent Hamlet but discovered him in the English language. In a more contracted and minor way, one can say that the English novel in India which began in the 1930s required, as well as the novelists, an idiom for its expression. All the more so must this be the case, when the medium is a second language which has to be learned from books and teachers rather than taken in with one's mother's milk.[10]

II

This book does not deal with the appropriateness of the use of the English language for our creative works. It is an art which gives us an illusion of reality even in a changed medium. Indians may not think in English, but the creative works written in it portray artistically the conditions of our mind. Like so many other foreign factors of our civilization, getting amalgamated with the Indian culture, English too has been "Indianized" and it is in this medium that the Indian-English writers write their works of fiction. The older generation of Indo-English novelists deals with the external climate, and not the climate of the mind. The Indian English fiction hovered round the theme of our national movement especially under the Gandhian impact. *Murugan the Tiller* (1927) and *Kandan, the Patriot: A Novel of New India in the Making* (1932) by K.S. Venkataramani (1891-1951) are novels on the Gandhian theme. Krishnaswamy Nagarajan also attempted two novels on the same theme in his *Athavar House* (1937) and *Chronicles of Kedaram* (1961). The Big Three of the Indo-English novelists, such as Mulk Raj Anand, R.K. Narayan and Raja Rao, were also influenced to write novels on the Gandhian theme. Mulk Raj Anand in *Untouchable* (1935), R.K. Narayan in *Waiting for the Mahatma* (1955) and *The Vendor of Sweets* (1967) and Raja Rao in *Kanthapura* (1938) deal with one or the other of the Gandhian themes. The three have respectively been called "the novelist as reformer... the novelist as moral analyst... (and) the novelist as metaphysical poet."[11] Bhabani Bhattacharya, again a novelist of the older generation, writes in the manner of Mulk Raj Anand. He shows some inclination for delineating the internal tensions, but by and large they are not much concerned with the individual crisis beyond the national and ideological one in their novels touching upon the theme of politics and nationalism.

It would, however, be far from the truth to state that the novelists of the pre-Independence India did not deal with the problem of the individual crisis of identity of character or consciousness. The theme of rootlessness is the chief problem in *There Lay the City* (1942) by D.F. Karaka. The same theme has been repeated in *Zohra* (1951) by Zeenat Futehally. Hamid, the heroine's husband's younger brother, is also Zohra's lover. He has been depicted as an outsider, a melancholy and a lonely man. As he himself assesses his character, he is "all out of tune, a kind of broken symphony."[12] He is not much different from Arun Joshi' s Sindi in *The Foreigner*. The theme of the loneliness of man as a factor in bringing out the crisis of character has been emphasized in some of the novels by R.K. Narayan. The crisis of character gives birth to the generation gap which has been treated in Narayan's *Swami and Friends*. Swaminathan's father is alienated both from his son's idealized world-view and his mother's myth. The central character in *Mr. Sampath* (1949) shuns his vanishing creation. Margayya's son in *The Financial Expert* (1952) is incommunicative and inarticulate and more so he develops into something of an upstart towards the close of the novel. In *The Bachelor of Arts* (1937) Chandran finds his friends "at grips with life, like a buffalo caught in the coils of a python."[13] Krishnan, a young college lecturer, the English teacher, finds a chasm between his aspirations and circumstances. The same theme is explicit in the author's *The Vendor of Sweets* (1967). The son, Mali, gets alienated from his father and Malgudi because people do not accept him in the society after his return from America with his foreign wife. Jagan's unhappy experiences are typical of Narayan's alienated characters. S. Nagarajan has rightly written that all his novels "in varying degrees convey this sense of unhappy frustration."[14] H.L. Williams has pointed out the presence of several aspects of alienation in R.K. Narayan:

> The young quarrel with the old, leave Malgudi for England or America, eat beef and marry foreigners, sometimes they return to vex and haunt and cruelly or comically disturb the still pools of Malgudi.[15]

Manohar Malgaonkar in several of his novels has taken up the theme of alienation and the crisis of identity. He has taken up this problem in his novels such as *Combat of Shadows, A Bend in the Ganges, Distant Drum* and *The Princes.* Ruby Miranda in *Combat of Shadows* is a study in rootlessness. She is a Eurasian young woman who sought to upclimb and become a member of the white English community. But she finds herself a stranger to both. Her English lover, Henry Winton, also suffers from loneliness. Gyan Talwar in *A Bend in the Ganges* represents those Anglicised Indians who have lost touch with Indian life and who fail to distinguish between the courage and cowardice, integrity and servility, truth and falsehood. Kiran Garud in *Distant Drum* is always cut off from the mainstream of life. The Maharaja in *The Princes* is cut off from Gandhianites to be closer to the British. V.S. Naipaul takes a particular notice of the Indian withdrawal and denial in this novel which, according to him, is "a part of the confusion of Indian Anglo-India."[16]

Kamala Markandeya probes the problem of identity systematically in her novels. She is concerned with the predicaments of identity faced by modern man. Dandekar in *A Silence of Desire* understands the precariousness of his position when he follows Sarojini to Swamy's house:

> His sense of identity began to slip; he knew who he was—I am Dandekar, he said to himself, but the words had no reality. The knowledge of time had gone.[17]

This experience is followed by his hectic search for identity which, however, is thwarted by his westernization. Sarojini tells him:

> ...you with your western notions, your superior talk of ignorance and superstition... you don't know what lies beyond reason and you prefer not to find out. To you Tulasi is a plant that grows in earth like the rest—an ordinary common plant.[18]

In her novel *Possession* she presents an account of de-Indianization and the resulting loss of identity. The protagonist of the novel Val is both culturally and psychologically conditioned by the West and also possessed by it. An English woman, Lady Caroline Bell, taking over him is symbolic of his condition. The hero is bought over for five hundred rupees from his parents. He is taken over to Madras where his English Lady Byer protects him at the cost of social recognition. After her exile to Switzerland she settles back in England where "she moulds him into a man, an artist and a lover after the image she has in mind, and in the process ruins him, depleting him of independence and spiritual strength and thus incapacitating him for a search for or an awareness of his identity."[19]

The protagonist's dilemma in *A Handful of Rice* is at the sociological level. The town in which it has been enacted has dark and desolate life. It is moreover "a jungle... a man-made jungle, full of snares and traps and unkept promises."[20] Ravi records all his sufferings, disillusionments and tragic experiences that are part of the predicament of identity. He has a terror of losing his identity in an indifferent city which he considers akin to death. He thinks of reverting to the role of an outsider who has opted to come out and declaring a war on the forces that grudged him a living. Her novel *The Nowhere Man* has a very significant title. It deals with the plight of lonely man in an alien land. It explores the crisis of alienation and a loss of identity of Srinivas, who is a figure of loneliness. Even after fifty years of stay in England he feels like a "nowhere man, looking for a nowhere country."[21] His eldest son Lakshman is even more alienated from his home; as against them Srinivas's wife, Vasanta, has no such crisis because she remains an Indian all along in every thing. On her death, her husband, Srinivas, sprinkles the Ganges water over her ashes and wishes that "he could have found some way to avoid consigning them to those alien waters."[22] Jasbir Jain suggests that "Srinivas's relations with the people around him are suspect and that his leprosy is indicative of his emotional isolation."[23] The end of the novel is a sorry one as the lifelong battle of an individual in pursuit of identity has a sad end.

In several of her novels Kamala Markandeya has taken up this problem and her novels

> ...contain a wide-ranging awareness of diverse factors responsible for the loss of identity and forces working for its quest and regaining. The sense of identity in them, however, is less predominant in the sociological sense than in the philosophical sense. These novels have aimed at working out carefully those philosophical issues which originate from the protagonist's search for identity. The nature and value of the sense of identity has been defined in them mainly in terms of traditional Indian values and norms. The persistent treatment of the loss of identity and struggle to regain it in her novels and others is a proof of the two English novelists' realization of the significance of a sense of identity, although it is a different matter whether he has been able to affirm it in a forceful and precise way.[24]

Balachandra Rajan, the academician, has also explored the predicament of the alienated heroes in his novels. As an academician he has, so to speak, been too long in the West. He has been charged with being incapable of expressing his inwardness and that his mixed sensibility has made him rootless. But these charges, according to him, "do not deserve serious thinking."[25] His fictional creations also are representatives of mixed sensibility. Krishnan in *The Dark Dancer* is alienated from his social surroundings. On his return from Cambridge after two years to India, he thought himself back to an indifferent sky. He did not seem to belong to the land. Looking at the village temple he felt

> ...no tide of emotion at returning. He had been born in its shadow, but he could have been born anywhere else, anywhere in that parched infinity where the roads narrowed and the gutters wormed among the congested houses, or wherever the scream filtered through the laboring rice fields, and the thatch was pierced by the anger of the first cry.
>
> He was coming back, but not to an identity, a sense of being rooted, nor even to an enmity like that of sun and

> earth, a struggle against circumstance, a creative confronting, which would open his mind to its depths of repossession.[26]

Krishnan is torn within owing to the warring elements in his personality because of his relations with Kamala and Cynthia. He thinks to revive the feeling of identity for the country and becomes aware of the differences of roots between Cynthia and himself. He thinks:

> England... was her background, just as India was his, and the mingling of backgrounds, creative though it might be, also involved an inevitable friction of dissent.[27]

Rajan's another novel *Too Long in the West* is a story of Nalini who studied at Columbia University for three years. Ever since her childhood her native village, Mudalpur, seemed oppressive and lonely to her. Her too long stay in the West worsens her impression and even her mother feels, as she has been "too long in the West, she'll never fit in."[28] One of Nalini's lovers points out to her:

> You won't fit in. You've joined the lost generation. Out of place everywhere and acceptable nowhere. You'll always be an exile and an alien, a self-created foreigner, a refugee from yourself. You can't belong. You'll live in two worlds and fall between two stools.[29]

These lines may remind one of the theme of Arun Joshi's *The Foreigner* (1968) which might have been influenced by B. Rajan's *Too Long in the West* (1961). The dominant impression of *Too Long in the West* is that of pervasive loneliness that tells upon the relations and happiness of various characters and adversely affects their identity.

Like Balachandra Rajan, Chaman Nahal is also an academic don who has written several novels such as *My True Faces* (1973), *Azadi* (1975), *Into Another Dawn* (1977), *English Queens* (1979) and *The Crown and the Loin cloth* (1981). As Professor O.P. Mathur says:

> The background may be domestic, inter-cultural or the movement of history, but they are all irradiated with emotional, spiritual luminosity of man, the potentiality of his being. His novels are celebrations of life and those of its qualities which give it meaning and its significance.[30]

Azadi in particular is much more than a "chronicle novel."[31] The character of Arun in it is a study in identity. He is determined to emerge a different figure in the changed context in which he has found "a new identity for himself."[32] One of the themes of the novel is the refugee problem. Lala Kanshi Ram, who has to leave Sialkot and live in an improvised settlement in Delhi, is faced with the problem of his "loss of identity,"[33] of "personality,"[34] of the loss of his "ability to communicate with his family."[35] Dr. Mohan Jha sums up:

> The greatest problem with Lala Kanshi Ram, even after his improvised settlement in Delhi, is his loss of "identity," of "personality," of the loss of his "ability to communicate with his family" and much though he feels like standing before a "tunnel" of which he could see no end, he wants a name for himself, and, thus cease to be either a stranger to himself or a "curiosity" to others. Judged from this standpoint, *Azadi* may be interpreted as a plea for realization and assertion of identity in a world that is cruel enough to push people into the oblivion of anonymity.[36]

The much talked of and controversial author Salman Rushdie has very sincere concern for the problem of roots and identity. There is much in his novels that is fantastic. Dilip Fernandes notices "the angst, loneliness and rootlessness"[37] of Rushdie. The novelist is concerned with his rootlessness. Rushdie has stated:

> And one such suspicious generalization may be that writers in my position, exiles or emigrants or expatriates, are haunted by some sense of loss, some urge to reclaim, to look back, even at the risk of being mutated into pillars

> of salt. But if we do look back, we must also do so in the knowledge—which gives rise to profound uncertainties—that our physical alienation from India almost inevitably means that we will not be capable of reclaiming precisely the thing that was lost; that we will, in short, create fictions, not actual cities or villages, but invisible ones, imaginary homeless, Indians of the mind.[38]

To Professor O.P. Mathur, Salman Rushdie's "sensibility is basically Indian."[39] Rushdie's statement affirms it: "...and to back to the root's idea I should say that I haven't managed to shake myself free off it completely."[40]

Most of the above novelists belong to the older generation. They are concerned with the problems of identity and alienation. But their involvement with the problem is more at the outer level than with the inner. As against them, the novelists of the younger generation such as Nayantara Sahgal, Anita Desai, Ruth Prawer Jhabwala are novelists concerned with the inner identity. Arun Joshi too belongs to this group. Kamala Markandeya who has been dealt with above is "an insider-outsider"[41] as against Jhabwala who is "an outsider-insider."[42] The alienated person is a stock figure in Nayantara Sahgal's novels. She deals with problems caused by a change in order which views everything in doubt. Her first novel *A Time to be Happy* is about the predicament of Sanad Shiv Pal whose problems are those of a West-educated boy coming home to India where he is torn between two sets of values. His main concern is how to regain his roots. The sense of his rootlessness results in self-pity. However, in the end he comes to realize the importance of healthy tradition. In another novel *This Time of Morning* Rashmi comes back to her parents after divorcing her husband, an I.F.S. officer. She is completely alienated and utterly distraught. Her other love affair does not alleviate her isolation. She craves for modernity and freedom. Replying to Neil's remark that she is "very conscious of past,"[43] the heroine says, "it is my identity."[44] In *The Storm in Chandigarh* and *The Day of Shadow*, the theme has been explored further. Vishal Dubey in *The Storm in Chandigarh* is aware of the discrepancy of communication between man and man. This has made society a kind of cave in which people live in total ignorance about what is happening to each other. Som in *The Day of Shadow* suffers from a mania of affluence. His views are elitist and he has no humanistic approach to life's problems. But such an attitude leads him to suffer and he gets eternally forlorn.

Ruth Prawer Jhabwala portrays various types of the determinants of, and threats to, identity. Her novels portray various types of seekers after the realization of the self. Her characters, as R.S. Pathak says:

> are in a perpetual quest for identity and have to face a series of crises in the process. Although her novels are littered with external manifestation of alienation, she is at her best while she portrays conflicts of individual and domestic friction. Her well-known story called "The Aliens" is a representative of her approach.[45]

In her novels she deals with urban middle class undivided Hindu families and ironic studies of the East-West encounter. In some of her novels the two themes coalesce.

Anita Desai is concerned with the life of young men and women in Indian cities. In *Cry, the Peacock* Maya's alienated psyche has been explored. Her sensibility has been rendered in terms of immeasurable human loneliness. It originates with the husband-wife alienation and culminates in a kind of schizophrenia. In *Bye Bye Blackbird* Anita Desai deals with the disturbing aspect of the loss of identity. It captures the confusion and conflicts of Dev. He is confronted with the initial problem of adjustment at the London School of Economics. His alienation and spiritual agony are objectified in his hellish experiences in the London tube. He is confronted with the problem of adjustment. The novelist writes:

> One of the eternal immigrants who can never accept their new home and continue to walk the streets like strangers

> in enemy territory, frozen, listless, but dutifully trying to be very unobtrusive and, however superficially, to belong.[46]

The blackbirds are the Indian coloured immigrants living in England facing hard times there. Desai focuses her attention on the disturbing aspect of loss of identity in marrying a wog, Sarah, who "had become nameless, she had shed her name as she had shed her ancestry and identity."[47] *Voices in the City* is a study in the character of a lean and hungry looking journalist, named Nirode, in Calcutta, a city of death. It explores the inner climate of youthful despair and is permitted by an existential angst. Camus, the existentialist writer, is upon his lips. Late Professor V.A. Shahane writes:

> The Indo-English novel, it seems to me, has become a primary instrument of art, to unfold the "self's emergence" as a historical entity and demonstrate art's dual connection with self and society. First, the self must define and unfold its existence in the form of fiction, and then relate its multiple relationship with the autonomy of art and fragmentation of social order especially after the Second World War and India's Independence.[48]

In the above extract late Shahane hints at the gist of the problem of identity. The Indo-English novelists are concerned not only with their milieu but also with their self-consciousness. This quest for identity has taken various forms. He has to take into consideration not only the problem of his national identity but also that of his individual identity. The following statement by C.D. Narasimhaiah makes the point clear:

> The individual artist has to "discover" as well as "create" his own identity. He does not find it readymade. Of course, in the process he discovers and creates his national identity too. Indeed... the two are connected and not mutually exclusive.[49]

The Indo-English novelists discussed so far deal with certain stock figures representing the need for national and individual identity arising out of the East-West encounter. Ignoring this aspect of the problem makes such figures rootless and alienated. The impact of the colonial expansion in the past and that of the cultural colonisation have fascinated many of the Indo-English novelists to write enthusiastically about the West, ignoring their ancient cultural heritage. This is a mistaken notion of internationalism. A writer and his fictional characters have to be aware of both the past and the present. The consciousness of both the past and the present is an important aspect of both national and individual identity.

As the Indo-English novelists follow the medium of a language brought to us by our alien rulers, it is bound to be influenced by the native variety of the language especially British and American. But in this respect too, the Indo-English novelists have tried to carve their own national identity. The English used by them has sentence structures based upon the native varieties but the idea, except in few of the authors and works, is Indian in spirit and imagery. There are frequent examples of not only code-mixing but also code-switching. All these emphasize the aspect of linguistic identity.

The Indo-English novelists are also concerned with the crisis of identity related to their race, culture, self and even sex which has given a trend towards feminism in literature.

With this background to the problem of identity in general and awareness of this problem in a few of the important works of the major Indo-English novelists, let us now move on to a brief survey of Arun Joshi's fictional works and his handling of the problems under discussion.

III

Arun Joshi (1939-93) has been classed with Indian-English novelists such as Nayantara Sahgal and Anita Desai, novelists of the post-Independence India. Arun Joshi has been concerned more with the dilemma of the human loneliness which has various manifestations in the forms of powerlessness, meaninglessness, formlessness, cultural estrangement, social isolation and self-estrangement. These aspects of alienation have been referred to in the article on Alienation in *Encyclopaedia Britannica* (1977). Susheel Kumar Sharma has drawn our attention to these variants of alienation with reference to *The Strange Case of Billy Biswas* in his article included in *The Novels of Arun Joshi*, edited by R.K. Dhawan (New Delhi, 1992). S.K. Sharma after Elizabeth B. Hurlock identifies three syndromes of alienation such as "recessive," "socially disinterested" and "socially ineffective."[50] He also quotes from Elizabeth B. Hurlock's book *Personality Development* in which she writes:

> In general, the alienation is marked by such unsocial behaviour as teasing and bullying, making unpleasant comments, being hypercritical, intentionally annoying people, lying and being sneaky, rising alibis and projecting blame on others, and being sullen, sulky and moody. People characterized by the socially ineffective syndrome are annoying to others, while those characterized by the recessive and socially disinterested are so distasteful that others have no desire to have anything to do with them.[51]

All these forms of alienation have passed into the psyche of modern man. The modern world is characterized by mechanization, urbanization, growing hostility due to changing values, depersonalization, self-misgivings, delusions, rootlessness, discontent, psychological and other maladjustments. All these taken together have made alienation a part of our life. We live in a world plagued by several forms of crisis in which we are even enmeshed in the crisis of our identity and consciousness.

The different variants of alienation, which are much larger than the crisis of identity, may be grouped into two:

> First with man's alienation from society which is the most prevalent kind of alienation, and, second his alienation from his own self. A non-conformist is alienated from society by rebelling against it, but a conformist is alienated from his own self by not following the voice of his

> conscience. It is this division of self which does not let man live in peace.[52]

Many of the novelists have withdrawn from the outer world to the inner world to explore the problem of human existence and to this Arun Joshi along with certain other novelists of his type is no exception. In an interview, Arun Joshi has confessed that he was prompted into writing to explore "that mysterious underworld which is the human soul."[53] In another statement Arun Joshi has said that he "essentially attempts towards a better understanding of the world and of himself."[54] In the fictional world of Arun Joshi, the questions of the self and its existence are the points to be probed. He delves deep into the dark recesses of the mind which are the inscrutable region of uncertainty and inscrutability. As R.K. Dhawan writes:

> Reading Joshi's novels is not always a smooth experience; there are moments when one is assailed by doubts and questions. There is "something" that attracts one's attention and then grips. Joshi delves into the inner recesses of human psyche where he finds instincts and impulses at work; he seeks a process of the apprehension of reality which may lead him to the world of the core of the truth of man's life. He realizes man's uniqueness and loneliness in an indifferent and inscrutable universe.[55]

Indian English fiction is now several generations old. The second generation novelists, to which Joshi belongs, stand on a different footing from older generation novelists like Raja Rao, R.K. Narayan, Mulk Raj Anand and Bhabani Bhattacharya. Arun Joshi does not propagate any social or political creed unlike Mulk Raj Anand; neither does he create the ironic vision of R.K. Narayan in his sense of place and the social realism and moral issues of Bhabani Bhattacharya. The philosophical concerns of Raja Rao are almost not to Arun Joshi' s likings. Joshi's novels may have philosophical reverberations, but they are not philosophical as such. Joshi is a child of the modern world both in its national and international contexts. His novels have an outer world, no doubt; but this is simply in the form of a background to his love for depicting the inner world which is psychological.

Arun Joshi's output in the realm of fiction is limited to five novels such as *The Foreigner* (1968), *The Strange Case of Billy Biswas* (1971), *The Apprentice* (1974), *The Last Labyrinth* (1981) and *The City and the River* (1990) along with *The Survivor,* a book of collection of his ten short stories published in 1975. Besides the ten short stories two other stories are published in different magazines.[56] There is also a work of biography entitled *Lala Sri Ram: A Study in Entrepreneurship in Industrial Management* (1975) which is more in the nature of domestic eulogy.

The Foreigner is a seminal novel of Arun Joshi. Its themes have been repeated in later novels. It has vast intercontinental area for its geographical expansion. Sindi Oberoi is a Kenyan-Indian, who is a globe-trotter. From his very childhood he is rootless and alienated and as such he suffers from a crisis of his identity. He is never at rest. Nairobi, London and Boston fail to give him any solace. His working in different capacities such as those of a dish-washer and a barman and a library assistant, leads him nowhere. His interest in religion, God and mysticism under the impact of a Catholic priest in Scotland, also gives him no indication as to the crisis of his consciousness. It is in India as Manager of Khemka's factory that there is something of his becoming close to the community of workers. His relationships with various European girls such as Anna and Cathy and the American June Blythe do not stop his worldly hungers. He comes to understand himself in his contact with Sheila, Khemka's daughter. The crisis of identity in the novel surfaces at various levels of plot and characterization. Baburao Khemka, the son of the industrialist, forgets his roots and is charmed by the promiscuity of the American life. But owing to his Indian psyche he makes no compromise with the fact that June Blythe was also in love with his Kenyan Indian friend Sindi Oberoi. The tension generated out of it is the cause of his losing balance in driving, which causes his death. *The Foreigner* has several thematic problems in it. But it is, above all, a study in the crisis of identity arising out of the different manifestations of alienation. The transformation of Sindi as rootless hedonist into an individual committed to social welfare is, according to M.K. Naik, "neither adequately motivated nor prepared for earlier,"[57] and that the ending of the novel "thus appears to be blotched up."[58]

Like the hero of *The Foreigner*, the eponymous hero of *The Strange Case of Billy Biswas*, is a man of cosmopolitan education. From the very beginning there is a schism in his soul. His parents send him to the U.S.A. to study Engineering, but he takes up Anthropology instead. In India he works as a teacher of Anthropology in Delhi University but here too from the subject of study he escapes into the object of it—the tribal world. The questions of his identity always plague him. His story may also be considered to be based upon the archetype of the Gautam Buddha who left his wife and child for the perennial quest. Like him Billy Biswas leaves his wife and even his beloved and marries a tribal girl, Bilasia. In all this "his interest in his own identity was aroused"[59] and he asked "Who was I? Where I had come from? Where I was going?"[60] R.K. Srivastava compares *The Strange Case of Billy Biswas* with John Updike's *Rabbit Run*:

> Like Billy, Harry Angstrom or "Rabbit" seems to be a victim of an all-encompassing alienation, feels terribly unhappy with his life and runs away. He comes back, is temporarily reconciled to his wife, but after the birth of a child, leaves her and runs again. In both cases there are no specific reasons but some kind of emptiness that rises in them from within and then affects their relations with others. Both Billy and Rabbit find the world horrible and decide to flee from it. Both are devoid of ambitions, and do not exploit others for their personal gains. They seem to be lost and terrified children in an unfamiliar crowd.[61]

Billy's interest in the primitive had been there from his very childhood. At Bhubaneswar he visited the tribals with a driver; and the sculptures at the Konark Sun Temple urged him on to think of his own identity. The civilized society was too much for him and his interest in the occult was due to "a great force, *urkraft,* a primitive force" in him.[62] The problem of the crisis of identity has its inkling in the epigraph of the novel, borrowed from line no. 41 of Matthew Arnold's *Thyrsis*: "It irked him to be here, he could not rest." The fate of Billy Biswas has affinity with that of *The Scholar Gipsy,* who, too, had a fascination for the primitive life. Billy may have got an answer to the crisis of his identity, but the civilized world considered him to be a misguided man and on the request of Billy's old parents, the administration in its search for Billy put an end to his life owing to the mistakes of an over-zealous constable.

The Apprentice psychoanalyses the mind of Ratan Rathor, who leaves the course prescribed by his nationalist father, who followed the footsteps of Mahatma Gandhi. The narrative strategy in it is that of dramatic monologue. The resulting narrative episodes read like a hymn to corruption. After his father was shot dead in the freedom struggle, Ratan Rathor seeks employment in the national capital, where after a lot of initial sufferings he is able to get it in the Department of War Supplies. It is a story of Ratan Rathor' s advancement in his service career; and the higher he is promoted, the greater is his moral downfall. Though he gets everything that money can buy, he wants more and more. In his moral downfall he becomes a wretched agent of unscrupulous politicians, officers and contractors and works against national honour, which causes the death of his Brigadier friend after the debacle in the Indo-China war in the North-East frontier region. Ratan does not confess his involvement in the heinous crime, but in the long last his conscience pricks him, and to atone for his guilt he wipes the shoes of the devotees visiting a temple.

The crisis of identity may take two forms. Modern man may abdicate his true self in trying to adjust to others or to society or to the system; or he may strive to keep and develop his individuality and thus alienate himself from society. V. Gopal Reddy states this from Ignace Fuerlicht's *Alienation: From the Past to the Future.*[63] Mr. Reddy finds both these types of alienation in the character of Ratan Rathor:

> Ratan begins his life with high ambitions and ideals to be honest, true to his self and make a mark in the world like his father. But he finds himself a misfit in the modern world. He had to abdicate his true self to fit in the corrupt society and eke out a living. He is thus alienated from his true self in the process.[64]

Ratan in his official career becomes "a sham and a fake"[65] and his work in the office leads him into striking several deals—"that is what the world runs on."[66] An expert manipulator of files, Ratan Rathor becomes in the end a shoeshine apprentice to expiate his sins. Ratan feels a terrible alienation in his soul and he is at a loss to get a meaning out of his life. His realization in the end that he has become a whore, a master-faker, a hypocrite, a scoundrel, thick-skinned, a liar, crooked, an upstart, spineless flunky and bogus, confirms that there is a schism in his soul regarding his acts and achievements. He sometimes feels with the Sheikh that "life is zero"[67] and that he is "abandoned on the planet."[68] The world of *The Apprentice* reveals that the crisis of character is dominant everywhere in the administrative world and it also engulfs Ratan Rathor, who feels emptiness within, restlessness, apathy, indifference that cover him "like a boil, like leprosy."[69] The crisis of his character gives him an impression that "his friends appeared no friendlier than a streetful of strangers."[70] Despite all his possessions and worldly achievements he feels that he is "going mad."[71]

The Last Labyrinth deals with Joshi's favourite theme and image in the fictional world. The novel is located in the labyrinths of Aftab's palace in Benares, but the scene goes on shuttling between Bombay and Benaras. Som Bhaskar, the hero of the novel, "is all appetite and want."[72] He is a type of a character who wants to become a business tycoon but he is never contented with his lot and reflects, "It is the voids of the world more than its objects that bother me."[73] A haunting cry within Som Bhaskar is, "I want, I want, I want."[74] Som Bhaskar was educated in foreign universities. At Harvard he studied not only Pascal but also Krishna and the Buddha. His scientist father researched on psychological truths and the First Cause of the universe. He is also a plastics manufacturer and after his death Som Bhaskar inherits the business. Som Bhaskar is married to Geeta, who is a chaste Hindu wife; but Som Bhaskar runs after several other ladies such as Leila Sabnis in Bombay and Anuradha in Benaras. Som Bhaskar's contact with Anuradha in Benares causes an upheaval in his life. Anuradha is a model of an antique life and is endowed with liberated views. She is a dancing girl living with Aftab who has no hesitation in allowing her to sleep with Som Bhaskar whom she tells, "You can't marry everyone you love. So why marry anyone at all."[75] *The Last Labyrinth* is a novel having several layers of interpretation; but for our present exploration it can be interpreted "as a fascinating exploration of the turbulent inner world of a successful young Indian urban."[76] Besides it, the novel also "plunges into a haunting world of life, love, God and death, the greatest of all mysteries... the last labyrinth."[77] Moreover, "the story's spiritual and sensuous dimensions are interwoven with great finesse."[78]

The Last Labyrinth deals with both the inner and the outer world of a westernized Indian aristocrat who has lost his spiritual roots. Yet he is never at ease despite his inherited affluence and the concept of materialism acquired from the West. He remains an alienated figure till the end. In the end Som Bhaskar attempts suicide by putting the revolver casually to his temple. But meanwhile his wife intervenes and shakes him "gently as though rousing a man from sleep."[79] The protagonists in Joshi's previous novels move from alienation to community but, according to Joshi himself, this hardly happens in the case of *The Last*

Labyrinth. In his reply to V. Gopal Reddy's questionnaire through his letter dated January 8, 1981, Joshi confirms that "Alienation of my characters in my novels that I have written so far ultimately leads them back to community. I realized that in my latest novel *The Last Labyrinth* for the first time this does not happen."[80]

Som Bhaskar in his search for roots discovers a haunting emptiness and void which makes him "mentally shattered, morally degenerated and physically exhausted with dreams and insomnia."[81] Som wants to obviate these with his business, but nothing comes to his aid. Som reflects:

> I looked at myself in the mirror: lean, crow-footed, graying, I could not, then see the hunger but there was the boredom and the fed-up-ness, endless depths of it....
>
> I woke up in the middle of the night, depressed, the taste of tranquilisers in my mouth.[82]

In his final work of fiction *The City and the River,* Joshi "continues to treat in its own ironical manner the predicament of his characters in a hostile world."[83] *The City and the River* is a novel amalgamating different modes and conventions. As a political novel it uses the form of a parable told through the mode of fantasy. Like the previous novels of Joshi, it has also an existentialist approach. Madhusudan Prasad has rightly pointed out about Joshi's novels that "they are singularised by certain existentialist problems and the resultant anger, agony, psychic quest and the like."[84] *The City and the River* is a story of endless repetition and periodic disintegration which can be prevented only if we achieve purity. The previous novels of Arun Joshi deal with the crisis of the individual which has been replaced in *The City and the River* by the "socio-political crisis of the city, which is a conglomerate of individuals and can be said to represent the whole humanity."[85] In *The City and the River* also Joshi "poses significant questions about identity, commitment and faith." But these questions are approached from the standpoint of politics. The novel also throws significant limelight on the meaning of life.[86] The city in it is a nowhere city and the river also is nameless, like the Nameless-One, great Yogeshwar's disciple. It is the great Yogeshwar who narrates the story of the city and the river to the Nameless-One.

The City and the River has the plot of power struggle. The Grand Master, who rules the city inherited from his forefathers, sees to it that he is crowned king, and son made his heir-apparent. He has a council of advisors which has an Astrologer as its prominent member besides having the Minister for Trade, his near relative, the Education Advisor and the Master of Rallies. There is a Police Commissioner who comes from the lower classes including the Master of Rallies. The Army is headed by General Starch. The Grand Master has befriended the brick people ignoring the boatmen who are poor people. The boatmen are deprived of their hearths and homes when the road from palace to the river-front is straightened. The boatmen headed by the woman headman rebel against the Grand Master and are not ready to owe their allegiance to him in lieu of the river. Bhoomiputra, popularly called Master Bhoma is a Mathematics teacher and a disciple of the Professor of Astrology. His brother and nephew are also on the side of the Grand Master. The power struggle makes the Grand Master despotic, as those who oppose him are put into the Gold Mines, which is a prison where the inmates are subjugated to personal afflictions such as blinding of the headman and the Astrologer's death due to Satyagraha.

The problem of identity is the core of the novel. The Grand Master and the persons associated with him want to domineer over others to make them feel their identity which is in a kind of crisis because they are ignorant of the reality of life. The boatmen and those who do not compromise with the Grand Master's regime suffer from weariness and loneliness. In the strange sorry tale of the city, even the Master of Rallies is not happy. It is reported about him:

> His misfortune lay in the fact that... instead of teaching him how to row a boat his parents had wanted him to join

> the ranks of the brick-people. The boatmen did not have money to hire him. The brick-people considered him an upstart.[87]

But this crisis of identity dominates more the characters who oppose the Grand Master. Both the Professor and his disciple Master Bhoma are weary and tired of the regime. In his wanderings in wilderness, "a sense of overwhelming futility filled him. At such times, so much so, that he saw no point in living."[88] Dharma's father suffers from a strange kind of disease: "The three Truths Syndrome, Stasis of the Soul. Atrophy of the brain and locomotor functions."[89] It increases to such an extent that he seems to be rotting within and as his existence is "reduced to zero," even the mirror fails to reflect his image. Even the Grand Master and his accomplices sometime or the other, think of the futility of life. The allegorical meaning of the fantasy is pointed out in the end by the great Yogeshwar to his disciple, the Nameless-One. The existential problem here takes on super-normal proportions of the endless repetition and destruction of life on the planet wrought by nemesis and retribution.

With this introductory background to the theoretical aspect of the crisis of identity and its different manifestations that we come across in the representative Indian English novelists in general and Arun Joshi in particular, we now move on to the different influences upon Arun Joshi and his fiction in Chapter 2.

NOTES

1. K.R.S. Iyengar, *Indo-Anglican Literature* (Bombay, 1947), 29.
2. R.S. Pathak, "Indo-English Novelist's Quest for Identity," in R.K. Dhawan (ed.) *Explorations in Indo-English Fiction* (New Delhi, 1982), 6.
3. Pathak 5.
4. Meenakshi Mukherjee, *Twice Born Fiction* (New Delhi, 1971), 5.
5. Pathak 1.
6. Pathak, "The Alienated Protagonist in the Indo-English Novel" in O.P. Saxena (ed.) *Glimpses of Indo-English Fiction,* Vol. I (New Delhi, 1985), 68.

7. Pathak 68.
8. Pathak 69.
9. Jawaharlal Nehru, *The Discovery of India* (New Delhi, 197l), 257.
10. William Walsh, "India and the Novel," in *The New Pelican Guide to English Literature,* (ed.) Boris Ford, Vol. 8, The Present (Penguin Books, 1983), 245.
11. Walsh 250.
12. Zeenat Futehally, *Zohra,* quoted R.S. Pathak, "The Alienated Protagonist in the Indo-English Novel," *Glimpses of Indo-English Fiction,* (ed.) O.P. Saxena, Vol. I (New Delhi, 1985), 73.
13. R.K. Narayan, *The Bachelor of Arts* (London, 1951), 154.
14. S. Nagarajan, "An Indian Novel," in Meenakshi Mukherjee (ed.) *Considerations* (New Delhi, 1977), 82.
15. H.M. Williams, *Studies in Modern Indian Fiction in English* (Calcutta, 1973), 55.
16. V.S. Naipaul, *An Area of Darkness* (1954), 71.
17. Kamala Markandeya, *A Silence of Desire* 80.
18. Markandeya 87-88.
19. R.S. Pathak, "Indo-English Novelist's Quest for Identity" in R.K. Dhawan, (ed.) *Explorations in Modern Indo-English Fiction* (New Delhi, 1982), 9.
20. Markandeya, *A Handful of Rice,* (New Delhi, 1966), 209.
21. Markandeya, *The Nowhere Man,* (New Delhi 1975), 47.
22. Markandeya 39.
23. Jasbir Jain, "The Novels of Kamala Markandeya," *Indian Literature,* April-June 1975, 40.
24. Pathak 10.
25. Balachandra Rajan, "Indian Virtue," *The Journal of Commonwealth Literature,* September 1965, 81.
26. Rajan, *The Dark Dancer,* (New Delhi, 1976), 1.
27. Rajan 164.
28. Rajan, *Too Long in the West,* (New Delhi, 1961), 24.
29. Rajan 55.
30. Prof. O.P. Mathur, *Modern Indian English Fiction* (New Delhi, 1993), 146.
31. Dr. Mohan Jha, "Chaman Nahal's *Azadi*: A Search for Identity," *Studies in Indian Fiction in English,* (ed.) Balram Gupta (Gulbarga, 1987), 36.

32. Chaman Nahal, *Azadi* (New Delhi, 1979), 227.
33. Nahal 347.
34. Nahal 362.
35. Nahal 363.
36. Jha 42-43.
37. Mathur, "Sense and Sensibility in Salman Rushdie's *Shame*," *The Indian Journal of English Studies,* Vol. XXVI, 1987, 19.
38. Salman Rushdie, "Reclaiming a City and a History," *Express Magazine* (*The Indian Express,* 11 March, 1984), 5.
39. Mathur 20.
40. Mathur 20.
41. M.K. Naik, *A History of Indian English Literature* (Sahitya Akademi, 1982), 236.
42. Naik 236.
43. Nayantara Sahgal, *This Time of Morning* (New Delhi, 1965), 137.
44. Sahgal 137.
45. Pathak 8.
46. Anita Desai, *Bye Bye Blackbird* (New Delhi, 1971), 208.
47. Desai 35.
48. V.A. Shahane, "Introduction:" *Explorations in Modern Indo-English Fiction,* (ed.) R.K. Dhawan (New Delhi, 1982), IX.
49. C.D. Narasimhaiah, *The Swan and the Eagle* (Shimla, 1969), 18.
50. Susheel Kr. Sharma, "*The Strange Case of Billy Biswas*: A Psychograph of an Alienated Hero," *The Novels of Arun Joshi* (ed.) R.K. Dhawan (New Delhi, 1992), 162.
51. Elizabeth B. Hurlock, *Personality Development* (New Delhi: Tata McGraw Hill, 1976), 41, quoted by S.K. Sharma in his article "*The Strange Case of Billy Biswas*: A Psychograph of an Alienated Hero" in R.K. Dhawan (ed.) "*The Novels of Arun Joshi*" (New Delhi, 1992), 162.
52. Ramesh K. Srivastava, *Six Indian Novelists in English* (Amritsar, 1987), 312.
53. Sujata Mathai, "I am a Stranger to My Books," *The Times of India,* July 7, 1983, 8.
54. Reply to M.R. Dua, dated September 3, 1971, quoted in *The Novels of Arun Joshi,* (ed.) R.K. Dhawan 8.
55. R.K. Dhawan, "The Fictional World of Arun Joshi," *The Novels of Arun Joshi* (New Delhi, 1992), 8.

56. M.G. Hegde, "The Short Stories of Arun Joshi: A Study" in R.K. Dhawan (ed.) *The Novels of Arun Joshi* (New Delhi, 1992), 201.
57. Naik 230.
58. Naik 230.
59. R.K. Srivastava, *Six Indian Novelists in English* (Amritsar, 1987), 316.
60. *The Strange Case of Billy Biswas* 122.
61. R.K. Srivastava, "Alienation in Arun Joshi's Novels," *Six Indian Novelists in English* (Amritsar, 1987), 319.
62. *The Strange Case of Billy Biswas* 23.
63. "*The Apprentice*: An Existential Study" in *Kakatiya Journal of English Studies*, Vols. V & VI, 1983-84, 10.
64. "*The Apprentice* 10.
65. *The Apprentice* 28.
66. *The Apprentice* 51.
67. *The Apprentice* 148.
68. *The Apprentice* 17.
69. *The Apprentice* 66.
70. *The Apprentice* 114.
71. *The Apprentice* 129.
72. Keki N. Daruwalla, "A Review of *The Last Labyrinth*," *Indian Literature*, Vol. 26, July-December, 1983, 136.
73. *The Last Labyrinth* 47.
74. *The Last Labyrinth* 11.
75. *The Last Labyrinth* 43.
76. The cover page blurb to *The Last Labyrinth.*
77. The cover page blurb to *The Last Labyrinth.*
78. The cover page blurb to *The Last Labyrinth.*
79. *The Last Labyrinth* 224.
80. V. Gopal Reddy, "A Note on the Novels of Arun Joshi," *Kakatiya Journal of English Studies*, Vol. VII, 1985-86, 90.
81. Reddy 90.
82. *The Last Labyrinth* 21.
83. R.S. Pathak, "The Quest for Meaning in Arun Joshi' s Novels" in *The Novels of Arun Joshi*, (ed.) R.K. Dhawan (New Delhi , 1992), 63.

84. Madhusudan Prasad, "Arun Joshi," *Indian English Novelists: An Anthology of Critical Essays,* (ed.) Madhusudan Prasad (New Delhi, 1982), 51.

85. Pathak 63.

86. Pathak 63.

87. *The City and the River* 71.

88. *The City and the River* 174.

89. *The City and the River* 133.

2

INFLUENCES UPON ARUN JOSHI: LITERARY, PHILOSOPHICAL AND LINGUISTIC

I

It is something in the nature of a platitude to say that an artist has been influenced, either directly or indirectly, by any particular writer or a set of writers. This is so because the term 'influence,' when examined in a strictly literary context, may and does have manifold ramifications. In the first place, an artist may be said to have been influenced by one particular writer or a group of writers in the sense that he has tried to imitate them, either successfully or otherwise, or has accepted him or them as his literary model or models. In this respect, the influence on a writer may be accepted as something direct and significant. Secondly, an artist may be supposed to have been influenced by one writer or a number of writers because his or their literary views and artistic execution strike us as something closely identical. In such cases, the term "influence" does bear a different kind of connotation, for in such cases what we find may be called the simple phenomenon of intellectual and artistic agreement. Thirdly, the term "influence" may also suggest a feeling of reaction or opposition because in several cases an artist may be said to have been influenced by one particular writer or several other writers chiefly in the sense of opposition or reaction. Negative influence is also a kind of catalytic factor that prompts or is likely to prompt an artist to take to literary creation. And lastly, the term 'influence' may imply part agreement and part disagreement, so that in view of this process of acceptance or rejection an artist's growth or development may be judged to a substantial degree. The moot point in this regard is that whenever we consider the case of a writer in terms of influences that have either worked or might have possibly worked on him, we lend ourselves both easily and readily to all kinds of speculation and suspicion.

Arun Joshi's fictional works are products of the various influences upon his mind and art. These relate to literature, philosophy and language. In his fictional themes and techniques, as also in view of life and language, Joshi has been influenced by the writers and philosophers from both East and West.

To trace the literary and other impacts upon Arun Joshi, a brief summary of his life, education and achievements would be helpful. Some of his biographical details have also their influences upon his literary achievements. Arun Joshi has had no mean intellectual heritage. His father, A.C. Joshi, was one of the eminent Botanists of the country. He served many prestigious institutions of the country and was associated with several national level learned committees. He was appointed one of the members of the committee set up by the U.G.C. in August 1961 "in order to undertake a systematic and objective investigation of problems relating to the standards of higher education in Indian Universities."[1] Professor A.C. Joshi was then the Vice-Chancellor of Panjab University and he was also later appointed V.C. of Benares Hindu University, where he had also worked as a Faculty Member of the Department of Botany. Arun Joshi was born as the youngest child of his parents at Benares on July 7, 1939. The city of Benares and its labyrinthine streets figure as the locale in Joshi's fourth novel, *The Last Labyrinth*, in which Benares is set against the business metropolis, Bombay.

During the freedom struggle, Arun Joshi was merely a child who might have occasionally heard the name of Mahatma Gandhi whom he refers to in a few of his novels, especially *The Apprentice*, which has for its theme the discrepancy between the idealism of national leaders during the freedom struggle and the decay of their ideals at the polling booths and administration in free India.

Arun Joshi was sent to the U.S.A. to receive his higher education where he studied at various centres of education. After passing his B.S. from Kansas University in 1959, he got his M.S. degree from M.I.T., U.S.A. in 1960. Like Arun Joshi many of his fictional characters as well are also trained in the U.S.A. Sindi Oberoi in *The Foreigner* has his degree in Engineering from the U.S.A. and professionally, like Arun Joshi, he also gets involved in an industrial and business concern. Arun Joshi's stay in the U.S.A. remained an influential factor in his life. He went on writing three of his novels with their major characters trained in the U.S.A. Billy Biswas in *The Strange Case of Billy Biswas* and Romesh Sahai became close friends during their stay for higher education in the U.S.A. Billy Biswas was sent to the U.S.A. by his parents to study Engineering, though without the knowledge of his parents he changed over to Anthropology. Som Bhaskar in *The Last Labyrinth* has also studied in the U.S.A., so has Leila Sabnis. The characters in *The Apprentice* as also in *The City and the River* and his short stories except Dr. Khanna in *The Only American from Our Village* and Rewal Kapoor in *The Survivor* are not fortunate in having the benefit of foreign education.

After receiving his higher education in the U.S.A., he joined the D.C.M. in 1961 as chief of its recruitment and training department. In 1964 he married Rukmani Lal, the daughter of a D.C.M. shareholder and subsequently held several positions in the company, such as in the D.C.M. Corporate Performance Assessment Cell; Secretary, D.C.M. Board of Managment; Executive Director of Sri Ram Centre for Industrial Relations and Human Resources. His association with the D.C.M. as an important executive and relative prompted him to attempt a domestic biography in 1975 of *Lala Sri Ram: A Study in Entrepreneurship in Industrial Management.* In 1965 he resigned from the D.C.M. but still continued to be Executive Director of

Sri Ram Centre for Industrial Relations and Human Resources, and he set up his own separate industrial establishments to manufacture diesel engines.

Arun Joshi's profession has been related to management and industrial relations. His avocation from the very beginning has been writing. Though he has never been a student of literature, he has been influenced by many of the authors and their works which were available in English translations, especially those of the French novelists such as Sartre and Camus. It is because of his literary influences that Arun Joshi has been writing ever since his student days and it is said the first drafts of *The Foreigner* (1968) had been written during the period of his American stay, where he had digested the works of the American and the European existentialist authors.

We gather facts of Arun Joshi's literary, philosophical and linguistic influences from various sources. These are by way of interviews or replies to questionnaires. Besides these we deduce many facts of influence on him from the scrutiny of the texts of his novels where there are many references to philosophical points borrowed from both East and West, linguistic aspects of the use of English as well as his knowledge of the crisis of modern man's predicament.

Arun Joshi has contributed a very short piece to *The Fictional World of Arun Joshi* edited by R.K. Dhawan (1986). In it he poses the questions and replies to them by quoting certain lines from Freud's lectures at the University of Vienna. The questions posed by him are:

> From time to time I am asked why I write? Why I pick the themes that I pick and why I treat them in the manner that I do?[2]

The answers to these are Freudian. Freud regards phantasy-life to be a thing of very general interest. Freud says:

> There is, in fact, a path from phantasy back again to reality, and that is—art. The artist has also an introverted

> disposition and has not far to go to become neurotic.... He longs to attain honour, power, riches, fame and the love of women; but he lacks the means of achieving these gratifications. So, like any other with an unsatisfied longing, he turns away from reality and transfers all his interests and all his libido to, onto the creation of his wishes in the life of phantasy.[3]

So phantasy and reality are important to Arun Joshi as well. Things of phantasy are realised through reality and the reality materialises phantasy. This psychological factor from Freud has a deep influence upon Arun Joshi's fiction. Harish Raizada in particular has traced this impact in Arun Joshi's fiction in his article "Double Vision of Phantasy and Reality in Arun Joshi's Novels."[4]

Arun Joshi's novels reveal his interest in both poetry and fiction as also philosophical writings from both East and West. The influences of Wordsworth and Arnold can be traced in *The Strange Case of Billy Biswas.* He quotes a line from *Thyrsis*, "It irk'd him to be here, he could not rest" as an epigraph of the novel. Moreover for Billy Biswas civilized society is too much. The philosophical concept elucidated in it has some affinity with the idea contained in Wordsworth's sonnet "The World is Too Much with Us." Billy escapes into the primitive life to become "a pagan sucked in the creed outworn."[5] Billy's restlessness of soul, because of the epigraph from Arnold, can also be traced back to the myth of *The Scholar Gipsy.*

Among the authors of the West, mention may be made of certain American and European writers advocating the philosophy of existentialism in their fictional works. In the words of Hari Mohan Prasad, Joshi is "a novelist in the tradition of Kafka, Camus, Sartre and Saul Bellow, Elison and Malamud."[6] G.S. Amur finds the influence of Camus on Joshi's novels and writes that "his affinities are more with novelists in American tradition like Saul Bellow and Bernard Malamud."[7] Elaborating this he writes:

> Joshi's vision of the modern world and man's place in it is Manichean and his heroes though rooted in the industrial civilisation have always been at odds with it. It is for this reason that the action of his novels takes the form of a search for an alternative. His novels take us to the heart of darkness—one of his most favourite metaphors is the labyrinth—but he is not a prophet of despair. All his novels hold out promise of regeneration and redemption.[8]

Joshi too has confessed to being influenced by few of the authors. In an interview to Purabi Bannerji he said:

> I did read Camus and Sartre. I liked the *Plague* and read *The Outsider*. I might have been influenced by Sartre I did not understand clearly or like. As for existential philosophers like Kierkegaard I never understood anything except odd statements.[9]

Joshi admits to have read Camus and Sartre and to have been influenced by them. He is also rather evasive about his understanding of Sartre and Kierkegaard. But their influences are definitely there in his novels. The existentialist novelists have definitely influenced Arun Joshi's themes and techniques. Like the heroes of Camus, Sindi Oberoi in *The Foreigner* passes through the crisis of the present. Camus's *L'etranger* literally means a foreigner or an outsider. Like the hero of the novel, Meursault, Sindi is also anti-ambitious and detached which he seems to cultivate as virtue. Meursault continues to be an outsider and indifferent to whatever he experiences. In the case of Sindi, cynicism and attachment seem to be a pose while these are built up into the texture of Meursault.

The fictional technique of *The Apprentice* and its thematic concerns have clear indications of the influence of Camus's novel *The Fall*. Like the long confession of Jean Baptiste Clemance in Camus's *The Fall*, Ratan Rathor, the protagonist in *The Apprentice* must tell all. Jean Baptiste Clemance, the protagonist of *The Fall*, sees the falsity of his existence like Ratan

Rathor and tries to salvage his fragmented self. He calls himself Judge-penitent. He confesses:

> He who clings to a law does not fear the judgement that puts him in his place within an order he believes in. But the keenest of human torments is to be judged without law. Yet we are in that torment. Deprived of their natural curb, the judges, loosed at random, are racing through their job. Hence we have to try to go faster than they, don't we? And it's a real mad house. Prophets and facts multiply; they hasten to get there with a good law or a flawless organization before the world is deserted. Fortunately, I arrived. I am the end and the beginning; I announce the law. In short, I am a judge penitent.[10]

Ratan Rathor in his psycho-narration does not call himself a penitent; but his calling himself sham, bogus, whore, fake, etc. "transforms penitence into prayer."[11] Ratan Rathor like Meursault, the protagonist in Camus's *The Fall*, exposes and ridicules his hypocrisy, servility and indifference in a mock heroic vein.

Joshi's fictional technique has also evidences of the impact of Joseph Conrad. R.K. Dhawan writes that "Arun Joshi's fiction conforms to Conrad's conception of the novel. Joshi recognises a reality beyond a mere phenomenal world, a reality which the artists could imagine and capture by giving a consistent form to the shapeless facts of human existence."[12] There are similarities between Arun Joshi's *The Strange Case of Billy Biswas* and a few of the novels by Joseph Conrad. Billy Biswas, like Kurtz in Conrad's *The Heart of Darkness*, forsakes civilized human society and adapts himself to the primitive and has a native mistress. Again like Conrad's *Lord Jim*, where Marlow narrates the story with the witness-narrator's point of view, Romesh Sahai in *The Strange Case of Billy Biswas* narrates the story of Billy Biswas in a similar vein. Besides it, like Conrad's narrator in *Under Western Eyes*, the witness-narrator, Romi says, "I had neither the imagination nor the obsessive predilections of Billy Biswas."[13]

R.K. Srivastava finds in *The Strange Case of Billy Biswas* some similarities with John Updike's *Rabbit, Run.* This may be by way of influence or a chance similarity. The themes in the two are almost identical:

> Like Billy, Harry Angstrom or "Rabbit" seems to be a victim of an all-encompassing alienation, feels terribly unhappy with his life and runs away. He comes back, is temporarily reconciled to his wife, but after the birth of a child, leaves her and runs again. In both cases there are no specific reasons but some kind of emptiness that rises in them from within and then affects their relations with others. Both Billy and Rabbit find the world horrible and decide to flee from it. Both are devoid of ambitions, and do not exploit others for their personal gains. They seem to be lost and terrified children in an unfamiliar crowd.[14]

Several other influences of either generic or specific nature might be traced in the novels of Arun Joshi. S. Rangachari finds T.S. Eliot's shadow on *The Foreigner* referred to by Joy Abraham in *The Novels of Arun Joshi*, edited by R.K. Dhawan, New Delhi, 1992 (160). But the point has not been elaborated. There are, however, many echoes of T.S. Eliot's themes and association of ideas in not only *The Foreigner* but also *The Apprentice.* Like J. Alfred Prufrock, Ratan Rathor also continues his dramatic monologue. In *The Foreigner* Arun Joshi has quoted from T.S. Eliot's *Love Song of J. Alfred Prufrock.* Commenting upon time, the narrator refers to "a business executive reciting T.S. Eliot in a bar."[15]

> There will be time, there will be time
> To prepare a face to meet the faces that you meet.

Sindi Oberoi retorts and in reply himself recites the lines from J. Alfred Prufrock:

> And indeed there will be time
> To wonder. "Do I dare?" "Do I dare?"
> Time to turn back and descend the stair.[16]

The creation of literature envisages the awareness of a healthy literary tradition in the author's mind. Arun Joshi is aware of so many aspects of literature in his works. The awareness of myths, symbols and archetypes is also a point of influence upon Arun Joshi. Arun Joshi has used a universal symbol of labyrinth in *The Last Labyrinth* and the archetypal figures in *The City and the River.* He is very fond of the symbol of labyrinth and uses it not only in his works of longer fiction but also in his short stories along with myth used "both as digressional methods and as structural parallels."[17] Mrs. Mukherjee views *The Strange Case of Billy Biswas* to be "a compelling novel about a strange quest drawing upon myth and folklore to reiterate its elementary concerns."[18] Joshi has used both the varieties of myth in his novels. In using myth as a structural parallel we come across mythical situations underlying the whole novel or part of it as in *The Strange Case of Billy Biswas* or *The Last Labyrinth* or even *The City and the River.* It has also been used as a digressional method in which a mythical story is woven within a story. In *The City and the River* the story regarding "the king is naked" is an example in point. Joshi uses not only the universal myth but also localized myths known as *Sthalapuranas* as also myths derived out of folk-tales.

The literary influences on Arun Joshi conform to K.R.S. Iyengar's analysis of it:

> Before 1947 (the year of the withdrawal of Britain's political connection), the English models were the major outside influence on the Indian novel. After independence, however, novelists in India have shown themselves susceptible to the influence of American and European (especially Russian) models, and also models from Oriental countries.[19]

In the case of Arun Joshi, the influences are greater with those of American and European models along with Oriental mythical situations.

II

Arun Joshi has clearly stated in an interview to Purabi Bannerji quoted above (ref. no. 9 on page No. 35) that he read Camus and Sartre and was also influenced by them. But he in a way contradicts himself when he says that he did not clearly understand or like Sartre. Among existentialist philosophers he refers to Kierkegaard whom he liked for his certain odd statements but never completely. He refers to Kierkegaard once in *The Last Labyrinth*: "Prayer doesn't change God, but it changes him who prays."[20] The influence of the existentialist authors and philosophers cannot, however, be denied. Hari Mohan Prasad has rightly pointed out that Joshi's characters "embody the theme of anxiety of which the existential writers of the West, Kierkegaard, Marcel, Jaspers, Buber, Paul Tillich have given concepts."[21] Like the existentialist writers and philosophers Joshi is also aware of man's feeling of anxiety and alienation. But Joshi's alienation is qualified by Indian philosophical optimism. Alienation and quest of identity of Joshi's heroes are not final; rather these are a step in the quest for meaning in life. As there is an undercurrent of existentialism in all the novels of Joshi, it will be useful as a sort of background to study in brief the main traits of the existentialist philosophy.

Existentialism is a highly subjective philosophy associated with such names as Sartre (1905-80) and Camus (1913-60). It is mostly a post-war movement associated with disillusion and a sordid view of life. It originates from the nineteenth century Danish philosopher, Soren Kierkegaard (1813-55) whose works in their German translation influenced Heideggar and Karl Jaspers. Heideggar is said to have commented that "Sartre is no philosopher,"[22] even if it is to his works that modern existentialists often turn.

Existentialism is not concerned with the nature of the universe or philosophical problems and individual's attitude to life and God is its main concern. Existence is basic and as such each self-aware individual can grasp his own existence on reflection in his own immediate experience of himself and his situation as a free being in the world. It is concerned with life itself and is suspicious of its logic. It believes in the supremacy of passion over reason. According to Margaret Chatterjee, "the existentialists are the romantics of the twentieth century."[23] The passions are the deep and dark powers in human life. But these are not cosmic but mundane. The solitary man who stands against the crowd becomes less a hero than an anti-hero. He is less a pilgrim than perhaps a hobo. Melancholy is no longer sweet; on the contrary it is indistinguishable from nausea. To quote Margaret Chatterjee:

> Man is no longer a fallen angel but a descendent of the apes. The paradoxes of human life are stark contradictions in society, contradictions which bring out alienation between man and man. The deep and dark powers are not in the stars but in ourselves.[24]

Existentialism may lean towards theism on the one hand or atheism on the other; but irrespective of the leanings it is an attitude of life concerning itself with the individual's ultimate problems, to be anti-idealists and anti-rationalists. The atheist existentialist, Sartre, believed that "hell is other people."[25] He said so to emphasize the subjectivity of the philosophy.

The crisis of identity as an offshoot of alienation is one of the agonising experiences of modern man. Some of the philosophers and thinkers have called the present age to be an age of alienation. Many agonising aspects of modern life such as the generation gap, the anti-war movement, the hippie phenomenon, the credibility gap, the compartmentalization of our life, the stunting of personal development and nagging sense of meaninglessness of life and others have made the modern man lose his confidence. This has resulted in his estrangement from the self, the family and the society. He is not able to grasp the meaning of his existence in a hostile world in which he is a stranger and an exile. There is something absurd about him. The absurd is that which is devoid of purpose. He feels lost and finds no solace in religion and philosophy which all thrust him towards becoming senseless, absurd and useless.

This age of alienation is also one of anxiety. It is paradoxical that despite scientific and industrial achievements, the contemporary man is doomed to find himself in a tragic predicament. Industrialization, urbanization, intergenerational tensions, the economic pressures due to the rising market economy and over-affluence have all taken man into their vice-like grip. In the rat race of life, man is a stranger not only from the outside world but also from his own self. This seems to be the root cause of crisis of identity which is one of the factors of the crisis of the present. Man has been plunged into uncertainty, perplexity and unsettlement. There is confusion, rootlessness, frustration, disintegration, disillusionment, meaninglessness prevailing in the human psyche. This is also true to the case of the Indian ethos which is perplexed by a gnawing sense of rootlessness maintaining itself as a crisis of identity. The condition of the luxurious and the overfed is no better. Living amid affluence they lead a joyless existence.

The typicality of modern life and that of the heroes of Arun Joshi's fiction are the existential encounter with nothingness. Man feels injured and his wounded psyche generates within him a cynical attitude towards the social norms and values which make him angst-ridden.

Crisis of identity may have its roots in both self-alienation and social alienation. Self-alienation is loss of contact of the individual selves with any inclination or desires not in agreement with the prevailing social pattern. Alienation from the self is the basic form of rootlessness. This is not only a sociological but also a psychological problem of contemporary man and literature.

Existentialism has influenced modern literature and as such this is the concern of the creative artists no less than that of the philosopher. The human existential condition is the perennial stuff of great literature. The basic existentialist categories as applicable to literature are contingencies, tragic necessity, unlimited freedom, loneliness and absurdity. To be alive is to be active. T.S. Eliot, in his essay, "Baudelaire," writes:

> So far as we are here what we do must be either evil or good; so far as we do evil or good, we are human; and it is better, in a paradoxical way, to do evil than to do nothing; at least, we exist. It is true to say that the glory of man is his capacity for salvation; it is also true to say that his glory is his capacity for damnation.[26]

To exist we have to act. It is just another matter that the action may be good or evil and through our action we can pave our way either for salvation or damnation. While the theists emphasize salvation, the atheists damnation. The atheists take recourse to their capacity of unfettered choice which motivates them to their final salvation in suicide which even Sartre took recourse to.

The tag of existentialism has come into currency in the twentieth century but the idea is as old as literature and philosophy. Traces of it have been found not only in the Biblical writings but also in Indian philosophical systems. Joshi believes Hinduism to be a "highly existentialist oriented philosophy, since it attaches so much value to the right way to live (to exist)."[27]

There is a very pronounced impact of existentialism on Arun Joshi's writings. All his novels from *The Foreigner* onwards to *The City and the River* have in them an undercurrent of the existentialist philosophy. *The Foreigner* is a study in the alienation in the soul of Sindi Oberoi. The crisis of his identity is concerned neither with geography nor with the roots. It lies within him and leads him from one crisis to another. In it Joshi also explores some of man's perennial dualities. The way out of these lies at last in the philosophy of attachment vs. non-attachment borrowed from the *Bhagawad Gita.*

The Strange Case of Billy Biswas explores the inner psyche of Billy who is not able to bear with the so-called civilized façade of modern life and as such he escapes into the unlimited freedom of choice that awaits him in the tribal world. *The Apprentice* is also an attack upon the post-Independence civilization with its scope for lying, hypocrisy, bribery, graft, drunkenness and womanizing. Ratan Rathor at last realises all this and to purify his conscience he performs a very humble job of a shoeshiner on the steps of a temple. In *The Last Labyrinth* the existential theme is that of the problem of life and death and God. Som Bhaskar is a multimillionaire at the age of twenty-five; but from the obsessive quest of the labyrinths of Lal Haveli at Benares he steps on for the quest of the last labyrinth which relates to the mysteries of life, death and God. One of the themes of *The City and the River* is related to how men in essence entirely free to choose, create by their choice the circumstances in which they have to live. It also explores the relevance of God to man's choices in which it is God and no one else who owns and governs the world. In the short stories also, included in *The Survivor* (1975), there has been an existential exposition of "the glittering flimsiness of the Indian affluent society."[28] In some of his stories as well, the image of the labyrinth has been used frequently. *The Gherao* in particular deals with "the agony and the hopelessness that divide one generation from another."[29] The principal of a college depicted in it is an alienated man whose son and daughter-in-law have become indifferent to him. The principal says, "I have a son but he doesn't answer to my letters. My daughter-in-law says, she doesn't want to see my face again. And all this because I did not give them the ten thousand rupees which is all that I have."[30] In his *gherao* by student leaders what the principal has to say "appeared to have got lost somewhere in the labyrinths of his enfeebled brain. It was as if an old railway engine were stuck on an incline and puffing vainly to gather enough steam to move ahead."[31] The lack of communion and loss of identity are the points emphasized in these statements of the story, *The Gherao*. In his short stories as well Arun Joshi is concerned with the same problem as we get in his novels. Hegde has rightly pointed out that "Arun Joshi's stories give a sure insight into the pseudo-westernized affluent society of India where decadence has set in."[32]

Besides existentialism and existentialist authors, Joshi has also referred to other philosophical systems of the West. His characters quote from, or comment upon, certain philosophical thinkers. The characters and their experiences are projections of the author's way of thinking which may be objectified in the creation. In *The Last Labyrinth*, in particular, several philosophers have been referred to or quoted from. Leila Sabnis, an expert in psychology and philosophy, was so fond of Descartes that the narrator refers to him as "her friend Descartes"[33] and refers to his opinion, "I think, therefore, I exist."[34] Again it has been said, "Of course, Descartes was no agnostic. He granted the existence of God since the idea of God existed in men's minds, he reasoned, it must have been God Himself who had put it there in the first place."[35] The narrator in his stream of consciousness thinks of the concept of people born with blank minds (the concept of tabula rasa of Locke). The philosophy of doubting everything has come from the West "along with Coca-cola, IBM, and the English language."[36] Som Bhaskar reflects on faith in reason and faith in God, as variations of Faith. The evolutionary philosophy of Darwin has also been referred to in *The Last Labyrinth*. Som Bhaskar in his curiosity regarding evolution states that "Darwin didn't say how we are supposed to evolve further."[37] Anuradha qualifies this statement with her, "May be Krishna begins where Darwin left off."[38] Som Bhaskar's father who researched on the First Cause finds and believes that "there are causes behind causes"[39] and he also states "I believe in science, yes, but science cannot solve the problem of the causes. Not many realize this paradox."[40] These are a few of the philosophical observations from *The Last Labyrinth* where lots of philosophical problems of both the East and the West have been referred to and quoted from.

Susheel Kumar Sharma identifies some traces of Marxism in *The Foreigner*.[41] Khemka's attitude to the workers of his factory highlights the applicability of the Marxian philosophy of class-consciousness and class-conflict. Mr. Khemka advises Sindi Oberoi, "Never trust these lower classes. They have to be made use of, but kept in their place."[42] Even Sindi is aware of Khemka exploiting his workers who suffer at his hand. In the class conflict it is the have-nots who suffer. Sindi tells Khemka:

> It is not I who should be ashamed of, Mr. Khemka, but you yourself. I have only been one of your victims. It is you who have swindled those miserable wretches in rags who push carts on your streets and die at twenty-five. It is you who have been telling lies and fabricating documents just so that you could air-condition this ostentatious house and throw gigantic parties for the horde of jackals who masquerade as your friends.[43]

All these ideas expressed in *The Foreigner* have the stamp of the Marxian philosophy which has its major role in industrial relationships.

Besides the western philosophical systems, Joshi has a good grounding of the Indian philosophical systems of the ancient times and even Gandhism of the modern times. Among the Indian philosophical systems, the traces of their influence on Arun Joshi's art and mind are there in the case of several of his novels such as *The Foreigner, The Strange Case of Billy Biswas, The Last Labyrinth* and also in his other works to some extent. His Hindu psyche seems to bubble up from the subconscious as he goes on referring to Hindu myths and philosophy. Sindi Oberoi, whose roots are hybrid, tells Sheila why her family did not want Babu to marry an American even though "Hindus prided themselves on their tolerance."[44] In *The Strange Case of Billy Biswas,* the narrator advises his friend, Billy, to get married and his persuasion was on the basis of the Hindu *dharma.* Besides Western pragmatism,

> I offered him the usual amalgam of western pragmatism (a wife is so necessary, socially, sexually, for a fuller life) and Hindu *dharma* (man's duty to marry and reproduce;

> there is a time for everything) that is the conventional wisdom of the Indian middle class.[45]

The novels of Arun Joshi do not reveal to us much about his knowledge of the Sanskrit learning. In *The City and the River* the ancient Indian language, Sanskrit, has been referred to as "the forgotten tongue"[46] and "the ancient tongue that no one understood."[47] The latter expression has been oft repeated in *The City and the River*. In *The Last Labyrinth* Som Bhaskar on the Ganga *ghat* refers nostalgically to the recitation by Pundits from the ancient texts: "A young Sanskrit scholar recited hymns on the top of his voice. I thought of my father and the little books of the Upanishads. Another boy equally young corrected him. Did Panini ever live in Benares?"[48] This is perhaps all that he has written about Sanskrit in his novels. But it is a certainty that being born and educated in early years at Benares, he might have schooling in it up to the secondary level. Whatever may be the reality he uses ideas from *the Bhagawad Gita, the Upanishads* and some other systems of Indian philosophy. The idea in *The Foreigner* relates to the problem of attachment versus detachment expounded in *the Bhagawad Gita*. Sindi Oberoi suffers from a wrong conception of detachment and as such does not want to get involved in action. But the presentation of detachment as panacea for life's problem as exemplified by Sindi Oberoi is erroneous. The plight of the factory worker, Muthu, and his exhortation makes Sindi realise his mistakes. It enables him to attain self-knowledge as he realizes:

> Detachment at that time had meant inaction. Now I had begun to see the fallacy in it. Detachment consisted of right action and not escape from it. The Gods had set a heavy price to teach me just that.[49]

The factory assistant, Muthu, impresses upon Sindi that "sometimes detachment lies in actually getting involved."[50] It is this advice which leads Sindi back from alienation to community.

Again in *The Strange Case of Billy Biswas* Arun Joshi has perhaps deliberately created a work of fiction on the concept of

Prakriti and Purusha on the Sankhya system of Indian philosophy. R.S. Pathak has explained the narrative of Bilasia and Billy on the Sankhya concept of the fusion of Prakriti and Purusha:

> As Billy's example testifies, if one is able to establish a rapport with the primitive forces in the world of nature, one can get rid of all problems of life. Bilasia, it is held, symbolises "the primitive culture," the untapped subterranean resources of psychic energy. It would be better to regard her as the matter (Prakriti), which according to the Sankhya system of Indian philosophy, is "one" and eternal, not an illusionary appearance but something real. Billy might be taken to represent the soul (Purusha), which by its mere presence excites Matter and illumines the process of evolution of the universe. Bilasia, we are reminded, is "the embodiment of the primal and invulnerable force that had ruled these Maikala hills; perhaps this earth, since time began." Her "enormous eyes," we are told, "poured out a sexuality that was nearly as primeval as the forest that surrounded them."
>
> In the Sankhya philosophy the material universe is traced to a First Cause.[51]

Som Bhaskar's father in *The Last Labyrinth* is a seeker after the First Cause and finds the answers of the life's problems in the Indian philosophical mysticism. Susheel Kumar Sharma in his article "Philosophical Reverberations in *The Foreigner*" in R.K. Dhawan (edited), *The Novels of Arun Joshi* (122 to 132) identifies the influences of not only *The Gita* but also other philosophical systems. Sindi Oberoi takes inspiration not only from the Jnanayoga but also Karmayoga preached about in *the Bhagawad Gita.* There are also traces on it of some of the Vedantic concepts. Sindi attaches importance to detachment because he considers this world to be illusion. He tells June Blyth, "Nothing ever seems real to me, leave alone permanent. Nothing seems to be very important."[52] Sindi wants to know the real and says:

> All love—whether of things, or persons, or oneself—was illusion and all pain sprang from this illusion. ...Birth and death are real. They are the constants. All else is variable. In the rest you see what you want to see. According to the Hindu mystics there is a reality beyond all this.[53]

In *The City and the River* as well, there are several philosophical and mystical reverberations such as to those of *Nada* or the music from the spheres[54] and to cosmic harmony and to "the endless repetition and the periodic disintegration"[55] of creation which can be halted only when men understand the relevance of God because "the world indeed belongs to God and to no one else."[56] This is a kind of adaptation of Sri Krishna's revelations to Arjuna that He manifests Himself to uphold the decline of law and order for the benefit of mankind.

Arun Joshi has imbibed knowledge of psychology and philosophy of both East and West. His narrative technique has been influenced by the psychology of the stream of consciousness which we find in several of his novels. He mentions Freud in connection with Leila Sabnis in *The Last Labyrinth.* She has behind her seat philosophers of America and Europe and "Freud as well bearded and saintly, indefatigable, groping in the night of man's mind, strewn with piss, excreta, struggling to put man together, the pervert and the insane but also those who, whole otherwise, walk the beaches at night and cry for the spirit."[57] This is a kind of summary of the Freudian psychology. Joshi also refers to certain other European philosophers such as Pascal, on whom Som Bhaskar did a paper at Harvard. A quotation from him has been given:

> Let us weigh the gain and loss in wagering that God is, let us estimate these two chances. If you gain, you gain all, if you lose, you lose nothing.[58]

As quoted and discussed earlier, Joshi believes in the Freudian motive behind literary creation, which grows out of fantasy and reality.

On many occasions in *The Last Labyrinth,* there are specific references to Krishna, Buddha, Tukaram and even Yajnavalkya whom he refers to in an Upanishadic quotation:

> When the Sun is set and the Moon is also set, and the fire has sunk down and the voice is silent, what, then Yajnavalkya, is the light of man?[59]

Som Bhaskar guesses what Yajnavalkya could have answered. Joshi's Hindu psyche makes him refer to Bhaskar's performing the last rites of his father at Hardwar. There are also references to several deities of the Hindu pantheon. Bhaskar recalls the statue of the Trimurti at Elephanta caves:

> Heavy lipped Brahma, Rudra with snakes and a third eye; Vishnu almost effeminate.[60]

Som Bhaskar also thinks of the dormant Kundalini power:

> I feel rage whipping at the end of my spine, and shooting up with the skull, to some dark hollows where the serpent slept, just waiting to be stirred.[61]

There are also several references to the Tantrik cult in *The Last Labyrinth.* Of all Joshi's novels *The Last Labyrinth* has perhaps the greatest number of reverberations from the different philosophical systems of East and West dealing mostly with the labyrinthine ways of life and death.

Perhaps no Indo-English novelist has ignored Mahatma Gandhi and the Partition of the country. He refers to his grandfather who during the troubled times of the Partition, when "rioters stalked the lanes and alleys,...carried a gun for protection and also out of a sense of humour."[62] In *The Apprentice* a contrast has been drawn up between the pre-Independence idealism preached by Gandhi and his followers and the post-Independence mockery of it at the hands of employees, officers and politicians. Ratan Rathor's father was a follower of the Mahatma who according to him was "a man of suffering."[63] He preached to his son, "To be good! Respected! To be of use!"[64] But all these get shattered when after his father's death Ratan

Rathor after a long wait gets employment in a government office.

In no other novel except *The Last Labyrinth* has Arun Joshi written anything on the Indian Muslim tradition. In New Delhi where Som Bhaskar sees Anuradha with Aftab at a Plastics Manufacturers' Conference, they all go to a *Dargah* where one Amzad Mian guides them through "the procession of tombstones."[65] The guide, Amzad Mian, narrates in his melancholy drone about Bustamy, Mansoor Hallaj, Khwaja Mu'inuddin, Khwaja Qutbuddin Bakhtiar, Baba Farid, Iltumish, Sheikh Nizamuddin, Mehboob-i-Ilahi and several others. The guide quotes from the song sung by mourners in ecstasy on the death of Khwaja Qutbuddin:

> *Kushtagane Khanjare taslim ra,*
>
> *Har zaman as ghaib digarast.*[66]
>
> and translated by the author as:
>
> When the dagger of submission has killed you, there will come new lives from unseen worlds.[67]

Amzad Mian, the guide, narrates Mansoor Hallaj putting to death raving to the end, "*Ana'l Haque, Ana'l Haque* (I am God)."[68] The guide guides the visitors through the gravestones addressing the buried:

> *Tariquat, Haqiquat, Tawakkul, Sabr, Khauf, Ishq, Rida, Fana.*[69]

Amzad Mian has been called "a learned man"[70] which can also be appended to the case of Arun Joshi who is the creator of the character and the episode.

Arun Joshi as a creative artist has used his knowledge of the facts of life, literature and philosophy to mould the fabric of his novels. Had these experiences not passed into his character he could not have used them.

III

Writing about Mulk Raj Anand, Meenakshi Mukherjee comments on the use of language:

> His endeavour to naturalize the English language depends on three devices. Most notable is the literal translation of Hindi or Punjabi idioms into English: thus, "my counterfeit luck" (*mere khota naseeb*), "is this any talk?" (*Yeh bhi koi bat hai*), "*nothing black in the pulse*" (*dal me kala*), "made my sleep illegal" (*neend haram kar dia*). Secondly, he interpolates Hindi words in an English sentence indiscriminately, sometimes as nouns ("Shut up *saley*, stop your *tain, tain*" or "These *angrez log* are crafty") sometimes more daringly in verbs ("*sisking*" or "*burburred*"). The third device is changing the spelling of English words to suggest uneducated speech: "yus" for yes, "notus" for notice, "poole" for police, "Girmany" and "Amrika" for Germany and America. The third device is patently false, because an Indian writer writing in English *prima facie* accepts the unreality of the characters speaking in English, since the characters would not do so in real life. Since it is understood that their speech is being recreated in another language, distorting the spelling of English words contributes nothing to the effect of verisimilitude. Even the device of interpolating Hindi words seems to be an unfair short-cut towards the solution of a problem that is essentially complex.[71]

All these devices except the last one have been used in Arun Joshi's fiction. Joshi has not corrupted the spelling of words in the Indian way. He has, however, translated Indian idioms into English sometimes with their Hindi equivalents as well, such as "*Manti Ke Putaley*,"[72] "*Soney Ka Dil*,"[73] "*Pagal Mat Bano*,"[74] "*Baal Nahin Banka Hogaa*."[75] The uses of such expressions are hardly justified because the writing of a novel in English located in a tribal belt is itself an act of translation.

In perhaps all the novels of Arun Joshi, Indian words in italics have been used in the texts. Some of the examples taken from *The Strange Case of Billy Biswas* are those like "Dharma,"[76] "Aarati,"[77] "Dhoop,"[78] "Vilayati,"[79] etc. In *The Last Labyrinth* several

Indian words printed in italics are such as, "Mantrajaap,"[80] "Namaskaar,"[81] "Salaam."[82] The last example "Salaam" has also been used as a verb with the addition of -ed- inflexional suffix "salaamed." "Cow-dust hour"[83] is a literal translation of Indian expression "*Godhuli Bela.*"

The characters in Joshi's three earlier novels are highly educated in British or American Universities. As such, in their use of English there is no unreality. Arun Joshi seems to convince us that some of his characters talk in English. When Sheila clarifies why her family did not want Babu to marry an American because of the language problem, Sindi retorts:

> "We all know English; don't we?" I asked. "Even now we are speaking English; aren't we?"[84]

Joshi writes this to convince us that his educated characters talk in English. But this may not be the case with tribals in *The Strange Case of Billy Biswas* and the boatmen in *The City and the River.* In *The Strange Case of Billy Biswas* Meena Chatterjee "talked almost entirely in English in that unique, rather flat, accent that is to be found in young ladies taught in convents."[85] Billy Biswas has received his education both in England and America. The narrator informs Mr. Rele that he can very easily know Billy Biswas because "He speaks English with a very pronounced accent, a British accent."[86]

Billy and Sindi Oberoi might be educated in Britain but the author himself is educated in U.S.A. So are many of his characters. English might originally have been the native language of England, but it is now a native language in so many countries including the U.S.A. and as a second or foreign language it is used by more people in India than the number of native speakers in the U.K. With different national varieties of English, certain national typicalities have been associated with it.

The core of English in perhaps all the varieties is the same model of British English. But in certain lexical forms, uses and idioms and the intonation in spoken English, the national varieties have certain differences from one another.

Joshi' s use of English may be said to be a fusion of British English with American and Indian varieties. It would be useful here to refer to G.P. Sarma's opinion who classifies Indo-English writers into two categories, such as those who are "more Anglian than Indian and those who are more Indian than Anglian in style."[87] While the distinction between the two is highly discerning, it is perhaps not appropriate to include Arun Joshi as a writer who is more Anglian than Indian. G.P. Sarma writes:

> The language of the new writers like Nayantara Sahgal, Anita Desai and Arun Joshi is therefore Queen's English, always impeccable in grammar, syntax and idiom.[88]

To include Joshi among the members of the group is unconvincing because the linguistic influences upon Arun Joshi as a writer are of not only American English but also Indian besides the core of British English.

Arun Joshi might have acquired British English during the period of his education in India where in the past the British model was prescribed. But during his higher education in Engineering and Management in the U.S.A., Arun Joshi also acquired the mannerisms of American English which he has also used in his novels. In *The Strange Case of Billy Biswas,* writing about the Indian Ambassadress in the U.S.A., Joshi writes, "It was strange that her English was Americanized."[89] But it is rather strange that in the case of Joshi despite his education in the U.S.A., his English is not highly Americanized. There are, however, several instances of American and Indian variants in Joshi's use of the English language. In this context it should also be noted that there are more Indian variants than the American. The novels of Arun Joshi recreate the experiences of the Indian characters either abroad or in India. They have naturally in them terms of expressions typically Indian. Arun Joshi tells Sheela about her father's aborted wish that "he could talk to friends at the club about the foreign-returned son."[90] In *The Apprentice* the author makes Ratan Rathor express: "I have come to kill you, I declared and felt a great upliftment."[91] Both *foreign-returned* and *upliftment* are expressions used in Indian English. Joshi also uses occasionally expressions that may be called Indianisms. He drops the indefinite article in "he was *in fever*"[92] where it is required in British English. Moreover, the expression "Anuradha was not to be cowed down by threats"[93] is Indian English because "cowed down" is not acceptable either in British or American English. Likewise the case of "went to sleep"[94] is an example of Indianism because in this case the native speakers prefer "went to bed." Joshi's love for Americanism is also illustrated in certain of his usages. The narrator in *The Strange Case of Billy Biswas* says that he met Billy in New York "where for one brief summer we *roomed* together."[95] The italicised expression is an example of Americanism. The use of "gotten" in "what has gotten into you"[96] is also typically American.

Joshi is not a conservative in his usage. He uses certain informal varieties of English as well. He freely uses the accusative case of personal pronoun after *than* and the use of "to" for "than" with the comparative degree of adjectives as in "He was younger to me by five years and had seen little of the world."[97] Besides, he uses *who* for *whom* as in "all those who I had respected."[98] Sometimes his usage can be hardly justified as the use of "most" for two as in "she said, she had two but she liked one of them the most."[99] The usage of *like* as conjunction, as in "I had noticed Anuradha like one notices a monument,"[100] and "as also" *e.g.,* "exaggerating no doubt in the process the importance of his activities *as also* the position he had occupied in the movement,"[101] are accepted ones in contemporary English. Joshi uses some of the informal forms of words such as "amidst the drink and the *eats*"[102] as a plural noun.

Arun Joshi favours the formal use of the English language in his dialogues and narrative passages. He sometimes ignores even the basic rules of syntax and punctuation as in the following:

> From time to time I am asked why I write? Why I pick the themes that I pick and why I treat them in the manner that I do?[103]

The use of the sign of interrogation in the first sentence and the omission of *do* in the second and the third are clear indications in favour of Arun Joshi's use of informal variety of English.

The influences upon Arun Joshi are literary, philosophical and linguistic as discussed in the three preceding sections. The literary influences are much more those of American existentialist novelists as well as the French existentialist philosophers and writers. The philosophical influences are those of the Indian philosophies as well as the Occidental. Among the Occidental philosophers he is indebted directly or indirectly to the existentialists and among the Indian systems to the *Jnanayoga* and the *Karmayoga* of the *Bhagawad Gita*, the theory of the communion of the *Prakriti* and the *Purusha* in the Sankhya system as well as to something from the Vedanta and to that of the Gandhian idealism and its practice. The linguistic influences relate to the core varieties of British English along with British and American variations in the use of certain forms, vocabulary and idiom.

NOTES

1. *Report on Standards of University Education* (1965), v (Preface).
2. Arun Joshi, "Towards Finding an Expression," R.K. Dhawan (ed.) *The Fictional World of Arun Joshi* (New Delhi, 1986), 15.
3. Joshi 15.
4. Joshi 69-103.
5. Wordsworth, "The World is Too Much with Us," Line No. 10.
6. H.M. Prasad, *Arun Joshi* (New Delhi, 1985), 112.
7. G.S. Amur, "A New Parable," *Indian Literature*, No. 144, July-August, 1991, 153-54.
8. Amur 154.
9. Purabi Bannerji, "A Winner's Secrets: An Interview with Purabi Bannerji," *The Sunday Statesman*, 27 February, 1983, iv.
10. Albert Camus, *The Fall* (Penguin ed. 1972), 86-87.

11. V.V.N. Rajendra Prasad, *Five Indian Novelists* (New Delhi, 1990), 158.
12. R.K. Dhawan, *The Fictional World of Arun Joshi* (New Delhi, 1986), 17-18.
13. *The Strange Case of Billy Biswas* (New Delhi, 1987), 152. All the subsequent references are to this edition.
14. Ramesh K. Srivastava, "The Theme of Alienation in Arun Joshi's Novels" in *Six Indian Novelists in English* (Amritsar, 1987), 319.
15. *The Foreigner* (New Delhi, 1972), 84. All the subsequent references are to this edition.
16. *The Foreigner.*
17. Meenakshi Mukherjee, *Twice Born Fiction* (New Delhi, 1971), 132.
18. Mukherjee 203.
19. K.R. Srinivasa Iyengar, *Indian Writing in English* (New Delhi, 1984), 314.
20. *The Last Labyrinth* (New Delhi, 1981), 180. All the subsequent references are to this edition.
21. Hari Mohan Prasad, *Arun Joshi* (New Delhi, 1985), 112.
22. *Pears Encyclopaedia,* 1968-69 edition.
23. Margaret Chatterjee, *The Existentialist Outlook* (New Delhi, 1974), 4.
24. Chatterjee 4.
25. Quoted in *Pears Encyclopaedia,* 1968-69 edition.
26. T.S. Eliot, *Selected Prose,* ed. John Hayward (Penguin Edition, 1958), 194.
27. R.K. Dhawan, *The Fictional World of Arun Joshi* 19.
28. M.G. Hegde, "The Short Stories of Arun Joshi: A Study" in *The Novels of Arun Joshi,* edited R.K. Dhawan, New Delhi, 1992, 201.
29. A. Joshi, *The Survivor* (New Delhi, 1975), 21. All the subsequent references are to this edition.
30. Joshi 26-27.
31. Joshi 27.
32. Hegde 208.
33. *The Last Labyrinth* 178-79.
34. *The Last Labyrinth* 179.
35. *Ibid.*
36. *Ibid.*

37. *The Last Labyrinth* 132.
38. *Ibid.*
39. *The Last Labyrinth*, 26.
40. *Ibid.*
41. Susheel Kumar Sharma, "Philosophical Reverberations in *The Foreigner*" in *The Novels of Arun Joshi*, (ed.) R.K. Dhawan (New Delhi, 1992), 130.
42. *The Foreigner* 140.
43. *The Foreigner* 227.
44. *The Foreigner* 60.
45. *The Strange Case of Billy Biswas* 42.
46. *The City and the River* (New Delhi, 1990), 9. All the subsequent references are to this edition.
47. *The City and the River* 10.
48. *The Last Labyrinth* 48.
49. *The Foreigner* 204.
50. *The Foreigner* 239.
51. R.S. Pathak, "Human Predicament and Meaninglessness in Arun Joshi's Novels," in R.K. Dhawan (edited), *The Fictional World of Arun Joshi* (New Delhi, 1986), 132.
52. *The Foreigner* 113.
53. *The Foreigner* 180.
54. *The City and the River* 52.
55. *The City and the River* 262.
56. The blurb, quoted in.
57. *The Last Labyrinth* 77.
58. *The Last Labyrinth* 11.
59. *The Last Labyrinth* 108.
60. *The Last Labyrinth* 23.
61. *The Last Labyrinth* 20.
62. *The Last Labyrinth* 154.
63. *The Apprentice* (New Delhi, 1974), 9. All the subsequent references are to this edition.
64. *The Apprentice.*
65. *The Apprentice* 20.
66. *The Last Labyrinth* 16.

67. *The Last Labyrinth* 16.
68. *Ibid.*
69. *The Last Labyrinth*, 17.
70. *Ibid.*
71. Meenakshi Mukherjee, "Beyond the Village : An Aspect of Mulk Raj Anand," in M.K. Naik, S.K. Desai, G.S. Amur, *Critical Essays on Indian Writing in English* (New Delhi, 1977), 240-241.
72. *The Strange Case of Billy Biswas* 163.
73. *The Strange Case of Billy Biswas* 227.
74. *The Strange Case of Billy Biswas* 228.
75. *The Strange Case of Billy Biswas* 163.
76. *The Strange Case of Billy Biswas* 42.
77. *The Strange Case of Billy Biswas* 97.
78. *The Strange Case of Billy Biswas* 97.
79. *The Strange Case of Billy Biswas* 114.
80. *The Last Labyrinth* 104.
81. *The Last Labyrinth* 201.
82. *The Last Labyrinth* 52.
83. *The Strange Case of Billy Biswas* 99.
84. *The Foreigner* 60.
85. *The Strange Case of Billy Biswas* 37.
86. *The Strange Case of Billy Biswas* 212.
87. G.P. Sarma, *Nationalism in Indo-Anglian Fiction* (New Delhi, 1990), 238.
88. Sarma 251.
89. *The Strange Case of Billy Biswas* 75.
90. *The Foreigner* 59.
91. *The Apprentice* 33.
92. *The Apprentice* 105.
93. *The Last Labyrinth* 146.
94. *The Last Labyrinth* 114.
95. *The Strange Case of Billy Biswas* 8.
96. *The Last Labyrinth* 148.
97. *The Strange Case of Billy Biswas* 218.
98. *The Apprentice* 111.

99. *The Foreigner* 189.
100. *The Last Labyrinth* 12.
101. *The Apprentice* 59.
102. *The Last Labyrinth* 12.
103. A. Joshi, "Towards Finding an Expression" in R.K. Dhawan (ed.) *The Fictional World of Arun Joshi* (New Delhi, 1986), 15.

PART-II
Exposition

3

The World of Business and Personal Relationships in *The Foreigner* and *The Last Labyrinth*

I

The Foreigner (1968) and *The Last Labyrinth* (1981) are respectively the first and the fourth novel written by Arun Joshi. These two works have been grouped together for the simple reason that they deal with the world of business relationships as well as the personal. In both these novels, the crisis of the present and that of identity of the major characters have been analysed in depth.

Arun Joshi is a novelist of the younger generation to which, besides others, belong the two women novelists such as Nayantara Sahgal and Anita Desai. All these are interested in exploring the inner soul of the characters who are not only globe-trotters, but also persons living on "the lonely planet."[1] The heroes of both these novels are trained in the U.S.A., and they come back to India to work in industrial concerns. While Sindi Oberoi in *The Foreigner* gets employment in the Khemka concern, Som Bhaskar in *The Last Labyrinth* runs his own plastics industry. Their day-to-day lives are guided both by their existence in the world of their business and also as individuals.

The present chapter examines and analyses the nature of the plot and the characters of *The Foreigner* first and then that of *The Last Labyrinth* before correlating the fictional concerns of the two novels of Arun Joshi. *The Foreigner* is a novel in which Arun Joshi has discussed several aspects of life on this disturbed planet dealing with "love versus hate; action versus inaction; possessiveness versus renunciation"[2]—"man's perennial dilemmas."[3] Associated with these are the aspects dealing with the themes of alienation, the absurd, the sordidness and seediness of the human existence. All the fictional works of Arun Joshi delve deep into these problems. *The Foreigner,* being the first novel of the author, is a seminal work in the sense that the above problems find a more in-depth study of these than in the other works where also all these problems recur in some form or the other.

In an interview with Purabi Bannerji, Arun Joshi said about his limitations:

> Thematically I would not like to handle a novel about the academic world which I do not know about;...the world which I know well is the industrial world which has not so far been handled in a novel.[4]

These two statements by Arun Joshi are rather half-truths. There is enough evidence in his novels of his acquaintance with the academic world. Joshi keeps on referring to the academic problems in not only *The Foreigner* but in his other novels also. In *The Foreigner* there is a very suggestive analogy of the system of education prevailing in India and the U.S.A. Both Sindi Oberoi and Baburao Khemka had been to the U.S.A. to qualify themselves as engineers from the prestigious M.I.T. in Boston. But while Sindi Oberoi gets through it with flying colours, Babu gets ploughed. Incidentally, the author himself had been a student of this prestigious institution. In *The Last Labyrinth* as well Leila Sabnis is no mean scholar, though otherwise very permissive, being divorced by her husband because of her too much academic pursuits. Som's father was a scientist, researching on the First Cause. Billy Biswas, the eponymous hero of the novel *The Strange Case of Billy Biswas*, is an American-educated scholar, working as Professor of Anthropology in Delhi University before his escape into the primitive life with the aboriginals of the Satpura hills. *The Apprentice* has no academic pretensions, though it is very much present in the final work of fantasy, *The City and the River*. Thus to state that Joshi does not know about the academic world is economical with the truth. Secondly, Joshi's assertion regarding his familiarity with the industrial world which, according to him, has not so far been handled in a novel, is also a half-truth. The heroes of both *The Foreigner* and *The Last Labyrinth* are engrossed in industrial relationships and, especially in *The Foreigner*, industrial problems have also been mentioned and solved. Among other themes, *The Foreigner* and *The Last Labyrinth* also deal with the problems related to the academic and the industrial world and hence an attempt has been made to study these together.

The plot of *The Foreigner* has been unfolded from the viewpoint of the omniscient protagonist narrator. Though Sindi Oberoi states very humbly, "I am not very good at remembering events, but for some reason I always remember the beginning and end of an affair,"[5] he is above all a good narrator and succeeds in communicating the very minute details of his life of both personal and business relationships. As Harish Raizada points out, "The narrative follows flash-ahead and flash-back technique."[6] The narrative, as R.K. Dhawan writes, "keeps moving from the recent past in Boston to the present in Delhi."[7]

The fictional plot of *The Foreigner* covers the locale of four continents—Africa, Europe, America and Asia. Sindi Oberoi is closely associated with all these geographical regions. The novel opens like a thriller in depicting the mutilated dead body of Baburao Khemka, son of a leading industrialist of Delhi. The scene is located in Boston. But it soon shifts over to New Delhi and then again to different continents in flash-back where Sindi

Oberoi had stayed in the course of his early life, education and profession.

Sindi Oberoi's life is a study in rootlessness. He is hardly Indian and this fact keeps on haunting him. His mother was an English woman and father a Kenyan-Indian. Thus he is a child of mixed parentage. Both his parents, settled in Nairobi, died early in an air-crash near Cairo. Being orphaned, he is brought up by his uncle, also settled in Kenya. Though Sindi had never to suffer the pangs of poverty, he felt starved of the parental love and on many occasions was compelled to think of the absurdity of his existence. Nevertheless his is a fit case of the lost childhood. Graham Greene wrote an opening essay under this title in his *The Lost Childhood and other Essays* (1951) which he has also used as the opening essay in his *Collected Essays*. Greene in his own turn has borrowed the expression from A.E. Russell's poem "The Germinal":

> In the lost childhood of Judas
> Christ was betrayed.[8]

Sindi too had lost childhood because of the death of his parents in his infancy. Being a product of a hybrid culture, and his education in Kenya, London, Boston and New York, cut him off from his racial roots. As he grows older, he is haunted by the gnawing sense of his rootlessness. He is always aware of the fact that he belongs to no culture and cannot confidently call himself either a Kenyan or an Indian. He is fed up with telling people of how his parents died in an air-crash and how he was brought up by his uncle. It is not that his uncle ignored his education but that it was the inner soul of Sindi Oberoi that always kept him in turmoils. The more he kept on flirting with the English ladies and American girls, the more conscious he became of his futile existence which sometimes even seemed to engulf the lonely planet. In this respect Sindi Oberoi has some affinity with Scobie, the Police Commissioner of the Gold Coast in Graham Greene's *The Heart of the Matter*. Though Scobie is not rootless, his abnormal sense of pity makes him think of the misery of the world, even of the heavenly bodies. Scobie sometimes thinks:

> What an absurd thing it was to expect happiness in a world so full of miseries?[9]

He thinks:

> Point me out the happy man and I will point you out either egotism, evil—or else an absolute ignorance.[10]

Moreover, he ruminates:

> If one knew, he wondered, the facts would one have to feel pity even for the planets? if one reached what they called the heart of the matter?[11]

Sindi Oberoi, too, thinks of the lonely planet, and the sense of pity and frustration also engulfs him. The heart of the matter with him is that he feels a foreigner wherever he goes and this is more psychological than physical.

Arun Joshi quotes certain lines from T.S. Eliot's *The Love Song of J. Alfred Prufrock*:

> And indeed there will be time
> To wonder, "Do I dare?" "Do I dare?"
> Time to turn back and descend the stair.[12]

Sindi Oberoi too is tossed up in his life of indecisions and rootlessness. The themes in Eliot's *Prufrock* are as various as "contrary pairs—youth and old age, work and idleness, spiritual life and death, commitment and indecisions, dreams and actuality, action and analysis, courage and fear, personal needs and social obligations, communion and loneliness, pride and disgust in the self, sincerity and hypocrisy, interest and boredom."[13] As Prufrock is an archetypal Everyman, the creation of the character of Sindi Oberoi is an evidence of Joshi's "contemporary sensibility etching out the inner wasteland of the archetypal modern Everyman."[14] The same scholar comments further that *The Foreigner* "takes us to the lower depths of human suffering and the inferno of existential agony."[15] The crisis of identity faced by the major characters in *The Foreigner* as also in the other novels of Arun Joshi has also some continental influences. Like the heroes of Camus, Sindi Oberoi in *The Foreigner* is involved in the crisis of the present. Sindi is devoid of emotion like Meursault in *The Outsider* by Camus. Arun Joshi has expressed indebtedness to the works by Albert Camus and Sartre:

> I did read Camus and Sartre, I liked *The Plague* and read *The Outsider*. I might have been influenced by them.[16]

The crisis of identity in the major characters of *The Foreigner* has been explored at various levels such as the cross-cultural, racial, national, international, individual, interpersonal, industrial and business relationships. There are various aspects of the plot, characterization and their interpretations. *The Foreigner*, as Dr. Mohan Jha writes,

> may as well be interpreted as a satire on man's exploitation by man in free India, on the corruptions corroding our social fabric, our population explosion and overcrowding in India, amidst poverty and hunger and disease and on the denial of rights to people in spite of our declared democratic and socialistic polity.[17]

While this is an accurate analysis of the situation present in the novel, thematically, too, the novel deals with different aspects on the basis of which the novel should be interpreted. To quote the same critic again:

> This novel may, by turns, be considered as a love-story, as a literary representation of rootlessness, or as an artistic triumph that unifies feelings and ideas, characters and events, the prose and the passion of life into an articulate whole.[18]

But all these interpretations of the plot, structure and theme emerge when we analyse the different episodes that make up the plot of the novel. Joshi's novels have not so much to convey at the level of the plot than at the psychological portraiture of character. The crisis of the present that has been projected in *The Foreigner* is not only faced by the protagonist, Sindi Oberoi, but also by the other characters who come in his contact. The crisis of identity dealt with in *The Foreigner* is mainly at the socio-psychological level. One of the main issues of crisis depicted in it is racial. This issue has been marginally touched upon in the episodes related to the reception to Indian students given by the Americans especially that at the International Students' Association. It is all a shallow formality:

> It was intended to bring foreigner in contact with Americans, but all it ever achieved was animosity; everybody ended up hating the Americans all the more. I don't know why it happened. It was not that the Americans showed off or misbehaved or anything. As a matter of fact they all were very courteous. Yet, something about it—a feeling that it was a bit of a charity or something—rubbed people the wrong way.[19]

Sindi also feels the pangs of the racial discrimination. He says, "Born an Indian, I had been spat upon; had I been a European, I would have done the spitting. What difference does it make? I would still die and be forgotten by the world. And spitting had not made the world's big shots any happier than we were."[20]

Sindi Oberoi is always faced with the crisis of his identity and quest for a solution which he gets in the end at the suggestion given to him by a low-paid employee, Muthu, of the firm. We have already hinted at the strain of lost childhood responsible for Sindi's psychological make-up. He feels a kind of rootlessness because of the fact that his hybrid birth did not place him anywhere. He did not receive the love of English mother and Kenyan-Indian father beyond the age of four when he hardly knew them and remembered them only through "a couple of wrinkled and cracked photographs."[21] He was deeply pained when people used to ask him about his parents. Mr. Khemka also posed him the same question when he visited him at Delhi after Babu's death. Sindi says, "I hated to talk about my parents. I hated the pity I got from people."[22] He had to repeat the episode of the death of his parents in an air-crash "for the hundredth time."[23] Sindi's life under his uncle in Kenya and his schooling there followed by his further studies in England and lastly in America made him all the more distanced from his roots, identity and a meaningful quest of life.

Sindi's crisis of identity rests in his soul. It has nothing to do with the geographical chasm. He feels himself a foreigner in Kenya, London, Boston and New Delhi. His American girlfriend, June Blyth, is the first one to point out to him of his being obsessed with the foreign complex:

> There is something strange about you, you know something distant. I'd guess that when people are with you, they don't feel like they're human beings. May be it's an Indian characteristic, but I have a feeling you'd be foreigner anywhere.[24]

In New Delhi also he is no different. Sheila tells him frankly "You are still a foreigner. You don't belong here."[25] When Babu in America accuses him of his ignorance of Hindu family in that "he was a perfect example of an Indian who pretended to be a foreigner and behaved as one."[26] Even Sindi hesitates in calling himself a Hindu. When June Blyth asks him whether as a Hindu he believes in God:

> Anyway I can't really be called a Hindu. My mother was English and my father, I am told, a sceptic. That does not seem like a good beginning for a Hindu. Does it?[27]

An asthmatic patient, Sindi Oberoi runs after seeking the pleasures of the flesh wherever he goes. But he dare not marry anyone as he feels himself "not really cut out for marriage."[28] Sindi considers life just meaningless and "death wipes out everything for most of us anyway. All that is left is a big mocking zero."[29] He considers his life to be a wasted one. Sindi thinks:

> My fifth Christmas on these alien shores. And yet all shores are alien when you don't belong anywhere. Twenty-fifth Christmas on this planet. Twenty-five years largely wasted in search of wrong things in wrong places. Twenty-five years gone in the search of peace and what

> did I have to show for achievement: a ten-stone body that had to be fed four times a day, twenty-eight times a week. This was a sum of lifetime of striving.[30]

He even speaks of the shocking absurdity of existence:

> Somebody had begotten me without a purpose and so far I lived without a purpose, unless, you could call the search for peace a purpose. Perhaps I felt like that because I was a foreigner in America. But then what difference could it have made for that matter? It seemed to me that I would still be a foreigner. My foreignness lay within me and I could not leave myself behind wherever I went.[31]

In his angst and ennui he thinks that he "existed only for dying."[32] Once he tells his uncle, "I was contemplating suicide since I was tired of living."[33] He convinces his uncle that his life in Nairobi had virtually ended; and consequently he leaves for London with no plans in mind except that he has to study engineering. He gets for sometime a strange sense of freedom to know the meaning of life. To compensate for his lack of experience he takes up certain jobs—first an evening job of a dish-washer in a nightclub in Soho where he meets Anna and has affairs with her. Later on he meets Cathy who after certain affairs with him for sometime goes back to live with her husband. Sindi also works for sometime in a library in a small village where he discusses religion, God and mysticism with a Catholic priest. Yet he is never satisfied:

> All love—whether of things, persons or oneself—was illusion and all pain sprang from this illusion. Love begot greed and attachment and it led to possession.[34]

It is from Scotland that Sindi goes to Boston to study Engineering at the MIT. It is here that he comes in contact with June Blyth whom Baburao Khemka also loves later on his arrival in Boston. Even his love for June Blyth is streaked with hatred and anger.

> And every passing day my love fell upon my anger and both grew stronger. It was as if two high voltage electrodes had taken root in my head and each of them kept splitting

> venom into my brain. The strain grew so great that I almost lost all ability to think logically for any length of time. Often I suspected I was going mad.[35]

It is rightly for all these that Meenakshi Mukherjee calls Sindi "a perennial outsider."[36] Even Sindi Oberoi is aware of all these. He tells Mr. Khemka in clear terms of the difference between the two:

> You had a clear-cut system of morality, a caste system that laid down all you had to do. You had a God—you had roots in the soil you lived upon. Look at me. I have no roots. I have no system of morality. What does it mean to me if you call me an immoral man.... I don't even have a reason to live.[37]

Sindi Oberoi is fed up with "the randomness of existence"[38] and does not accept the offer of a job at the MIT. He wants to go back to Nigeria or India which also is decided by "the flip of a coin."[39]:

> Head for Nigeria, I said.
> The coin showed tails. New Delhi.[40]

It is this which changes the course of his life and he comes first to New Delhi, the land from where his forefathers had settled in Kenya.

Sindi never feels at home during his stay either in the U.K. or U.S. At Boston the episode with June Blyth is also marked by her feeling of emptiness all the time. After Babu reaches Boston, June is closer to him because Sindi does not find himself cut out for marriage. June's separation from him makes him realize that she had become a part of him. "It was as if somebody had given me a big dose of anaesthesia."[41] And that their "separation had been like an unforeseen abortion."[42] His professor found him lost and though Sindi was offered a teaching assignment on the faculty, he did not accept it and shifts to New York for an assignment where he develops with his team "a machine that will throw twenty thousand people out of work and make them feel so small that they would go home dead drunk."[43] In his inner crisis Sindi finds the past haunting him like a ghost, yet as he says, "Like a castrated bull I returned to the yoke of everyday life for whatever it was worth."[44] The tragedy with Babu and later on with June Blyth is all due to Sindi's wrong notion of detachment. Babu drives himself to his death after learning that Sindi too had been June's lover. June died in the act of abortion of the foetus that was Babu's. All these deals make Sindi lost in the phantom of his past. Sindi's initial life in New Delhi also is one of chasm. Though he accepts a job in Mr. Khemka's factory, he does not see eye to eye with him. Mr. Khemka "is a modern Maharaja"[45] who makes electric kettles. He has three houses in New Delhi and a villa in Mussoorie and he earns thirty thousand per day, while the daily wage-earners in his factory get only three rupees per day. There is a chasm of misunderstanding between him and his employees. There was a reign of servility syndrome in his office and works. His employees looked upon both Mr. Khemka and his daughter with "the mortal dread."[46] Sindi narrates:

> The workers cringed before them as if the man and his daughter were malevolent spirits whose curse could be all-consuming. My life had carried me through strange places and I had seen men act from the end of the tethers but the servility I came across in Khemka's office is quite new to me.[47]

Khemka has only one end of his life to build an empire by flouting the company and tax laws which in the end puts him behind bars and factory under lock-out. Even Sindi has plans to leave it to get a new job either in Calcutta or Bombay but at the intervention of Muthu, Sindi becomes aware of his meaningful existence. It is this low-paid employee who teaches him the positive meaning of life that "sometimes detachment lies in actually getting involved."[48] It is this message that clicks him and he surrenders himself wholeheartedly to reviving the factory with close affinity with Sheila, Babu's sister. And he even changes his name from "Surinder Oberoi to Surrender Oberoi."[49] Thus at last he is able to emerge out of the crisis of the identity and gets a new motivation on his being aware of the true meaning of life which he derives from the philosophy of *the Bhagawad Gita.*

The Khemka household may be stinking rich, but it, too, is not immune from the crisis of existence. The Khemka household stands for life of affluence with the money earned by the sweat of the brow of workers leading a subhuman existence. He is a man of the world and has around him only successful men. The parties that he throws regularly, are attended by the people of his sort. He, however, talks "so sweetly, so disarmingly"[50] with Sindi Oberoi that he could hardly refuse anything he asked for. He had himself been to America to sign a collaboration agreement for the manufacture of air-conditioners and was proud of the deal because "ours would be the first air-conditioner plant in the country."[51]

Mr. Khemka is very strict. His son Babu has been brought up under his strict supervision. But Babu too had experienced a lost childhood because there is no mention in the novel about the mother. Thus being devoid of the love of one of the parents and having been brought up under the strict supervision of his father, his instincts had been suppressed. It is for this reason that in the U.S. he experiences unfettered freedom and begins flirting around with American girls. He makes it clear to Sindi Oberoi "What's the good of coming to America if one is not to play around with girls."[52] Babu is sent to America to be an engineer and after coming back with a degree to India to manage his factories, but all this remains a dream.

Sindi had been there at the M.I.T. much before Babu's admission and, therefore, he was active in receiving Babu at the airport and in the reception to newcomers hosted by the International Students' Association. Sindi could sense "something eerie about Babu."[53] He had lack of experience and it was his innocence that brought about the crisis of his life. At

New Delhi Sindi cannot reconcile himself to the manner in which he is received at the Khemka household. They knew him through Babu's letters and it was he that had cabled the news of Baub's death in car-crash. Despite it all, they greeted him with a calm resignation with no sign of grief and offered him drinks. Sheila, moreover, kept on pestering him to tell her of Babu's affairs in Boston. He had written about a few of them to her but not to his father.

Babu failed all his exams at the M.I.T. and was removed from it. He then applied in about two dozen engineering institutions for his admission. He was never serious with his studies; and incidentally he compared the American system of education with the Indian. In India he could be serious at the time of the end-of-the-term examination and pass it, whereas in America he had to be serious from the beginning itself as teaching and testing went together. He wrote of it to his sister Sheila. Babu was conscious of his shortcomings, especially in failing his examinations and in his belying the hope of his father. He plans his marriage with June Blyth but postpones it fearing what his father might say. Meanwhile when he learns that June had also been in love with Sindi, in his tense mood and reckless driving he puts an end to his life.

Sheila, Babu's sister, is very harsh with June and she calls her "a harlot and a witch,"[54] who laid snares for her brother. It is Sindi who points out to her "that codes of morality differ from country to country. Girls do certain things in America, women never do here."[55] When she insists that June had never been a virgin, Sindi retorts her, "So you think one of these Marwari girls is really superior merely because of a silly membrane between her legs."[56] He even accuses Mr. Khemka who wanted to marry Babu to a fat Marwari girl in which dowry might bring him half a dozen new factories.[57]

Sindi analyses the genuine point in the character of Babu that caused a crisis of his identity which he could not face or solve:

> It was his innocence that killed him, Sheila. Innocence concocted by you and his father. He lived in a world of dreams, in a world with sculpture in drawing-rooms. In the end, the hard facts of life prove stronger than his flimsy world of dreams. His death could have been heroic. But the pity of it was that even the dreams were not his own. They were products of the turbid flotsam of a rotten social class he was supposed to perpetuate.[58]

Sindi may be confused in personal life, though not in the academic, yet he has been able to identify the root cause of Babu's tragedy in America. It is for his immaturity and innocence that Babu gets ready to give up his Indian roots where he may not be accepted with his American wife. Babu thinks America to be a wonderful country and says, "I would never go back to India if I had a choice."[59] He is afraid, his father could never agree to his marrying an American, because he is a terrible sort of a father and also orthodox, though sister is comparatively very progressive. Babu sometimes wishes to have "been born in America. Not that I have anything against India but there is nothing to beat America."[60] There was a strange contradiction in Babu's character: "On the one hand he loved his father, on the other he was mortally afraid of him."[61] Sindi realizes later after seeing him:

> Mr. Khemka, I suppose, is one of those fastidious persons who are so often found among big people. He was clever and successful and he seemed to expect everybody whom he loved, to be clever and successful. And if they failed he became so emotionally involved that he destroyed what little capability they had. That, I suppose, had happened to Babu.[62]

He did not even know his father and sister. He blows hot and cold about him and says that far from being afraid of his father, he had deep respect for him. About his sister he says that "she is very broadminded and all."[63] Even June comments to Sindi about Babu's father that he "seems to be an awful bully,"[64] because after receiving a letter from him Babu used to get worried. June analyses that matters with Babu would have been much simpler if father "were not there in the background, sending long sermons of telling him what's wrong with him and how he should carry himself."[65] June too gets disillusioned with Babu for his strange behaviour in postponing the marriage and in not having the courage to bear that before him some other could have also loved June. All these drive Babu to the edge of a breakdown. He sometimes even tries to domineer over June by referring to his father's property. Sindi, too, feels responsible for Babu's death. It is his detachment that causes all this:

> All along I had acted out of greed, selfishness and vanity and had heard nobody very much. When I had come close to gaining through detachment and had acted out of goodness, I had driven a man to his death.[66]

The sight of Babu's mutilated dead body in the morgue left him a broken man and later on that of June's death in abortion.

There are a few characters in *The Foreigner* who are not alienated from something or the other. While it is in the make-up of Sindi Oberoi who is a bundle of contradictions in being "cynic,"[67] "an eternal joker,"[68] "saint,"[69] "a sage,"[70] "a honey-brown Indian"[71] who goes on betraying his anxiety, loneliness, emptiness, absurdity and misplaced detachment as a lost individual. His Austrian room-mate Karl also feels the void within: "To all appearances he seemed to have abandoned his homeland."[72] He was always terribly hungry for one thing after the war. As he says, "Then I hated the way my step-mother brought lovers home after my father died. And one day when she got drunk and tried to seduce me, I left."[73] Karl has harrowing experiences of the war and as such no philosophy is anodyne to him. He talks with his friend Arun on the problem of freedom and non-cooperation and believes that under a foreign rule "despite everything you lose your freedom all the same."[74] But his friend Arun tells him that there is no question of losing freedom when it is never present:

> All freedom is illusion. You had no choice in your birth nor do you even choose your death.[75]

To this June Blyth intervenes:

> "But you can always choose your death. You can always kill yourself."
>
> "That is not freedom, it only shows the lack of it. Suicide is the end of a battered old road not the beginning of a new one."
>
> "If everything is beyond control, then how do you suppose you live from day to day."
>
> Arun said dreamily, "Random events happen around you, forcing you to make decisions, propelling you on through life. It is only vanity that makes us imagine that we are leading our own destiny."[76]

All this is in the mode of stock-opinions of existentialist philosophers and writers who have had their influences upon the authorial voice of Arun Joshi.

II

The Last Labyrinth is a quest for meaning in life. The narrative, located mainly in Bombay and Benares, is an account of Bhaskar's business deals and love-story. Running alongside is Bhaskar's crisis of identity.

Like *The Foreigner, The Last Labyrinth* is also concerned with both the business and personal relationships. In *The Foreigner* the world of business relationships is marginal to the hero of the novel. Sindi Oberoi is an engineer by profession who has to manage Mr. Khemka's business. But Som Bhaskar in *The Last Labyrinth* is himself a businessman. At the age of twenty-five he has amassed a huge fortune and everything that is needed for worldly success. He is highly educated in the world's most famous universities. His wife, Gita, is well-bred, beautiful and trusting and remains loyal to husband despite his erratic love-affairs with Leila Sabnis in Bombay and Anuradha in Benares. Som Bhaskar is descended from a very intellectual father who was professionally a scientist interested in solving the problem of the First Cause. He spent over a quarter of a million on his son's education in the prestigious American institutions. Som Bhaskar writes a research paper on Pascal at Harvard. He is also deeply aware of the philosophical implications of the teachings of Krishna and sermons of the Buddha at Sarnath. Though he also runs after material prosperity, his attitude to it is rather cynical. His concern as an industrialist is to grab failing industries to add to his empire. He thinks cynically, "that money was dirt, whore. So were houses, cars, carpets."[77] In his personal life he is a seeker after pleasure and hungers for the joys of life. In both the worlds of business and love he explores possibilities of new experience. But his indulgences have also an inner contradiction in that the more he runs after the material needs and sensual pleasure, the more dissatisfied he becomes with his existence and cries, "It is the voids of the world, more than its objects that bother me."[78] Yet he is always haunted by an insatiable cry of "I want, I want, I want."[79]

Leila Sabnis is herself a philosopher and psychologist and a polyglot, divorced by her executive husband for her reading too much. She has rightly analysed the character of Som Bhaskar when she refers to his problem of identity. Som Bhaskar gets engulfed in the following conversation:

> "I didn't think problems of identity existed for people of my age."
>
> "You would be surprised. There are people whose sense of identity at the end of life doesn't go beyond: I own this house; earn so much; have four children; drive this car; have so much in the bank and so on. Maybe such identity is not enough for you."
>
> "I don't see why not."
>
> "I suppose you can't take your identity from your caste."
>
> "What caste?"
>
> "You are a brahmin, after all."

> "A Bhaskar, what is a Bhaskar doing in business?"
>
> A pain, as physical as of a wound, shot through me every time I thought of Anuradha or heard her name. Leila said:
>
> "Or, may be the identity of an extended joint family." I kept quiet, sipping coffee, thinking vaguely of ill-defined things. Leila meant well but she was always seeking explanations, immediately, fiercely. She could be a pain in the neck.
>
> We went on like this for another half hour.
>
> "Or, maybe," she was saying, "maybe what you want is a mystical identification, identification with a godhead, as most Hindus want, sooner or later."
>
> I want no such thing.
>
> "You haven't got the stamina for that, I know, you haven't got the faith. You have always been a sceptic. You always will be."[80]

All that is clear from this dialogue is that Som Bhaskar is little aware of the problem of his identity and if he has any, he does not go beyond his being attached with his business, his inheritance and the family. But the identification is more at the level of the inner personality than the outer. Som denies having any quest of his for mystical identification as a Hindu.

Som Bhaskar psychoanalyses his own character in the context of his family background and his upbringing. His father was perturbed by the perennial questions of science and philosophy regarding the First Cause and this gave father melancholia. His grandfather had been a contrast to his father. The former had been "a man-about-town, gourmet, fond of women and drink."[81] Som Bhaskar reminisces "anything to do with God embarrassed him."[82] But Som's father was unlike his (Som's) grandfather:

> He knew things beyond anything grandfather could imagine. Was it his knowledge, then, a knowledge of verities sparsely known among ordinary men, that had pushed him over the brink, had convinced him that there

> were no verities at all? And where did I fit in? I was a womanizer all right, and a boozer, but my womanizing and boozing had not settled anything. I had inherited the afflictions of both of them—for what were they if not afflictions, afflictions that had let us into unbearable entanglements.[83]

In business life Som has little of his father's character. His mother died of cancer when he was just fifteen. She relied more upon Krishna than drugs for cure. His father too did not live long after Som established himself in business. Som is neither devout like his mother nor inquisitive like his father. The quest for the unknown labyrinths touches him in his associations with Anuradha and Gargi. He suffers from certain contradictions of his life and seeks someone to resolve them. He is in lookout for an escape and a safety-valve. It is with this motive that he comes in contact with two ladies, Leila Sabnis, and Anuradha at Aftab's Lal Haveli in Benares. The two ladies are contrasted ones. Like Som Bhaskar himself Leila Sabnis too is well-trained in philosophy and psychology. She had been a student of both Descartes and Freud. She says:

> She had ideas of her own that she catapulted with singular ferocity, charging them with the electricity of brain. You couldn't say she hadn't worked at her thoughts. She had slogged. She had studied and understood and memorized. Oh yes, Leila Sabnis knew a lot. Even if she had experienced little and suffered even less.[84]

She was a polyglot who knew a number of languages from the East and the West, such as Marathi, Sanskrit, French, German besides Hindi and Tamil. Her husband, an executive in an oil company, divorced her for reading too much. Freud in her library "was bearded and saintly, indefatigable groping in the night of man's mind, strewn with piss and excreta."[85] She had an M.A. and Ph.D. degrees from Michigan and some other degree also from London. Yet she realized that Michigan "was crumbling; the West itself was crumbling."[86] Yet Leila Sabnis is to Som

Bhaskar, "a muddled creature. As muddled as me. Muddled by her ancestry, by marriage, by divorce, by too many books."[87] Leila Sabnis has an obsession with explanations like Som's father. She is an analyst. As a psychologist she psychoanalyses Som Bhaskar's character as follows: "You are much too high strung. Without reason. You are a neurotic. A compulsive fornicator."[88] Though she prescribes Som Bhaskar to read the philosophy of Descartes, she is not impressed by his philosophy because he kept the two worlds of matter and spirit separate. Som's encounter with Leila Sabnis fills in his erotic urges, but beyond this he does not learn anything else to fill in the voids of his personality. His next encounter with Anuradha becomes a kind of an obsession and has an abiding influence upon him. Som sees her at a Delhi hotel at a party hosted by Aftab Rai for the Plastic Manufacturers' Association. Som Bhaskar is by then thirty-five. He finds himself attracted by her magnetism. She is a symbol of antique beauty. The demon of love so overpowers him that he visits Aftab's Lal Haveli in Benares. This mansion is built like a labyrinth which is a central symbol of life and death in the novel. In the words of Gabrial Josipovici, "from the cunning passages, contrived corridors and issues of 'Gerontian,' through the mazes of Kafka, Proust, Borges and Robbe Grillet, the labyrinth has been the favourite image of modern literature."[89] Many of the post-modern writers of the East and the West have used in their works the metaphor of the labyrinth. Joshi too, who is fond of it, has used this image several times before *The Last Labyrinth* where it is a central symbol. The structure of Lal Haveli is a maze within a maze in the maze-like structure of the city of Benares.

Aftab Rai's family has a great ancestry. His great-grandfather had been a courtier of Wazid Ali Shah and after the mutiny he settled in Benares where Lal Haveli was erected. Aftab Rai is a man of culture arid refinement. He is more rooted in the Oriental culture than western. He has also in him both business instinct and finer feelings of life. He lives with Anuradha as man and wife, but does not claim any possession of her.

Anuradha's history is a variegated one. She was born in Biharsharif of an insane mother who earned her livelihood by singing for her customers. She (Anuradha's mother) was once taken away by one of her customers who killed her in his drunken state with a broken whisky bottle. Anuradha, known in her childhood as Meera, was brought up and educated by one of her aunts. She suffered many humiliating experiences. As a child also she was sexually abused and as such she experienced many moments of privation. She joined the film world where also she was seduced by her producers. It was Aftab Rai who extricated her from the film-world and gave her an honourable place in his Lal Haveli though they were not married. Though to Som Bhaskar, "it seemed a pity that she should be nobody's wife,"[90] Anuradha was proud of her indiscriminate status: "It is better not to be anybody's wife...you can't marry everyone you love. So why marry anyone at all."[91] This is very amazing to Som Bhaskar whom Anuradha says, moreover: "I can imagine I am married to Aftab. I can imagine I am married to you. My mother used to imagine she was married to Krishna."[92] One of the reasons why her mother had been killed by her lover might be that she refused to marry him on her logic that she was married to Krishna.

Som Bhaskar considers everything about Lal Haveli to be enigmatic. Like the building, the persons and places also become symbols in *The Last Labyrinth.* This has been a very favourite device with some of the English novelists such as Emile Bronte in *Wuthering Heights* and E.M. Forster in his novels especially *Howards End* and *A Passage to India.* To Som Bhaskar, not only the Lal Haveli but also the streets and the bank of the Ganga in Benares and inhabitants of the maize-like structure become labyrinthine. Anuradha is as mysterious to him as her sudden disappearance from Lal Haveli.

Aftab Rai once takes Som Bhaskar to the other side of the Ganga where in a lonely cottage he is introduced to Gargi who is deaf and mute and communicates by writing on her pad. She is a forty-year-old ascetic woman. Her father was a prince who later became a Sufi Pir who used to live with Aftab's father. He had also supernormal powers and restored eyesight to Aftab but Som Bhaskar did not believe in it. Anuradha even admonishes him for it, "You are wrong about many things. You are wrong even about yourself. You think you know a lot, when, in fact, you don't."[93]

Som Bhaskar hungers for possessing not only Anuradha for ever from Aftab Rai but also to acquire his shares in the plastics market. Anuradha is in the beginning indifferent to Som's offer of love, but in his next visit to Benares he finds Anuradha by his bedside at night in the Lal Haveli and she acquiesces to him. Som develops a kind of obsession for her and to obviate it he tours Europe, America and Japan with his wife but this too does not remove Anuradha from his mind. He seeks the blessings of Gargi in Benares who encourages him by saying, "God will send you someone to help... someone who has known suffering."[94] She also asks Som not to quarrel with Anuradha because "she is your *Shakti.*"[95] He also realizes that Anuradha is indispensable to him and keeps on visiting Lal Haveli for her sake and enjoys "the nourishment of the shades thrown by her naked body under the chromatic shower."[96]

In his hectic business life in Bombay Som suffers a massive heart attack. On his mysterious recovery from it he contacts Anuradha who expresses her inability to see him any more. This infuriates Som Bhaskar who gets determined to take revenge on her and Aftab by ruining the latter's business. He buys not only all the shares of Aftab but also employs private detectives to gather information regarding the shares transferred to Anuradha by Aftab's father.

It is in this context that Som Bhaskar, accompanied by his doctor friend Kashyap, goes to a high mountain to visit the temple of Krishna to acquire the shares of Anuradha. Som risks his life in ascending the high altitude of the mountain where the temple is situated. To his surprise, he sees Gargi at the temple.

It is through her words that Dr. K. learns how Som survived his massive heart attack when medical science had given up all hope for his survival. Anuradha went to Gargi after Som had suffered a heart attack. Dr. K. reports:

> She [Anuradha] begged you to save him. He laughed her away saying he was in good hands and what could you do that the doctors could not. You said you could not perform miracles. Anuradha persisted, wept, begged and threatened. She said to you she could not live without Som and she would eat poison if something happened to him. She said your father had given Aftab his eyesight so why could you not save Som's life. She said she would not go home until you did something for Som.[97]

Gargi in the end agrees to do the miracle on the condition that Anuradha would give up Som for ever. This intrigues Som Bhaskar who is still after her shares to settle a score with her because she had deserted him. Som tells it frankly to Gargi "In the absence of evidence I intend to challenge the whole thing: I want to take not only the shares but also Anuradha. It scares me but I have no choice."[98] Gargi advises Som against it and writes on her pad, "God does not work in the simple manner, God does not seek revenge,"[99] and completes the next sentence by looking up a Hindi-English dictionary, "man's vanity (*ahankar*) brings him revenge enough."[100] Som denies being vain to Gargi and out of curiosity he wants to take away Gargi's share with him. Yet Som searches for Anuradha in Lal Haveli where Aftab advises him against it:

> You don't understand us. You work by logic. By your brain. You are proud of your education or what you consider education. There is an understanding that only suffering and humiliation bring. Anuradha has that. Even I have a bit of it. You are empty of that understanding.[101]

Yet Aftab allows Som to see Anuradha who advises him to leave Lal Haveli for his safety. He acts up to her advice for his night stay but again comes back in the morning to see her, but he is bewildered to find her absent from Lal Haveli and even takes police help to rescue her but they also fail. Anuradha's disappearance is a mystery. Though it may be a ploy to separate the two, Gargi had done the miracle of saving Som's life on the condition that she would never see him. Som Bhaskar comes back disappointed to Bombay where he sees Tarakki, Aftab's driver who used to kill snakes at Lal Haveli. Aftab had once written about him to Som Bhaskar that Tarakki was a snake. Aftab's letter is full of his inner anguish due to Anuradha's disappearance and he too vows revenge upon Som and curses him, "While you live you will rot.... When dead you shall not find peace... from one graveyard to another you will wander... a million years."[102] When Som gets confirmed of the presence of Tarakki in Bombay with some evil designs against his life, both Aftab and Som experience "this terrible, terrible, hatred in common."[103] It is thereafter that "like a curse I carry my grandfather's gun whenever I go,"[104] Som's life becomes a big mess and strange mad thoughts carom around his skull. In one of his frenzied outbursts he reflects:

> Anuradha, listen. Listen to me wherever you are. Is there a God where you are? Have you met Him? Does He have a face? Does He speak? Does He hear? Does He understand the language that we speak?[105]

The opening sentence of the novel hints the revenge motive in Som Bhaskar, "Above all I have a score to settle. Forget nothing, forgive no one."[106] But instead of acting against Aftab, he acts against himself and taking his grandfather's revolver from the cabinet he takes it casually to his temple. His wife Geeta prevents it from getting fired, "shaking me gently as though rousing a man from sleep."[107]

The case of Som Bhaskar, according to Dr. H.M. Prasad, is that of "the crisis of consciousness."[108] According to the same critic Bhaskar is:

> a modern anti-hero embodying chaos and uncertainty. He possesses a Pascalian passion to know, and perhaps

> to believe, but he cannot believe, and torn by doubts he walks tight-roped between life and death, illusion and reality, body and spirit. He suffers from an undefinable hunger, restlessness, a Hamlet-like incertitude, an inherent sickness.[109]

The character of Som Bhaskar, as revealed in *The Last Labyrinth*, is that of the turbulent inner world of an industrialist. He has respectable inheritance, education and accomplishments. At the age of fifteen he loses his mother and at the age of twenty-five his father. But at the early age of twenty-five he is a millionaire, married to an ideal wife, true to him in every respect. Yet Som Bhaskar "goofed it all up."[110] He is never satisfied with his possessions and is always after acquiring more and more shares. Though he has become a chronic patient of insomnia and is always accompanied by his family physician Dr. K., he runs after satisfying his undefined hungers and it is this that leads him through a haunting world of life, love, God and death, the greatest of all mysteries and the last labyrinth. The novel, according to R.S. Pathak, "raises some pertinent questions about life and its meanings and tries to unravel the still unresolved mysteries of God and death."[111] The protagonist of the novel is tormented by a great roaring hollowness inside his soul. His life of affluence has simply added to the "boredom and the fedupness."[112] There is within him "orchestras of discontent"[113] instead of heavenly harmony. At an early age he becomes "a worn-out weary man incapable of spontaneous feeling." He feels "like a hare chased by unseen hounds."[114] He once confides to Anuradha, "I am dislocated. My mind is out of focus. There is something right in front of me and I cannot see it."[115] Som feels that inside him "there was nothing but an empty roaring, like the roar of the sea in a conch."[116]

It is not that he contracted this feeling later in life. The futile activities of life upset him as student and once he wanted his headmaster's wife "to explain the meaning of it all."[117] He feels void both within and without and the physical labyrinths existing in Lal Haveli at Benares and its lanes as also the intricate allies of life make him conscious of the labyrinthine ways of life and death, which is also the last labyrinth. The images of the labyrinth, maze, void, vanity, along with certain sordid imagery associated with the animal life emphasize this point in Bhaskar's life.

The life is a complicated maze, "a labyrinth within a labyrinth."[118] Like the lanes of Benares, the ways of life could best be compared to "meaningless flights of stairs"[119] "or a fisherman's net."[120] Like the Biblical preacher Ecclesiastics, life to him is "Vanity of vanities."[121] Som thinks, "It is the voids of the world, more than its objects, that bother me. The voids and the empty spaces within and without."[122] The burning ghats of Benares also communicate to him the sense of "voids with a bang. Both within and without... voids all."[123]

There is a strange contradiction in Som Bhaskar's character. There is discrepancy between his principles and action. He is hungry to know of the secrets of life. Yet he is not able to achieve it because of his obsessive desire to have more and more. Even the ascetic woman, Gargi, fails to satisfy his questions regarding the voids of the world and despite her warning that he should not take Anuradha's shares, he insists on having it:

> If God existed, if a miracle had taken place, and if I now walked off with the shares—and with Anuradha—I should perhaps die.
>
> That was a hell of a thought to be burdened with but I didn't think I had a choice. All I knew was that I wasn't prepared to give up Anuradha on these grounds.[124]

Despite all this awareness Som Bhaskar walks away with Anuradha's shares and also goes to Benares to possess her which is foiled by her sudden mysterious disappearance from Lal Haveli which also adversely affects Aftab Rai.

Several critics of Arun Joshi have pointed out to the existence of the labyrinth at the various levels in the novel. Dr. R.K.

Shrivastava suggests that "The title of Arun Joshi's *The Last Labyrinth* can be operative on many levels."[125] At one level it is physical in which Lal Haveli and Benares are both included. Som Bhaskar views Lal Haveli to be the "sepulchral, sensual den of Aftab's amidst the labyrinths of Benares."[126] Being a descendant of Wazid Ali Khan, he considered his ancestors to be "the true rulers of Hindustan."[127] His ancestors erected the structure of Lal Haveli on the idea of Bhul Bhulaiyan. It was built either with no plan or with the most meticulous plan, though directed at an elusive objective. The structure, however, fitted in the labyrinths of the city. At the symbolical level, the Lal Haveli stands for the maze of life and *The Last Labyrinth* of the title is death itself which is even more mysterious than existence itself.

The narrative of *The Last Labyrinth* is mostly a tale of two cities represented respectively by Aftab and Bhaskar. While the former was "a child of Benares,"[128] Bhaskar was that of Bombay. Anuradha's on the other hand, was "a city without a name, a city set in an oasis, plundered a thousand times and waiting to be plundered again,"[129] by men like Aftab and Bhaskar. Everything about Lal Haveli and its inhabitants seems a fantasy to the sceptical Bhaskar. The pock-marked antique beauty Anuradha is as much a mystery as her relations with Aftab. Coupled with the intricacies of the city and the building is the presence of the experiences of voids and spirituality. Gargi's cottage on the other side of the Ganga, the burning ghats and the bulls in the narrow alleys produce a picture of the complexity of life itself. While Bhaskar's life in Bombay has simply matter, the life in Benares has both matter and spirit.

In the labyrinth of life and death in both Bombay and Benares, Som Bhaskar fails to get an exact identity of his character in consonance with his caste, ancestry, education, upbringing, family relations and profession, business relationships as well as personal relationships. Leila Sabnis has very rightly pointed out to these discrepancies in him which have been discussed previously in this chapter.

Som Bhaskar is aware of the roaring hollowness, terrible loneliness and the overpowering void about himself. He poses questions and he has also given answers. Yet he is not satisfied. His father used to say, "I believe in science, yes, but science cannot solve the problem of the causes. Not many realise this paradox."[130] He delved deep beneath the causes behind causes with reference to geological periods to establish the First Cause in the cycles of birth, growth, decline and death. He also got some of the questions and answers from the *Upanishads* of which he had a copy. At Benares he listens to the hymns recited by a young boy at the top of his voice and an equally young boy correcting him, Panini-like. The problems of life posed by Pascal, Krishna, the Buddha, Yajnavalkya, Kierkegaard, Darwin, Descartes, etc. crop up. But none of these is able to alleviate the inner crisis of Som's life. There may be a crisis of identity in his life, yet he has never experienced suffering which ennobles the person as has been in the cases of both Anuradha and Aftab. The *mantra* that resounds within him is not that of his identity with any godhead but with "I want, I want, I want."

Som Bhaskar's anguished soul has no cure in the medicines prescribed by Dr. Kashyap or psychiatrists. He is torn between unbelief and belief and even Gargi, who at Anuradha's request, had saved his life with a miracle, fails to convince him of the existence of divinity and miracles. Gargi wrote for him on the pad, "There is no harm in believing that God exists" and he was reminded of Pascal whom he had studied. Pascal also says in a similar vein. Still Bhaskar persists,

> It is easier to believe that He does not exist. It is more convenient that way.[131]

The crisis of identity in *The Last Labyrinth* is not due to the confrontation "with society but with forms and forces beyond the recurrings of reason and science."[132] The paradoxes emerging out of faith and reason, miracle and explanation give the novel some of the features of fantasy "because of the intriguing juxtaposition of the sensual and the spiritual weird locales crumbling Haveli,...."[133] We have seen how Leila Sabnis attributes Som's problems to that of identity. Som Bhaskar is not ready to associate himself with any mystical identification.

All along his life Som Bhaskar suffers from an inner crisis and, as R.S. Pathak writes, "is apparently at war with himself."[134] Som Bhaskar analyses himself:

> If I believed in God I could pray, maybe run a rosary through my fingers. But that's out. Sitting around, I get into arguments: with the living, with the dead, with myself.[135]

Som Bhaskar finds no solace in his education which makes him all the more melancholy. Even Anuradha tells him of his lack of self-knowledge, "You are wrong even about yourself. You think you know a lot, when, in fact, you don't."[136] Aftab too finds him empty of that understanding that only suffering and humiliation bring. This kind of understanding is there in the personality of Anuradha who had to pass through harrowing tales of lost childhood, suffering and humiliation. Dr. K. refers to these very pointedly:

> I know enough. Illegitimate child, insane mother, no home. Molested as a child. Witness to murders, suicides, every conceivable evil of the world. Can you imagine what a childhood she must have had?[137]

In his anguished soul Som Bhaskar addresses the missing Anuradha:

> Anuradha, if there is a God and if you have met Him and if He is willing to listen, then Anuradha, my soul, tell Him, tell this God, to have mercy upon me. Tell Him, I am weary. Of so many fears; so much doubting. Of this dark earth and these empty heavens. Plead for me, Anuradha. He will listen to you.[138]

Leila Sabnis earlier had psychoanalysed Som Bhaskar's lack of stamina for mystical identification on the basis "You haven't got the faith. You have always been a sceptic. You always will be."[139]

The text of *The Last Labyrinth* has predominance of use of images associated with labyrinth and void. Moreover as R.S. Pathak writes, "Words like 'dream,' 'mystery,' 'doubt,' 'reality' and 'understanding' seem to serve as recurrent motifs in the novel. All these are related to Som Bhaskar's crisis of identity and of consciousness. The woman characters such as Anuradha, Geeta and Gargi are the persons who know. Even Aftab has deep faith in spiritual matters. But it is Som Bhaskar who lies outside. He himself thinks of the wanters and the givers "and often, the wanters, I know, don't recognise the givers, or the givers the wanters."[140] The crisis with Som Bhaskar is that he is always a wanter and never a giver. Aftab Rai points out to him of this discrepancy:

> You have to sacrifice before you are given. You can't have your cake and eat it too. You want to have faith. But you also want to reserve the right to challenge your own fate when it suits you.[141]

Som Bhaskar does not even believe in Kierkegaard's saying, "Prayer does not change God but changes him who prays."[142]

The Last Labyrinth does not seem to close with any positive progression of ideas and as Joshi has himself written in a letter to V. Gopal Reddy, "Alienation of my novels which I have written so far, ultimately leads them back to community. I realise that in my latest novel *The Last Labyrinth* for the first time it does not happen."[143] The heroes of both *The Foreigner* and *The Last Labyrinth* suffer from the malady of the crisis of identity. But while in *The Foreigner* it is at the mundane levels of existence, rootlessness, loneliness and lack of identity with the problems of existence, in *The Last Labyrinth* the crisis of identity is at the cosmic level besides the physical one. Till the end Som Bhaskar fails to get reconciled with the problems of life and death, science and religion, miracle and reason. The novel opens with the vow of revenge and closes with Som Bhaskar's abortive suicidal gesture as Geeta intervenes.

NOTES

1. *The Foreigner* 186.
2. Blurb to *The Foreigner* 1.
3. Blurb to *The Foreigner.*
4. "A Winner's Secrets": An Interview with Purabi Bannerji, *The Sunday Statesman,* 27th February, 1983, iv.
5. *The Foreigner* 33.
6. Harish Raizada, "Double Vision of Fantasy and Reality in Arun Joshi's Novels," *The Fictional World of Arun Joshi,* (ed.) R.K. Dhawan (New Delhi, 1986), 74.
7. Raizada 24.
8. Quoted in "The Lost Childhood," Graham Greene, *The Collected Essays* (London, 1969), 19.
9. Graham Greene, *The Heart of the Matter* (Penguin ed. 1971), 123.
10. Greene 123.
11. Greene 124.
12. Quoted in *The Foreigner* 94.
13. Joseph Margolis, "The Love Song of J. Alfred Prufrock" in John Wain (ed.) *Interpretations* (London, 1965), 183.
14. Hari Mohan Prasad, *Arun Joshi* (New Delhi, 1985), 28.
15. Prasad 28.
16. "A Winner's Secrets": An Interview with Purabi Bannerji, *The Sunday Statesman,* 27th February, 1983, iv.
17. "*The Foreigner*: A Study in Innocence & Experience" in R.K. Dhawan (ed.) *The Fictional World of Arun Joshi* 168.
18. "*The Foreigner* 168.
19. *The Foreigner* 24.
20. *The Foreigner* 30.
21. *The Foreigner* 12.
22. *The Foreigner* 11.
23. *The Foreigner* 12.
24. *The Foreigner* 33.
25. *The Foreigner* 149.
26. *The Foreigner* 159.
27. *The Foreigner* 35.
28. *The Foreigner* 111.

29. *The Foreigner* 114.
30. *The Foreigner* 98.
31. *The Foreigner* 68.
32. *The Foreigner* 65.
33. *The Foreigner* 174-75.
34. *The Foreigner* 180.
35. *The Foreigner* 137.
36. *Quest, No. 60,* January-March 1969, 101.
37. *The Foreigner* 143-44.
38. *The Foreigner* 195.
39. *The Foreigner* 186.
40. *Ibid.*
41. *The Foreigner* 150.
42. *Ibid.*
43. *The Foreigner* 172.
44. *The Foreigner* 150.
45. *The Foreigner* 128.
46. *The Foreigner* 16.
47. *The Foreigner* 16.
48. *The Foreigner* 239.
49. *The Foreigner* 242.
50. *The Foreigner* 15.
51. *The Foreigner* 12-13.
52. *The Foreigner* 23.
53. *The Foreigner* 20.
54. *The Foreigner* 59.
55. *The Foreigner* 58-59.
56. *The Foreigner* 60.
57. *The Foreigner* 59-60.
58. *The Foreigner* 69.
59. *The Foreigner* 95.
60. *The Foreigner* 97.
61. *The Foreigner* 119.
62. *The Foreigner* 119-20.
63. *The Foreigner* 120.

64. *The Foreigner* 130.
65. *The Foreigner* 130.
66. *The Foreigner* 184.
67. *The Foreigner* 108.
68. *The Foreigner* 125.
69. *The Foreigner* 146.
70. *The Foreigner* 203.
71. *The Foreigner* 78.
72. *The Foreigner* 28.
73. *The Foreigner* 28.
74. *The Foreigner* 80.
75. *The Foreigner* 81.
76. *Ibid.*
77. *The Last Labyrinth* 11.
78. *The Last Labyrinth* 47.
79. *The Last Labyrinth* 11.
80. *The Last Labyrinth* 112-13.
81. *The Last Labyrinth* 156.
82. *The Last Labyrinth* 156.
83. *The Last Labyrinth* 156-57.
84. *The Last Labyrinth* 79.
85. *The Last Labyrinth* 77.
86. *Ibid.*
87. *Ibid.*
88. *The Last Labyrinth* 80.
89. Quoted in A. Ram Krishna Rao, "The Image of Labyrinth in Borges, Durrell and Joshi," *Glimpses of Indo-Anglian Fiction*, Vol. III, (ed.) O.P. Saxena (New Delhi, 1985), 22.
90. *The Last Labyrinth* 43.
91. *The Last Labyrinth* 43.
92. *The Last Labyrinth* 128.
93. *The Last Labyrinth* 61.
94. *The Last Labyrinth* 118.
95. *The Last Labyrinth* 121.
96. *The Last Labyrinth* 121-22.

97. *The Last Labyrinth* 205.
98. *The Last Labyrinth* 213.
99. *Ibid.*
100. *The Last Labyrinth* 214.
101. *The Last Labyrinth* 217.
102. *The Last Labyrinth* 222.
103. *Ibid.*
104. *Ibid.*
105. *The Last Labyrinth* 222-23.
106. *The Last Labyrinth* 9.
107. *The Last Labyrinth* 224.
108. "The Crisis of Consciousness: *The Last Labyrinth*" in Dhawan (ed.) *The Fictional World of Arun Joshi* (New Delhi, 1986), 238.
109. Dhawan 232.
110. *The Last Labyrinth* 40.
111. "Human Predicament and Meaninglessness" in R.K. Dhawan (ed.) *The Fictional World of Arun Joshi* (New Delhi, 1986), 122.
112. *The Last Labyrinth* 21.
113. *The Last Labyrinth* 12.
114. *The Last Labyrinth* 12.
115. *The Last Labyrinth* 107.
116. *The Last Labyrinth* 115.
117. *The Last Labyrinth* 24.
118. *The Last Labyrinth* 29.
119. *The Last Labyrinth* 34.
120. *The Last Labyrinth* 37.
121. *The Last Labyrinth* 32.
122. *The Last Labyrinth* 47.
123. *The Last Labyrinth* 48.
124. *The Last Labyrinth* 211-12.
125. "Intricate Alleys in Arun Joshi's *The Last Labyrinth,*" *The Indian Journal of English Studies*, Vol. XXVIII, 1989, 5.
126. *The Last Labyrinth* 23.
127. *The Last Labyrinth* 39.
128. *The Last Labyrinth* 37.
129. *Ibid.*

130. *The Last Labyrinth* 26.
131. *The Last Labyrinth* 213.
132. O.P. Bhatnagar, "The Art and Vision of Arun Joshi" in R.K. Dhawan (ed.), *The Fictional World of Arun Joshi* (New Delhi, 1986), 62.
133. Harish Raizada, "Double Vision of Fantasy and Reality in Arun Joshi's Novels" in R.K. Dhawan (ed.), *The Fictional World of Arun Joshi* (New Delhi, 1986), 96.
134. "Human Predicament and Meaninglessness in Arun Joshi's Novels" in R.K. Dhawan (ed.) *The Fictional World of Arun Joshi* (New Delhi, 1986), 134.
135. *The Last Labyrinth* 10.
136. *The Last Labyrinth* 61.
137. *The Last Labyrinth* 190.
138. *The Last Labyrinth* 223.
139. *The Last Labyrinth* 113.
140. *The Last Labyrinth* 62.
141. *The Last Labyrinth* 166.
142. *The Last Labyrinth* 118.
143. Quoted, R.K. Dhawan (ed.) *The Fictional World of Arun Joshi* (New Delhi, 1986), 47.

4

THE PRIMITIVE WORLD *VERSUS* THE CIVILIZED WORLD IN *THE STRANGE CASE OF BILLY BISWAS*

I

The Strange Case of Billy Biswas is chronologically Arun Joshi's second novel published in the year 1973. Like the first novel *The Foreigner* as well as like the fourth *The Last Labyrinth*, which have been dealt with in Chapter 3, *The Strange Case of Billy Biswas* too delves deep into the problem of the quest for identity and the crisis of consciousness. The title of the novel is itself a pointer in this regard. It is the only novel by Arun Joshi that has an eponymous hero, Billy Biswas; and the narrator delves deep into the psychological problem of the crisis of Billy's identity.

The narrative point of view of the novel is that of "the witness-narrator's,"[1] while in *The Foreigner* it is that of "the protagonist narrator's point of view"[2] in which the narrative follows both flash-ahead and flash-back technique. In *The Strange Case of Billy Biswas* it is Billy's friend, Romesh Sahai, known as Romy to his friends, who is the omniscient first person narrator. He had been with Billy Biswas in the U.S.A. and as such he knew everything of his life and deeds in America. Coming back to India on his father's death, Romy sits at the I.A.S. competition and gets through it. It is in this capacity that as Collector of Jhansi, Romy has to be actively involved in the Strange Case of Billy Biswas. From the very beginning the narrator lays stress on the point that it is difficult to know the mind of Billy Biswas:

> As I grow old, I realise that the most futile cry of man is his impossible wish to be understood. The attempt to understand is probably even more futile. If in spite of this I propose to relate Billy's story, it is not so much because I claim to have understood him as it is on account of a deep and unrelieved sense of wonder that in the middle of the twentieth century, in the heart of Delhi's smart society, there should have lived a man of such extraordinary obsessions.[3]

It is amply clear from it that human nature is inscrutable, more so that of the man like Billy Biswas. Yet despite this disclaimer, Romesh Sahai along with Tuula Lindgren, a Swedish researcher, understands the nature of Billy Biswas and they have no confusion regarding the root cause of the crisis of identity in the character of Billy Biswas. D. Prempati finds the point of view in *The Strange Case of Billy Biswas* to be immensely helpful in the fictional technique of the novel:

> What gives *The Strange Case* its basic irony is the device of a point of view carefully focused through the vision of the narrator Romesh Sahai, one of the two characters to have had a measure of sympathetic understanding of the enigmatic Billy. Arun Joshi made a deft use of memory-monologues, and largely through the central vision of the point of view protected the monologues from being one-sided affair, an egotistical narration of only one dimension.[4]

Though Arun Joshi has divided the novel into two parts: Part-I up to 98 pages and Part-II from pages no. 99 to 244, it could have been better, as Harish Raizada suggests, if it could have been divided into three parts designated respectively as "the Civilized World," "the Primitive World" and "the Impingement of the Civilized on the Primitive World."[5] In the fantastic structure of the novel, Billy's disappearance into the world of tribals sounds "a bit like Scheherazade"[6] or "like Scheherazade alright."[7] It is in this respect that Arun Joshi may be looked upon as a fantasist. His final fictional work, *The City and the River,* is a true specimen of Joshi's interest in fantasy.

Except for *The Apprentice* and *The City and the River,* Joshi's novels are full of characters trained in foreign universities. *The Strange Case of Billy Biswas* has three characters who were together during their educational career in the U.S.A. The novel opens in New York's Harlem, a black ghetto of America, where no man of dignity would have preferred living. But Billy Biswas preferred this for his residence. In this choice of Harlem there is the spirit of his taking refuge from the white dissipation around. Billy has a decisive liking for the black American aboriginals to white cultured citizens of the U.S.A. Even the experiences of Billy's childhood suggest the turmoil in his soul for the primitive. This is, however, kept in suspense because of the external forces. He belongs to the privileged minority of the well-fed and the well-educated. His grandfather had been Prime Minister of the Princely State in Orissa, while his father was a Judge in the Supreme Court of the Union and also for sometime Ambassador to a European country, when Billy was just a boy of fifteen. As such owing to his school education in England, Billy had almost as good command of English as that of a native speaker.

Billy is always plagued by some kind of inner crisis and duality in his character. He was sent to America for an engineering degree and the parents never knew that their Bimal had switched over to Anthropology in which he got a Ph.D. degree from an American University. As a student of Anthropology Billy was a thorough explorer. He makes it clear to his room-mate Romy: "All that I want to do in life is to visit the places they describe, meet the people who live there, find out about the aboriginals of the world."[8] It is this love for the aboriginals of the world that inspires Billy to give up Engineering in favour of Anthropology.

Billy once reminisces in one of his memory-monologues how he used to visit Bhubaneswar as a schoolboy of Delhi and Dehradun. When once his uncle's driver took him to a hamlet of Oriya aboriginals, their uninhibited life had left its deep obsessive impression upon his mind. Billy himself says:

> It was as though a slumbering part of me had suddenly come awake. You know, this happens with almost everybody at the time of adolescence. Strange passions are roused. Some get fascinated by music, others by painting or literature or the sciences. Your life starts to take the final mould, so to speak.[9]

This made Billy deeply interested in the problems of the crisis of his own identity in the fashion of the Upanishadic questionings such as—"Who was I? Where had I come from? Where was I going?"[10] Billy ascribes this to his experiences with the Oriya tribals near Bhubaneswar that had brought these on to him. Billy also reminisces his impressions of the sculptures of the Konark's Sun Temple. He tells Romy about his experiences of the Konark:

> But I know it was not the exoticness of the sculptures that appealed to me: as a matter of fact, even though I had not had any training in the matter, except for a few pieces I found most of the sculpture rather unaesthetic. No, what appealed to me was the shades of the same spirit that I spoke of although I knew them, as I know now, that the spirit was a much, much older force, older than the time when man first learned to build temples. If anyone had a clue to it, it was only the adivasis who carried about their knowledge in silence, locked behind their dark inscrutable faces.[11]

Billy finds that it is the tribals which know the spirit behind the erotic sculptures of Konark. Billy, as he says, is impressed not by the exoticness of sculptures but the spirit behind them which was much older than man's knowledge to build temples. Billy himself possesses this urge which a few of his friends know. It is his urge for the primitive that in a music party in George's apartment at a black ghetto in New York that Billy plays a pair of banjo drums creating a strange hush on the scene. Among a few friends who understand Billy is the Swedish researcher, Tuula, who like Billy is interested in Anthropology and the occult. She has been able to fathom the inscrutable character of Billy Biswas. As for herself she is strongly interested in "India especially in the tribal people."[12] She is in search of finding "a psychiatric explanation of the concepts of the ritual and the taboo"[13] as she talks "in one breath of religion and yoga and Gandhi"[14] and she is also in search of finding "Freudian explanation of Gandhi's non-violence."[15] She tells Romy of a great dormant force lying suppressed in the personality of Billy Biswas who has within him:

> A great force, urkraft,...a...a primitive force. He is afraid of it and tries to suppress it.... But it is very strong in him, much stronger than in you or me. It can explode any moment.[16]

Tuula's assessment of Billy's character is very correct and it is what she terms in German *urkraft* which explodes in Billy's life and he escapes into the tribal world deserting the world of civilization and the members of his family including wife and son. In this respect Billy's case is not on all fours with the Buddha who too left his wife and son but he did not live in any tribal world engrossed in the tribal totems. Yet the Buddha is a kind of an archetypal figure upon which Billy has been moulded in some respect in the context of the urban society versus the tribal world.

Back home in India Billy Biswas gets a teaching assignment at the Department of Anthropology of Delhi University, but the restive soul of Billy Biswas never allows him any inner rest. Billy does not confine his studies to the books alone but also mixes with the tribals to explore their lives. It is in course of such an expedition that Billy disappears into the wilderness of the Maikala hills.

Billy's parents and relatives had also tough time in persuading Billy to accept the traditional Hindu way of life. He was persuaded to marry on the logic of:

> the usual amalgam of the western pragmatism (a wife is so necessary, socially, sexually for a fuller life) and Hindu *dharma* (man's duty to marry and reproduce: there is time for everything) that is the conventional wisdom of the Indian middle class.[17]

Billy remained indecisive in his choice between Rima Kaul who understood him better and Meena whom his parents favoured. Though he gets married to Meena who bears him a son, his adulterous affair with Rima Kaul also continues. With the passage of time, the misunderstandings between husband and wife get the form of the crisis of character. Their relationship gets "stranger and stranger with every passing day."[18] Meena even makes a clean breast to Romy, "He... he doesn't want me any more. He hasn't touched me for six months. Not once."[19] The crisis of identity between them goes to the extent of making a hell of their lives and perhaps to escape the hell of this relationship Billy Biswas escapes from the civilized world to the tribal shelter. He had once given an inkling of it to Romy, "I will, if I do come back. He laughed."[20] But the omniscient narrator comments:

> As a matter of fact he never did. On the second day of the expedition, Billy Biswas disappeared from the face of the earth, simply vanished into the *saal* forests of the Maikala hills.[21]

Billy's escape from a civilized society to a primitive world is not for the sake of his becoming a Yogi, but because the phoney atmosphere of the modern society which is nothing more than "the making and spending of money"[22] is not to the liking of Billy Biswas. O.P. Bhatnagar rightly points out that Billy "renounced this materialistic society and civilization not to be an ascetic but to fulfil all the demands of his self to the perfection of participated joy."[23] When after his escape into the tribal world, Romy in one of his official visits of the district meets him by chance and asks him to give an explanation, Billy Biswas tells him about Delhi society getting on his nerves; and in this respect perhaps all city societies are not much or less the same. Billy speaks out rather a long explanation of the so-called glories of the modern civilized society:

> What got me was the superficiality, the sense of values. I don't think all city societies are as shallow as ours. I am, of course, talking mainly of the so-called upper classes. I didn't really get to know the others. I don't think I have ever met a more pompous, a more mixed-up lot of people. Artistically, they were dry as dust. Intellectually, they could do no better than mechanically mouth ideas that the West abandoned a generation ago. Their idea of romance was to go and see an American movie or to go to one of those wretched restaurants and dance with their wives to a thirty-year-old tune. Nobody remembered the old songs, or the meaning of the festivals. All the sensuality was gone. So was the poetry. All that was left was loud-mouthed women and men in three-piece suits dreaming their little adulteries. May be it is different now.[24]

Thus Billy Biswas prefers leading a life with the primitives to that of a city society where one has no time to stand and stare. The tribals are not interested in the mundane affairs but only in the rhythms of nature. The alternatives before Billy were limited, "I had two clear choices: I could either follow this call, this vision, whatever the cost, or be condemned to total decay."[25] Bilasia, the essence of the primitive force, becomes the beacon light of his tribal life. In his contact with her he gets a kind of *tantric* spirituality. Their union revives the glow of the *Chandtola* peak, extinct since the death by poison of the tribal king and queen long ago. The revival of this miracle makes the tribals think of them as reincarnations of their old king and queen. They deify Billy who, according to them, is capable of creating miracles including reviving the dead and turning the ferocious tiger away.

While on the one hand the tribals hail the emergence of Billy, the administrative machinery of the city society is geared up to investigate the whereabouts of Billy. In their investigations they come out with different explanations of his disappearance, the most prominent being that he fell prey to a man-eater. The village headman Dhunia feigns ignorance of the whole affair. It is just accidentally that Romy encounters Billy in his loin-cloth speaking impeccable English. Billy leads a life close to nature and knows of the curative values of herbs and even cures Romy's wife's nagging migraine with one of the wild herbs and makes him promise that he would never divulge the secrets of his whereabouts which, however, Sitoo, his wife in her zeal leaks out to the concerned family, who again set the administrative machinery rolling to find out Billy.

It is during the course of the search led by the S.P. Mr. Rele himself that an overzealous constable shoots Billy dead. Romy, the Collector of the district, because of his apprehensions of something untoward had joined the search party, but he could not prevent the tragic end from occurring. The strange case of Billy Biswas and the drama of his life come to what has been termed as "an epic end"[26] which is both a "catastrophe"[27] and "the great tragedy."[28] "The surly Havildar"[29] is suspended for his indiscriminate firing and is later killed by Dhunia in revenge. When Meena sees the handful of ashes of Billy, she had at last "a glimpse of the phantoms that had driven Billy out of her life and now out of the world."[30] Romy, the District Collector, has at last to file a brief report of the case:

> The Strange Case of Billy Biswas had at last been disposed of. It had been disposed of in the only manner that a humdrum society knows of disposing its rebels, its seers, its true lovers.[31]

II

Professors O.P. Mathur and G. Rai state that *The Strange Case of Billy Biswas*, like *The Foreigner* "develops the theme of man's feeling of anxiety and alienation."[32] Billy's alienation from civilized society including his family is responsible for his escape into the tribal world. The feeling of alienation and anxiety and the crisis of identity is not at the physical level but at the spiritual and mental. Billy comes out of the upper crust of the society and has everything that post, power and privilege can give. Yet he is not only indifferent but hostile to all these. Interesting anthropological explorations in India also urge him on to search for identity. It is not that this was a later development of his life. It was in the make-up of his personality. His tribal urge on his visit to the Odisi tribals and the Konark during his childhood and his preference for the Negroes in Harlem to the American whites are all offshoots of his inner urge of being a tribal.

The crisis of Billy's identity has roots different from those of Sindi Oberoi in *The Foreigner*. Sindi's problem is that of rootlessness but it is not so with Billy Biswas. The narrator Romy reminisces:

> In spite of somewhat longish stay in America, neither of us had lost our roots in India or in the city of Delhi; nor did we suffer much, except for passing spells of loneliness, from that alienation that many other Indians seemed to be burdened with.[33]

Billy may thus be hardly called a rootless man. He is conscious of his Bengali roots, though educated abroad. He only alienates himself from the civilized life to escape into the so-called uncivilized tribal life. A pioneer critic of Indian English literature, K.R.S. Iyengar, has probably missed the point when he writes:

> In *The Strange Case of Billy Blswas*, Arun Joshi has carried his exploration of the consciousness of hapless, rootless people a stage further and has revealed to our gaze new gas-chambers of self-forged misery.[34]

Billy Biswas may be hapless but is not rootless; and unlike Sindi Oberoi he does not create gas-chambers of self-forged misery. It is just another matter that though Billy Biswas is among family members, "yet he does not feel integrated with them. He is not in harmony. He is alone. He is isolated... a stranger."[35] Billy himself writes to Tuula about his predicament, "We are swiftly losing what is known as one's grip on life."[36] As a narrator Romy himself says, "Billy is interested not in the glossy surfaces of our pretensions but in those dark, mossy labyrinths of his soul that languish for ever, hidden from the dazzling light of the sun."[37] What he does is to seek it "more doggedly"[38] than others and "having received a signal, abandoned himself so wrecklessly to its call."[39] Billy desperately "pursued the tenuous thread of existence to its bitter end"[40] and did not think of "what trails of glory or shattered hearts he left behind in his turbulent wake."[41]

The Strange Case of Billy Biswas is, to Thakur Guru Prasad,

> Yet another variation on the paradigmatic pattern of the doomed existential quest for values in a mad, bad, absurd world. It holds forth the added attraction of the dark, mysterious forces of the universe like Bilasia, the tribal girl and the moon rising out of the dark night that magnetise the protagonist and drive him to a dross of death, the last labyrinth that life holds for man in the existential vision.[42]

Even before *The Last Labyrinth*, Arun Joshi is aware of the implications in the use of the labyrinth symbolism which has been used both in *The Foreigner* and *The Strange Case of Billy Biswas*. Billy Biswas wanders through the labyrinths of the civilized life and finding a dead end in it, goes to seek the simple ways of the life of the primitive people. White America is "much too civilized for him"[43] as the aboriginal black America is more to his liking. As an anthropologist he has an urge for travel, a little bit in America, but mostly in India, to explore fascinating societies existing there. The interest in the primitive man is the quest of his existence. In the quest of primitive force he makes a quest of the anarchy of the wild which he tames. Billy in his letter written to Tuula Lindgren considers himself "a visitor from the wilderness to the marts of the big city and not the other way round."[44] In his tirade against the civilized society he writes to her:

> I sometimes wonder whether civilization is anything more than the making and spending of money. What else does the civilized man do? And if there are those who are not busy earning and spending—the so-called thinkers and philosophers and men like that—they are merely hired to find solution, throw light, as they say, on complications caused by this making and spending of money. What need would there be of psychiatrists, research foundations, learned societies, great scholars, scientists, ministerial advisers, ambassadors, generals, had the world not initially been hung on this peg of money.[45]

Thus Billy is very critical of the organised society and its so-called measures of civilization. It is the peg of money, as he says, upon which everything rests. The problem hinted at by Billy is that of the existential problem of reality, identity and absurdity of the human creation. When Billy thinks of the absurdity of family relationships and the crisis of identity arising out of the problem of thinking, the identity of the self and other members of the family, Billy "cannot decide who they are or what accident of creation has brought us together."[46] In a series of letters written to Tuula Lindgren, Billy amply justifies the crisis of identity, the mesh of which has engulfed him. All these letters she refers to the narrator Romi Sahai. In one of them Billy speaks of the impossibility of perfect communion: "To speak, I am afraid, if you address the deaf."[47] Billy also reveals himself in his comments upon his visit to a temple in the evening *aarti* time. He becomes sceptical even of the existence of the divine:

> As I stood there, my eyeballs restive behind the quivering lids, it suddenly dawned upon me that it was all a great waste, that the god who awaited me now was one to which no temples could be built. What awaited me now, I realized, was Fate.[48]

All these statements from Billy's letters go to prove that Billy is lost in the labyrinth of a civilized life out of which he wants an escape.

Arun Joshi's choice of the epigram for the novel is a pointer to his way of thinking about the restive soul of Billy. Joshi quotes from Matthew Arnold's *Thyrsis* (line no. 41):

> It irk'd him to be here, he could not rest.

Arnold's friend, Arthur Hugh Clough, being fed up with the Victorian wasteland, wanted to escape out of it and died at Florence in 1861. It is in his memory that Arnold wrote *Thyrsis*, a monody to commemorate his friend. The epigraph borrowed from Arnold is a pointer to the existential theme of alienation and the crisis of life and identity dealt with in the novel. Joshi may also have on his mind the case of the scholar gipsy celebrated in the poem after this very title. The spirit of the letters written by Billy to Tuula Lindgren reminds us of the unrest in the soul of the scholar gipsy. What Arnold writes of the gipsies is possessed of by the tribals. The scholar gipsy once replies to two of his Oxford scholars who met him:

> ... that the gipsy-crew,
> His mates, had arts to rule as they desired
> The workings of men's brains,
> And they can bind them to what thoughts they will.
> "And I," he said, "the secret of their art,
> When fully learned, will to the world impart;
> But it needs heaven-sent moments for this skill."[49]

Comparing the leaden present with the golden past, as applied to the case of the scholar gipsy's life at Oxford and with the gipsies, Arnold writes:

> O born in days when wits were fresh and clear;
> And life ran gaily as the sparkling Thames;
> Before this strange disease of modern life,
> With its sick hurry, its divided aims,
> Its heads o'ertax'd, its palsied hearts, was rife—
> Fly hence, our contact fear!
> Still fly, plunge deeper in the bowering wood!
> Averse, as Dido did with gesture stern

> From her false friend's approach in Hades turn,
> Wave us away, and keep thy solitude![50]

The comparison has its relevance in its application with the tribal world and the civilized society. Billy Biswas gets fed up with the civilized society and as the narrator says, "Aside from knowing a few headline facts, Billy was woefully out of touch with what had been happening in the country, leave alone the world."[51] Instead of being left alone for meditation, Billy was given dozens of promises to be fulfilled to Meena. It resulted in, as Billy says, "communication between us was soon reduced to zero."[52] It is not that Billy shirks responsibilities. As he says, "I had greater responsibilities towards my soul."[53] Billy calls these greater responsibilities *the Other Thing* which he writes about as follows:

> It gradually dawned on me that a tremendous corrupting force was working on me. It was as though my soul were taking revenge on me for having denied it for so long that Other Thing that it had been clamouring for. "Here, you swine, if you haven't the guts to break away from this filth, well, then, I am going to wallow in it until it makes you stick." You see what I mean.[54]

Billy declares that *Other Thing* to be the be-all and end-all of what his life is all about. "Becoming a primitive was only a first step, only a means to an end. Of course I realized it only *after* I ran away."[55] Billy is not sure whether he is seeking God because he thinks it to be "too big a word"[56] but yields to the suggestion that he was seeking "something like that."[57] Billy's fantastic life may sound like an "odd tale,"[58] a "folklore"[59] and "a ballad,"[60] yet on the whole it has in it the proportionate blend of both fantasy and reality. The story of his life should not be taken as "a stereotype childish escapade."[61] He is a searcher after "a God, apart from the gods of civilized India."[62] Jasbir Jain thinks that "Billy, like Sindi, is in search of a human world of emotional fullness... a world of meaningful relatedness."[63]

R.S. Pathak does not perhaps overstretch the point when he finds in the story of Billy a fictional representation of the *Sankhya* concept of the fusion of *Prakriti* and *Purusa*:

> As Billy's example testifies, if one is able to establish a rapport with the primitive forces in the world of nature, one can get rid of all problems of life. Bilasia, it is held, symbolizes "the Primitive culture, the untapped subterranean resources of psychic energy." It would be better to regard her as the Matter (Prakriti), which according to the Sankhya system of Indian philosophy, is "one" and eternal, not an illusionary appearance but something real. Billy might be taken to represent the Soul (Purusa), which by its mere presence excites Matter and illumines the processes of the evolution of the universe. Bilasia, we are reminded, is "the embodiment of that primal and invulnerable force that had ruled these (Maikala) hills, perhaps this earth, since time began." Her "enormous eyes," we are told, "poured out a sexuality that was nearly as primeval as the forest that surrounded them." In the Sankhya philosophy the material universe is traced to a First Cause.[64]

Joshi also hints at the concept of the First Cause in *The Last Labyrinth*. In *The Foreigner* there has been a kind of gloss on the interpretations of the concepts of attachment *versus* detachment. As regards *The Strange Case of Billy Biswas* we have to realize that Billy as Purusa is in the grip of the crisis of identity until his union with Bilasia as a symbol of *Prakriti*. Though the union takes place, it is cut off by the meddling intellect of the organisers of the civilized society. Billy, moreover, had much more affinity with the black forest, representing the *Prakriti* than the artificialities of the so-called city societies. *The Strange Case of Billy Biswas* as Professor O.P. Mathur and Professor G. Rai interpret, represents "the universal myth of the primitive in the heart of man ever alienating him from the superficial and polished banalities of modern civilization."[65]

Billy Biswas suffers from a strange kind of crisis of identity. He has no feeling of rootlessness either in India or in U.S.A., though he has much more affinity with the tribal world than with the civilized. This may be said to be a variation of alienation and the crisis of consciousness and identity. Even in the U.S.A. he prefers living in the black ghetto of Harlem and is led into the world of ecstasy while playing musical instruments of the tribals. Back home in India he does not muster moral courage in the beginning to rebel against his parents in not marrying the girl of their choice. He does not even tell them to leave him alone or get him married to Rima Kaul, the girl of his choice. He is persuaded to marry Meena by an appeal to the sense of pragmatism of the West and that of the life being incomplete without marriage in the Indian context.

Billy Biswas is lost in posing questions about the nature of reality and that of the identity of man and his real descent. Before being a refugee from civilization Billy Biswas quests for such queries as:

> "Who am I? Who are my parents? My wife? My child? At times I look at them, sitting at the dinner table, and for a passing moment I cannot decide who they are or what accident of creation has brought us together."[66]

But Billy in his practical life is hardly after solving these problems even though he realizes that "becoming a primitive was only a first step, a means to an end."[67] He is actually never in search of this end in his life with the tribals. In the Maikala hills, living with Bilasia, a tribal widowed lady he becomes a godhead for them; but even in this capacity he hardly solves questions which he has posed regarding the identity and the existence of individuals on earth. As an anthropologist, "he wasn't just some hairy-fairy academic."[68] He was deeply interested in his area of specialization in the tribal affairs which took him on study tours with his disciples to the tribal world of the Maikala hills into which he escapes and identifies himself with the tribals shedding off all his associations with the civilized world where lived his parents, wife and child. The root cause of Billy's crisis of consciousness is what a Swedish researcher Tuula Lindgren calls *urkraft*. The dormant tribal urge explodes out of him as he leaves the civilized world to take refuge in the tribal world.

Billy's soul is never at rest. Even as a student in America where he goes to study engineering, he switches over to Anthropology and becomes an anarchist. Tne novelist as an omniscient commentator writes about Billy that "he was one of those rare men who have poise without pose."[69] This seems to be a true appreciation of Billy's character. But this is hardly completely true. His tribal sympathies are hardly due to any pose in him. He is instinctively attracted towards the tribals. There does not seem to be the presence of traits in his character that could be said to constitute the element of poise in him. He is a man given over to obsessions and fixations. There might be certain analogues in the life of Billy Biswas to the Scholar Gipsy as exemplified in Arnold's poem on him or the Buddha who renounced the palatial pleasures for the sake of the guest for finding solutions to mystical and philosophical problems. But Billy has no such quests though he poses such problems.

NOTES

1. Harish Raizada, "Double Vision of Fantasy and Reality in Arun Joshi's Novels" in *The Fictional World of Arun Joshi,* (ed.) R.K. Dhawan (New Delhi, 1986), 82.
2. Harish Raizada 74.
3. Arun Joshi, *The Strange Case of Billy Biswas* (New Delhi, 1987), 7.
4. "The Strange Case of Billy Biswas: A Serious Response to a Big Challenge" in *The Fictional World of Arun Joshi* (ed.) R.K. Dhawan (New Delhi, 1986), 191.
5. "Double Vision of Fantasy and Reality in Arun Joshi's Novels" in *The Fictional World of Arun Joshi,* (ed.) R.K. Dhawan (New Delhi, 1986), 83.
6. *The Strange Case of Billy Biswas* 128.
7. *The Strange Case of Billy Biswas* 129.
8. *The Strange Case of Billy Biswas* 14.
9. *The Strange Case of Billy Biswas* 122.

10. *The Strange Case of Billy Biswas* 122.
11. *The Strange Case of Billy Biswas* 23-24.
12. *The Strange Case of Billy Biswas* 17-18.
13. *The Strange Case of Billy Biswas* 18.
14. *Ibid.*
15. *Ibid.*
16. *The Strange Case of Billy Biswas* 23.
17. *The Strange Case of Billy Biswas* 44.
18. *The Strange Case of Billy Biswas* 75.
19. *The Strange Case of Billy Biswas* 78.
20. *The Strange Case of Billy Biswas* 83.
21. *Ibid.*
22. *The Strange Case of Billy Biswas* 96.
23. "Art and Vision of Arun Joshi" in *The Fictional World of Arun Joshi,* (ed.) R.K. Dhawan (New Delhi, 1986), 55.
24. *The Strange Case of Billy Biswas* 178-79.
25. *The Strange Case of Billy Biswas* 190.
26. *The Strange Case of Billy Biswas* 229.
27. *The Strange Case of Billy Biswas* 236.
28. *The Strange Case of Billy Biswas* 243.
29. *The Strange Case of Billy Biswas* 223.
30. *The Strange Case of Billy Biswas* 238.
31. *The Strange Case of Billy Biswas* 240.
32. "Arun Joshi and the Labyrinth of Life" in *The Fictional World of Arun Joshi,* ed. R.K. Dhawan (New Delhi, 1986), 144.
33. *The Strange Case of Billy Biswas* 25.
34. *Indian Writing in English* (New Delhi, 1984), 514.
35. *Ibid.*
36. *The Strange Case of Billy Biswas* 97.
37. *The Strange Case of Billy Biswas* 8.
38. *Ibid.*
39. *Ibid.*
40. *Ibid.*
41. *Ibid.*
42. "The Lost Lonely Questers in Arun Joshi's Fiction" in *The Fictional World of Arun Joshi,* ed. R. K. Dhawan (New Delhi, 1986), 161.

43. *The Strange Case of Billy Biswas* 9.
44. *The Strange Case of Billy Biswas* 96.
45. *The Strange Case of Billy Biswas* 96-97.
46. *The Strange Case of Billy Biswas* 97.
47. *The Strange Case of Billy Biswas* 96.
48. *The Strange Case of Billy Biswas* 98.
49. Matthew Arnold, *A Selection of His Poems,* (ed.) Kenneth Allott (Penguin Books, 1954), 208.
50. Arnold 208.
51. *The Strange Case of Billy Biswas* 108.
52. *The Strange Case of Billy Biswas* 186.
53. *The Strange Case of Billy Biswas* 186.
54. *The Strange Case of Billy Biswas* 189.
55. *Ibid.*
56. *Ibid.*
57. *Ibid.*
58. *The Strange Case of Billy Biswas* 132.
59. *The Strange Case of Billy Biswas* 161.
60. *The Strange Case of Billy Biswas* 162.
61. *The Strange Case of Billy Biswas* 206.
62. *The Strange Case of Billy Biswas* 227.
63. "Foreigners and Strangers: Arun Joshi's Heroes"—*The Journal of Indian Writing in English,* 5/1 January 1977, 54.
64. "Human Predicament and Meaninglessness in Arun Joshi's Novels," *The Fictional World of Arun Joshi,* (ed.) R.K. Dhawan (New Delhi, 1986), 132.
65. "The Existential Note in Arun Joshi's *The Strange Case of Billy Biswas* and *The Apprentice,*" *Commonwealth Quarterly,* V/17 (December, 1986), 35.
66. *The Strange Case of Billy Biswas* 97.
67. *The Strange Case of Billy Biswas* 189.
68. *The Strange Case of Billy Biswas* 131.
69. *The Strange Case of Billy Biswas* 11.

5

The Innocence and Experience of The "Homespun" World of *The Apprentice*

I

The Apprentice (1974) is chronologically the third novel by Arun Joshi. The two novels preceding it, *The Foreigner* (1968) and *The Strange Case of Billy Biswas* (1973), and the one following it, *The Last Labyrinth* (1981), deal with heroes who are in some way or the other globe-trotters. Moreover, the heroes in these novels have all been educated in British or American universities. *The Apprentice* is, however, distinct from these novels. The action of the novel takes place in India, though there are references to the British rule. Educationally, Ratan Rathor, the hero of this work of fiction, is a "home-spun" one. He has received no higher education beyond the frontiers of the Punjab. No character in it has received any foreign degree.

In *The Apprentice*, as Mr. H.M. Prasad writes, "The tone is almost Pascallian. Through self-mockery he exposes the world. Self-remorse will rehabilitate him. The fall contains recovery; it is a necessary process of his individuation."[1] It is through his vein of self-mockery that Ratan Rathor exposes hollowness of the Indian political and social systems. Professor Prasad has rightly pointed out that "the novel is both a social document and threnody of a tormented soul."[2]

The main thrust of the novel is a contrast between pre-Independence idealism preached by Mahatma Gandhi, "a man of suffering"[3] and post-Independence disillusionment. This Christ-like figure taught our national leaders how to use the weapon of non-violence to drive away the British, our alien rulers. But with the achievement of Independence, the Indian rulers and the ruled forgot what Gandhi had taught them. The democracy that came in the wake of the Republic was only in name, because with every subsequent election it was throttled at the polling booth, election being "five-yearly farce of the ballot-box."[4]

Ratan, the son of a freedom-fighter, has been an eye-witness of his father being shot dead while leading a procession, shouting patriotic slogans such as *Inquilab* and *Sarfarosi Ki Tamanna.* Ratan is the child of double inheritance. His father, an ardent patriot, gives up his lucrative practice as a lawyer to join politics at Gandhi's call. He donates his income and property to the national cause, without thinking of the difficulties faced by his wife in running the family. She is herself tubercular. She coughed and spat blood. Ratan reminisces that in living with his tubercular mother "it is like living with death."[5]

> Well, she lay there spitting blood, and my father called her several times without getting a response. Finally, she answered. You should go to a sanatorium, he said, all upset and excited. I'll be all right, my mother said, taking my hand in her own. No, you must, he persisted. Where's the money, my mother snapped at last. I'll go back to my practice, he said. Who'll lead the processions, said my mother, mocking. I don't care about the processions, he said.[6]

It is but natural that this lady should be disillusioned about the sacrifices made by patriots during the freedom struggle. A woman suffering all the time physically, mentally and economically becomes almost cynical about money as it is the only thing needed to make a man's life happy in the world. Even Ratan Rathor in his bureaucratic career thinks of the discrepancy between the ideals dreamt by the pillars of the freedom struggle and the condition of India under the leadership of the politicians reaping the fruits of free India. Ratan Rathor reminisces that in free India our politicians are worse substitutes for the alien Englishmen: "Could it be that the Englishmen had been merely replaced? And many times over? Could it be that *nothing* else but this has happened?"[7] This problem becomes so nagging that Ratan Rathor is compelled to think that it has simply given us a new slavery: "Yes, a New Slavery with new masters; politicians, officials, the rich, the old and new. Swindlers in fancy cars."[8] This problem of freedom and the new slavery in place of the British imperialism have been one of the fertile topics in the Indian English fiction. Bhabani Bhattacharya is one of the prominent of the Indian English novelists to deal with this kind of situation in a few of his novels, especially *A Goddess Named Gold*, where also he speaks of the throttling of our democracy at the polling booth: "Free India will die a hundred deaths. Beware, lest one such death takes place at the polling booth of this village."[9] Thus, Ratan Rathor is torn between the world of his father's idealism and mother's pragmatism. He takes an extreme course to amass money for him by compromising all the idealist lessons given to him by his father.

Besides the freedom struggle, the 1962 Indo-China war also figures as one of the main issues involved in the deteriorating situations of those people who control the war from their Secretariat chambers and are always bent upon grinding their own axe even at the cost of the national honour. The Indian debacle in the North-East led by a Brigadier, Ratan's childhood friend, is due to the defective war supplies because of the connivance of the Minister and the Secretary of the Department, not to speak of the lower cadre officers.

The Apprentice deals with Ratan Rathor's adolescent innocence, manly experience and saintly expiation. It is the protagonist, Ratan Rathor, who narrates the story of his life and times to an N.C.C. cadet come to New Delhi to participate in the Republic Day parade. Ratan narrates the episodes ranging from his childhood to his apprenticeship as a shoeshiner on the steps of a temple as a sort of expiation for his sins. The narrative, however, is not straightforward, as it keeps on swinging between the past and the present. The tone of the narration is that of self-mockery and the narrative impresses us in the end to be a kind of Horatian satire upon the abuses of position and power in the context of the Indian political system. The references to politicians and officers, however, are generic; yet persons behind them can be traced by an ardent political and historical researcher; but to obviate it Arun Joshi cautions us of such an approach and therefore he writes:

> The characters in this novel as well as the personality of the narrator are all inventions and bear no resemblance whatsoever to persons living or dead.[10]

But this is simply Joshi's non-controversial pose mingled with his gentlemanly poise. As we go through the novel, it is not difficult to find the references to shady deals undertaken by political executives and bureaucrats. *The Apprentice* reads as a cynical hymn to corruption which has a biting and corrosive edge.

Ratan presents before us a background of his childhood life both before and after the death of his father. Ratan has been an eye-witness to the sight of his father lying dead, while shouting in a procession, at the hands of a British sergeant. He had simply been a ten-year old boy at that time. Ratan's mother, after the death of her husband, had to sell away the remaining of the family property to meet the expenses of her son's education up to the graduate level. As a student Ratan also had high ideals and hoped that free India will bring a new light to the citizens of the Republic. But with the achievement of Independence all these hopes of Ratan get shattered:

> ... the death of my father had meant only one thing to me. That it was stupid to get killed like that. Stupid and meaningless. It served no one. Those who thought you served forgot you within the month. No life, I had thought sitting by the woman, no life had been more pointlessly spent than that the life of my father.[11]

While Ratan tries to live up to his father's expectations of him "To be good! Respected! To be of use!"[12] his disillusioned mother keeps on persuading him not to be influenced by his father's crazy ideas of his joining the freedom struggle. She wants him to be pragmatic and to realise the importance of money: "Man without money was a man without worth. Many things were great in life, but the greatest of them all was money."[13] She exhorted Ratan of this pragmatism:

> It was not patriotism but money, she said, that brought respect and bought security. Money made friends. Money succeeded where all else failed. There were many laws, she said, but money was law unto itself.[14]

In search of means of livelihood after his graduation, Ratan comes to Delhi, "a city of opportunities."[15] It is here that Ratan gets disillusioned when he goes to seek help from certain of his father's lawyer friends. In his search for employment he realises that though the posts are advertised, most of them are "filled by people, who had, in some manner, been pre-selected."[16] During his stay in Delhi Ratan gets shelter in an inn beside a mosque where several others also occupy the same room with him. A stenographer living at the same inn, manages a job for him in a Government office, dealing with war purchases. Thus begins Ratan's life as an apprentice clerk. Ratan keeps his eyes upon careerism despised by his father as bourgeois filth. But Ratan ignores this and works hard to please his Superintendent. The first thing that he does after employment is that he leaves the inn to settle elsewhere and even tries to keep away from the stenographer who had been instrumental in securing a job for him. In a very short time of six months, on the recommendation of the Superintendent, he gets confirmed in the service on his assurance that he would marry the Superintendent's niece. Henceforward he never looks back and on the Superintendent's retirement gets this coveted post which brings for him every comfort in life, denied to his parents. Ratan realises the practical importance of negotiations and deals in life:

> Deals, deals, deals, my friend, that is what the world runs on, what it is all about. If men forgot how to make deals, the world would come to a stop. It would lose its propelling power. Men would not know what to do with themselves. They would lose interest. It is not the atom or the sun or God or sex that lies at the heart of the universe; it is deals. DEALS. It is a bit like my mother's prophecy, about money. It is not whether you like making deals or you like money. They are simply there, like air.[17]

In this Ratan has grasped the pulse of the time and this makes him rise upward, though it is through his corrupt practice in which he is just a cog in the corrupt official machinery. Sometimes he gets so fed up with the corrupt practices that he thinks of deliverance through death, like a few of the existentialist characters. During the time of the nation's adversity, he is not the only one to gain prosperity by clearing substandard war-materials supplied by the Sheikh Himmat Singh. Ratan's own case is an instance of irony of fate. There is nothing unethical about the fact that the son of the freedom fighter runs after a bureaucratic career, but it is highly illegal and unethical and unscrupulous that he should get corrupt and act against the national interest. What is important in the character of Ratan is that he is fully aware of it. But he cannot escape the situation because all around him there is, what he calls, the crisis of character. He even writes an essay on the topic which, after it is rejected by so many papers, is circulated in the cyclostyled form. Ratan calls this essay a "comic document"[18] but tragic, too. He gives a resume of it to his silent listener, a student from the Punjab. He begins it with a quotation from Mahatma Gandhi, borrowed from a book on him and followed by the one from *the Bhagavad Gita*. Ratan paints in it the golden history of India's past, often referred to in the tourist pamphlets. To do it he refers to the landmarks of the ancient Indian civilization such as Harappa and Mohenjodaro, the conquests of Kalinga by Asok and the rule of *dharma* and truth.

Then he describes the dark ages of the country when with the falling night the sun of *dharma* set. This was followed by a "twilight in which what hope was left dwindled."[19] This was again followed by the night like that of "*amavas*"[20] which lasted "the span of twenty generations, a night that led us into slavery and ended only with the dawn of Independence."[21] But the crisis of Indian character comes to the forefront even after Independence which made "a display of greed before which the plunderings of a Ghaznavi paled. Freedom did not bring that elevation of the spirit that the great leaders had hoped for."[22] The country is chained by corruption. Ratan Rathor emphasizes this aspect of the crisis of Indian character in his article and he shows it to so many of his colleagues that they nickname him Mr. Crisis of character. But despite all this, Ratan Rathor confesses:

> You see, to cut a long story short, just before the war started I took a bribe. An enormous bribe. Yes, Mr. Crisis of character took an enormous bribe. No more, no less.[23]

Ratan goes on to explain how he had to accept the bribe. The situation now shifts to the freedom struggle and to the time of the Chinese invasion. The Minister and the Secretary associated with war supplies passed Sheikh Himmat Singh on to Ratan, the Superintendent of the section who had refused to pass the defective war materials. But he had to accept the bribe from the Sheikh "for some obscure reasons,"[24] thus selling away his soul to the devil. The Sheikh operated in a way that nothing could be proved as all the documents regarding the deal were to be destroyed. The Sheikh teaches Ratan the Machiavellian philosophy of life and he tells Ratan that only a fool and hypocrite likes getting killed. The Sheikh also impresses upon him that the rulers of the country are "phoney people who knew only how to make speeches,"[25] and that "the ruled were brainless."[26] In his official rise to success Ratan never gives up magnanimity. He donates freely to charitable funds and writes patriotic letters to the editors of certain papers. He even donates blood to Red Cross for the national cause and inspires all

Indians to rise as one nation. Yet Ratan goes on to the primrose way of pawning his heart and soul for the cause of the worship of the Mammon. Sometimes he reminisces why he began taking bribes even though he did not "need the money."[27] Besides the war purchases, hectic purchases for the refugees also brought prosperity to the persons dealing in it. Ratan is amazed to see duplicity all around. All those who matter are master-fakers. Rulers of free India became worse substitutes of the British. Ratan is very eloquent about the role of bribe in free India:

> If I had taken a bribe I belonged rather to the rule than the exception. Peons were frequently taking bribes. So were government officials and traffic policemen and railway conductors. A bribe could get you a bed in the hospital, a place to burn your dead. Doctors had a fee to give false certificates, magistrates for false judgements. For a sum of money politicians changed sides. For a larger sum they declared wars. Bribery was accepted by factory inspectors, bank agents and college professors; by nurses, priests and chartered accountants; by all those who acted in the public interest. Men took the bribes to facilitate the seduction of their wives; women for seduction of other women. All this I knew and had known for twenty years. And now if I had happened to have accidentally indulged in a little slip-up, the sky was not going to fall.[28]

This is a fine justification of why Ratan starts taking bribes though he does not need the money for any one of his needs. With the accumulation of riches, Ratan also gets engulfed in the vices associated with wealth such as taste for wine and woman. In Bombay he once gets engrossed in "fantasies of pleasures."[29] The world of Bombay, however, also reminds him of the contrast between the simple life led in the village and the life of city carrying on commerce and business and bargains. Ratan's crisis of character always keeps on pricking him. He realizes that he is after wrong things but he cannot avoid being an accomplice in the official misdeeds. His case is striking in that the son of a freedom fighter has become engrossed in the anti-nationalist and nefarious designs.

Ratan has deep anguish in his heart at the fate of his childhood friend who as Brigadier in the North-Eastern front has been responsible for the nation's debacle at the hands of the Chinese army. The real culprits, however, play in the corridors of power in the Defence Ministry. The politicians and bureaucrats acting in the interest of the self do not even think of the national honour and clear the defective war materials supplied by the Sheikh who is a kingpin in the deal. The war operations are guided by people who have no experience of the field and from places far away from the operation site. All the guilt of the national defeat falls upon the head of the innocent Army Brigadier who is helpless as ammunitions do not work and as such the guns misfire.

A reverse of this kind of situation has been mocked at by Bernard Shaw in *Arms and the Man* where Captain Sergius, betrothed to Louka, leads his battalion forward into desperate action without much ammunition in which, however, because of the defective ammunition in the enemy camp, he becomes a hero in the battle of Slivnitza only because the enemy's guns misfired:

> And there was Don Quixote flourishing like a drum major, thinking he'd done the cleverest thing ever known whereas he ought to be court-martialled for it. Of all the fools ever let loose on a field of battle, that man must be the very maddest. He and his regiment simply committed suicide; only the pistol missed fire: that's all [*Arms and The Man* (Orient Longman, 1983), 17].

With reference to the Chinese invasion, the same thing happened to them. They got the better of the Indian Army whose weapons misfired because of the defective ammunition.

Ratan feels for his Brigadier friend, who, in his school days, had saved him from being thrashed at the hands of hooligans. He is now baited and court-martialled for the Army's debacle, though the real culprits are those who are responsible for the war purchases.

Even though intelligence people have information regarding the shady deals, the Superintendent of Police conducting the enquiry, has no substantial papers to prove it. Ratan in the police lock-up for a night sometimes decides to confess, and even makes a clean breast of everything in writing, which, however, he does not pass on to the S.P., who has to leave him scot-free in the absence of any documentary proof.

For this anti-national act on the part of the Minister and the Secretary, the Brigadier suffers a nervous breakdown and commits suicide. Despite this Ratan views his misdeeds to be "little adulteries of the soul that did not count."[30]

Sometimes Ratan, in his guilty conscience, tries to cleanse himself with the help of worship in temples. But to his great amazement he finds that even the temple is a den of corruption. The pujari of the temple thrives on it. His son has been booked for constructing buildings which had all crumbled down because of the use in the construction work of substandard building materials. The priest, knowing of the high position of Ratan in the department, offers him bribe to help his son escape from this enquiry. It is only after this that Ratan takes up a novel way to expiate himself. He does not enter the temple to worship the deity there; rather he sits outside on the stairs to wipe the shoes of devotees either in the morning or evening while going to or coming from office, while his expensive car is parked outside. It is here that Ratan comes across a student from the Punjab coming to Delhi to participate in the Republic Day parade. He also shines his shoes:

> HERE you are! Almost the last. Let me get your shoes. Would you care for some tea, if you are not in a hurry? It is already dark. But I forget it is November.[31]

II

The Apprentice is a self-analysis by Ratan of his own crisis of identity and consciousness. He narrates the story of his life in the form of a dramatic monologue in which time and again he dwells upon his character. He is conscious all the time that he has not been doing the right things, yet he goes on with his affairs and not till his Brigadier friend commits suicide on being court-martialled, does he feel anguish. It is after this episode that he seeks to get solace in the rituals of religion which also repel him as being no less corrupt than the official world. As a substitute he takes to the job of shoeshining to expiate the sins committed. The following lines make it clear how bruised Ratan's soul is:

> And all these years this terrible loneliness, something that you may not suspect by looking at me, something that none has ever suspected. How, all these years, I have been alone, so horribly alone in my failures, carrying them in secret, like a thief, close to my heart, until their blazes have turned upon me and turned me to ashes. Believe me, I have seen it happen. I have seen my soul turn to ashes.[32]

But Ratan' s soul is not yet dead. There is hope for him yet. Even the Sheikh confesses, "My soul was killed, you put yours to pawn. But souls that were pawned could perhaps be retrieved.... Maybe souls are like muscles, Ratan Rathor. Maybe to develop them one has first to put them to use."[33] Shoeshining devotees' footwear puts his soul to use. His pawned soul is retrieved in its expiation. But even before he is conscious of it, he is all the time concerned with a schism in his soul. Speaking to the N.C.C. cadet he wonders that the capital is "a no-man's land."[34] In his loneliness Ratan Rathor finds himself "abandoned on the planet"[35] and even finds the world "a place without law, a planet turning in the darkness, going heaven knew where."[36] The anarchy prevailing in the world seems to rock him "through some dark dungeons of the world."[37] Like Graham Greene's Scobie in *The Heart of the Matter*, Ratan, too, feels a kind of pity for the planets. Sometimes Ratan's agonizing alienation leaves him face to face with cosmic problems. Ratan Rathor uses phrases and terms of expressions using device of variation plus repetition, so important in creating rhythm in the novel, as expounded in Foster's *Aspects of the Novel.* Such expressions are scattered throughout the novel, to stress Ratan's tormented soul. The loss of discrimination between good and bad makes Ratan conscious of the fact that life without it is "panic and foolishness. Panic and foolishness."[38] This pestilence is a common weakness in our nation. Unemployment is what Ratan calls "my biggest dread"[39] but even after getting an employment he is not free of it.

Ratan, in his introspection, feels that the most striking aspect about his life is a discrepancy between idealism and realism. He had high hopes as the son of a freedom fighter; but in his practical life he associates himself with the biggest of the frauds. But what is commendable in Ratan Rathor is that he confesses everything to lighten the burden of corruption on him. He calls himself, or others call him, "a master-faker,"[40] "a sham,"[41] "a sham and a faker,"[42] "an upstart,"[43] "a thick-skin and a washout,"[44] "a whore,"[45] "a scoundrel,"[46] "a fool or a great hypocrite,"[47] "spineless flunkey and bogus,"[48] "a pile of dung,"[49] "a bundle of shams,"[50] "a trickster"[51] and "a betrayer of the spirit."[52] Such expressions have been integrated into the syntactic patterns of the sentences. But in many of the cases they form part of verbless sentences or simply stray noun phrases. Ratan sometimes even gets disillusioned with the concept of, and the word, freedom. He speaks in the monologue:

> Freedom. Freedom. What is freedom but a word, my friend? Freedom of men, of nation. No more than a word. We thought we were free. What we had, in fact, was new slavery. Yes, a New Slavery with new masters;....[53]

Ratan is fed up with the flow of words:

> Words, words, words. Speeches, editorials, resolutions, handouts, slogans, posters, banners, proceedings of the numerous assemblies, exchanges with foreign countries, memoranda of the chambers of commerce, manifestos of

> trade unions, draft five-year plans, books extolling our past. An endless barrage of words, very few of which, I soon realised, meant anything, just as they mean nothing today.[54]

Ratan, in the course of his rising corruption, feels not only restlessness but also apathy and indifference within himself: "Upon me. Inside me. Like a boil. Like leprosy."[55] His role in the treachery at the national peril makes him realise that he "was a liar, as crooked a liar as any common thief."[56] He tries to get out of "the crookedness of the world;" "the crookedness of oneself"[57] and after a great deal of deliberation he decides in favour of wiping the shoes of the congregation.

III

The Apprentice is very close to existentialist philosophy. As Thakur Guruprasad says:

> Ratan Rathor, the protagonist of the novel, conforms to the dot to the dictionary definition of "existential": the doctrine that man forms his essence in the course of his life he chooses to lead. He is born a good man, the son of a martyr in the national movement. But when he goes out of his village to graduate in life of the crooked world, honesty does not get him even the lowest job, and he makes his essence, as he goes choosing the life he leads.[58]

In his life full of compromises and deals Ratan's conscience is restless and he spends sleepless nights. He admits, "To sleep is a privilege not given to all. As long as you can sleep, all is well."[59] Ratan wallows in the bourgeois filth, and even though his position gets higher in the official hierarchy, he feels no aggrandisement, rather he shrinks. Dr. Hari Mohan Prasad hints at the point when he says about Rathor, "He gets isolated and incommunicative. He becomes an island."[60] His soul is smothered by the seedy life all around and even though his father's idealism smoulders within him, it is not allowed to burn up till the end of his final realization after the Brigadier's death.

Adapting an idea from Ignace Fuerlicht's *Alienation: From the Past to the Future* (Connecticut: Greenwood Press, 1978, 41), V. Gopal Reddy writes:

> Modern man may either try and adjust to "others, to society, to the system, abdicating his true self, or he may strive to keep and develop his individuality and alienate himself from society.[61]

In the case of Ratan Rathor we come across both these types of alienation. Ratan Rathor, in his efforts to mould himself after his father's idealism, becomes a misfit in the modern world and as such he has "to abdicate his true self to fit in the corrupt society and eke out a living. He is alienated from his true self in the process."[62] Caught in the web of these two types of alienation, Ratan becomes a prisoner of his own self which builds a labyrinth for him. This is true not only to *The Apprentice* but also to Joshi's other novels as well. V.V.N. Rajendra Prasad states, "The core of Joshi's fictional theme consists in viewing the self as labyrinth, and any kind of assessment that the self makes of itself is a therapeutic process."[63] It is difficult for Ratan to get out of the labyrinth and get lost in the ways of life which leads to the corruption of his self which is itself corrupt. According to C.N. Srinath, *The Apprentice* is "tale of conscience-torn man, with a curious mixture of idealism and docility, a vague sense of values, a helpless self-deceptive effort to flout them for the sake of a career—in short with a deep awareness of the conflict between life and living."[64]

In the absence of any demarcation between right and wrong, success and failure, loyalty and betrayal, love and hate, Ratan Rathor finds himself "reduced... to the status of those leaves of autumn that are blown here and there, at the mercy of the wind. Why be surprised if one of them falls into the sewer."[65] Ratan Rathor suffers from an agonised soul. It keeps him tormenting. Ratan Rathor refers to one of his friend's definition of zero, life as zero and his own amendment of the concept of zero:

> Life is zero, he would say, and, he would add, you can take nothing away from a zero. He was a persuasive man and I must confess I used to be much impressed, at least, for the duration of his talk. Of late, however, I have begun to see a flaw in the argument. You see, you can take things out of a zero! You can make it negative. And if my colleague were alive today I should ask him this: Would he prefer a negative to a zero? Life might well be a zero, for all I know, but it seems to me that it need not be negative. And it becomes negative when you take out of it your sense of shame, your honour.[66]

Ratan's distinction between zero and negative contains in it a subtle point of life's philosophy. The last sentence of the indented quotation above makes the distinction very meaningful. Applied to Ratan's case this holds out well. Before the idealism preached by his father, Ratan's life might have been a zero; but as he feels ashamed of his misdeeds and expiates it, he upholds honour, so that his life should not degenerate into a negative one. Moreover, Ratan gets aware of the need of a positive attitude to life. He affirms:

> There is hope as long as there are young men willing to learn from the follies of their elders. Willing to learn and ready to sacrifice. Willing to pay the price.[67]

Ratan's confessional mode of the narrative is also an affirmation of his real quest of identity which had been a sort of abominable crisis which tempts him on to act as dishonourably as he could with his other accomplices in this official hierarchy. Ratan's confessions make it evident that *The Apprentice* as a sarcastic hymn to corruption is also a satire. Through the narrative Ratan goes on to expose a duplicity in the Indian character. This is to be seen at the top political and bureaucratic levels. Its presence at the lower official level is a reflection of the top-rank people around us. They may talk of "religion,"[68] "politics,"[69] "culture,"[70] but "nothing connects"[71] and "chaos"[72] and "panic"[73] engulf us. The freedom that has been achieved at the cost of great sacrifice is no more than a word because we have been dominated by a system of new slavery:

> Yes, a new slavery with the new masters: politicians, officials. The rich, old and new. Swindlers in fancy cars. Some of these men I recognised; others I only heard about.[74]

This sometimes makes Ratan feel a strange kind of "restlessness,"[75] "apathy[76] and "indifference."[77] He also feels "run down"[78] and "used up."[79] Even in his affluence he feels disturbed and depressed and darkness within and without. The situations in the country seem as if the blind were following the blind. It is natural that he should feel as one of the "frustrated men sailing about in a confused society, a society without norms, without direction, without even, perhaps, a purpose."[80]

The Apprentice is a narrative told in a flash-back. The narrative concentrates upon the "brainwashing"[81] of Ratan's "clerical mentality."[82] This results in Ratan's alienation and loneliness which turn his soul into ashes. But his realization of "the sorrow of a wasted life"[83] makes Ratan come clean out of the purgatory of national melting pot which goes on amalgamating things for the nation's amelioration.

NOTES

1. Hari Mohan Prasad, *Arun Joshi* (New Delhi, 1985), 77.
2. Prasad 65.
3. *The Apprentice* 9.
4. *The Apprentice* 74.
5. *The Apprentice* 9.
6. *Ibid.*
7. *The Apprentice* 63.
8. *The Apprentice* 63-64.
9. Bhabani Bhattacharya, *A Goddess Named Gold* (New Delhi, 1984), 114.
10. *The Apprentice* 6.
11. *The Apprentice* 83.

12. *The Apprentice* 19.
13. *The Apprentice* 20.
14. *Ibid.*
15. *The Apprentice* 31.
16. *The Apprentice* 30.
17. *The Apprentice* 51.
18. *The Apprentice* 58.
19. *The Apprentice* 59.
20. *Ibid.*
21. *Ibid.*
22. *Ibid.*
23. *The Apprentice* 60.
24. *Ibid.*
25. *The Apprentice* 84.
26. *Ibid.*
27. *The Apprentice* 61.
28. *The Apprentice* 112.
29. *The Apprentice* 78.
30. *The Apprentice* 117.
31. *The Apprentice* 7.
32. *The Apprentice* 74-75.
33. *The Apprentice* 146.
34. *The Apprentice* 8.
35. *The Apprentice* 17.
36. *The Apprentice* 44.
37. *The Apprentice* 103.
38. *The Apprentice* 23.
39. *The Apprentice* 27.
40. *The Apprentice* 28.
41. *Ibid.*
42. *Ibid.*
43. *The Apprentice* 36.
44. *The Apprentice* 41.
45. *The Apprentice* 49.
46. *The Apprentice* 70.

47. *The Apprentice* 83
48. *The Apprentice* 136-37.
49. *The Apprentice* 137.
50. *Ibid.*
51. *The Apprentice* 139.
52. *The Apprentice* 142.
53. *The Apprentice* 63.
54. *The Apprentice* 64.
55. *The Apprentice* 66.
56. *The Apprentice* 108.
57. *The Apprentice* 148.
58. Thakur Guruprasad, "The Lost Lonely Questers of Arun Joshi's Fiction" in *The Novels of Arun Joshi,* (ed.) R.K. Dhawan (New Delhi, 1992), 99.
59. *The Apprentice* 8.
60. H.M. Prasad, *Arun Joshi* (New Delhi, 1985), 78.
61. V. Gopal Reddy, "*The Apprentice*: An Existential Study," *The Novels of Arun Joshi,* (ed.) R.K. Dhawan (New Delhi, 1992), 217.
62. V. Gopal Reddy, "*The Apprentice*: An Existential Study," *The Novels of Arun Joshi,* (ed.) R.K. Dhawan (New Delhi, 1992), 217-18.
63. V.V.N. Rajendra Prasad, "*The Apprentice*: Self as Labyrinth," *The Novels of Arun Joshi,* (ed.) R.K. Dhawan (New Delhi, 1992), 211.
64. "Fiction of Arun Joshi," *The Literary Criterion,* XII, 2-3, 1976, 127.
65. *The Apprentice* 73.
66. *The Apprentice* 148.
67. *The Apprentice* 149.
68. *The Apprentice* 60.
69. *Ibid.*
70. *Ibid.*
71. *Ibid.*
72. *Ibid.*
73. *Ibid.*
74. *The Apprentice* 63-64.
75. *The Apprentice* 66.
76. *Ibid.*
77. *Ibid.*

78. *The Apprentice* 67.
79. *Ibid.*
80. *The Apprentice* 74.
81. *The Apprentice* 106.
82. *The Apprentice* 85.
83. *The Apprentice* 140.

6

PEOPLE AT STRIFE IN *THE CITY AND THE RIVER*

I

The City and the River (1990) "strikes an entirely different theme from Arun Joshi's earlier novels."[1] Yet there are certain striking parallels with Joshi's previous novels as well. In his earlier novels as well Arun Joshi had been interested in the mode of fantasy and satire especially in *The Strange Case of Billy Biswas* and *The Apprentice*. But whereas in the previous novels, fantasy and satire had been incidental, in *The City and the River* these constitute the basic fictional technique.

The City and the River is the only fictional work by Arun Joshi bearing a title conjoined by the cumulative conjunction "and." This serves to juxtapose the first noun phrase "the City" with the second "the River." Both these are inanimate objects which have been used as symbols of the two ways of life. The city represents the city state governed by the Grand Master, who runs it with the assistance of a Council of Advisers. The river passing by the city symbolizes the endless flow of life. The real sons of the river are the boatmen living in mud-houses that lie scattered by the river on the outskirts of the city. The city had its elite living in "the neat rosy pink, oval of the brick colonies."[2] The brick-people have all lost their authenticity and are not concerned with what goes on in their city state. The mud-people, on the other hand, are all deeply involved in the anti-repressive measures adopted to subjugate them. The Grand Master with his advisers creates a reign of terror and the state terrorism is let loose. The Grand Master assisted by his son and advisers use the latest scientific equipment to suppress boatmen's rebellion. Boatmen are tortured; their head person, who is a woman, is imprisoned and blinded. There is much destruction of life and property including the Grand Father's Rose Garden and the inmates in it. Finally, nature has its own revenge as the river rises to an unprecedented level and washes away the entire city including its buildings and inmates, leaving no trace of any habitation. Yet out of the ruins of the old city a new one rises up; and it has all the ways of life that had been there in the old city. Out of the flood only one person survives, and he has been simply called Nameless-One, who is an illegal child and who is sent to the city with the mission to re-establish it.

The novel opens with *Prologue* and ends with *Epilogue.* In between the two it has nine chapters narrating the rule of the Grand Master, his becoming king, the perpetuation of the reign of terror, people's rebellion, the declaration of an Era of Ultimate Greatness, which is tantamount to the clamping of the rule of Emergency, the repressive measures adopted by the king, and lastly, the destruction of the city with the great flood.

Prologue and *Epilogue* inform us of the narrative strategy of the novel. The great Yogeshwar is an ageless seer and teacher at whose feet several persons of the novel such as Astrologer, the Minister for Trade and the Hermit of the Mountain also received education. The agelessness of the teacher is borne up by the fact that "a hundred years ago, as young students, the Astrologer and the Hermit had long debated this particular Parallelogram."[3] Both of the disciples have crossed much more than a century of their lives and their teacher, the great Yogeshwar, must have been almost ageless. The *Prologue* tells us about the last day of Nameless-One with the great Yogeshwar. The great Yogeshwar celebrates his pupil's thirtieth birthday by revealing to him who he is. Moreover, he points out to him the mystery of the world and how to "keep the grain and the chaff apart."[4] The great Yogeshwar also teaches him the secret of the body and that of the spirit and how the spirit gained the control of the body. He also teaches his pupil the way of the pilgrim and the way of the warrior, and cautions him "about the ways of the tyrant and how to wait."[5] The great Yogeshwar teaches him everything but tells him nothing about who he is. The great Yogeshwar reads out something from a book of yellowed sheets, containing "a strange, sorry tale."[6] To celebrate his thirtieth birthday the teacher offers him elixir which is "the colour of the peacock's feathers."[7] It makes the Nameless-One aware of the music and the dance prevailing in the infinite spaces of the cosmic night and he feels "as vast as sky and as tall as a mountain."[8] The teacher is satisfied that his disciple also sees the dancing of a god and then he tells him:

> I shall tell you now a tale and in my telling, perhaps, you will know who you are. Listen, this is how it goes.[9]

Then follows the narrative of the novel in about two hundred and fifty pages describing the city and the river. This is crowned by *Epilogue* beginning with the question posed by the Nameless-One "and then what happened?"[10] The great Yogeshwar then goes on to tell him of the fate of the periodic disintegration and regeneration of the city and its different activities. All this had happened thirty years ago when the Nameless-One, an illegal child, had been placed on a raft floating on the river. The great Yogeshwar himself comes by him and not only rears him up but also educates him. In *Epilogue*, the great Yogeshwar sends him back to the city in the same raft which had taken him to the great Yogeshwar. The great Yogeshwar tells the Nameless-One of the endless repetition and periodic disintegration and sends him back to the city "to prevent this endless repetition, this periodic disintegration,"[11] but cautions him that "to achieve that we need purity."[12] The sage means thereby that he should purify himself "of egoism, selfishness, stupidity."[13] Its acquisition is a question of trying "but purity can come only through sacrifice."[14] By way of telling him who he is, the great Yogeshwar teaches him that "God resides as much in a Grand Master as in you or in me."[15]

The sage tells him, moreover, "it is what you are inside that governs what you are outside."[16] The sage also promises to him that he would be with him as an instrument "of the great God in the highest heaven who is the master of the universe."[17] The Nameless-One in his journey to the city finds a casket of burnished brass containing within a prophecy which had also been there with the previous city and which had been a topic of much debate by the great Yogeshwar's former disciples. Regarding the fate of the city the great Yogeshwar elaborates:

> On the ruins of that city as always happens, a new city has risen. It is ruled by another Grand Master, which, of course, need not always happen. In the new city is another Professor, another Bhumiputra, another tribe of boatmen. There is also another Council and another set of Councillors. The men have other names but the forces they embody remain unchanged. And into all this when you go you will, perhaps, be known as another hermit of the Mountain, and it is possible you will have a disciple whose name will be Little Star. To someone this replay, this repetition of things, might appear as a charade, a joke. But, then, whoever said the good Lord did not have humour.[18]

Prologue and *Epilogue* bring out the cyclic motion of the novel. As Usha Bande says, "the story ends where it begins and begins where it ends."[19] She rightly compares it with T.S. Eliot's lines in *The Four Quartets*:

> In my beginning is my end. In succession
> Houses rise and fall, crumble, are extended,
> Are removed, destroyed, restored.[20]

Prologue and *Epilogue* tell nothing palpable or concrete about the narrative, but these prepare us for the interpretation of the novel as a whole. The paragraph quoted from the text is related to the continuation of "the psychic march of humanity"[21] in which "a new city is reborn like the phoenix on the ruins of the old."[22]

Prologue and *Epilogue* read like extracts from some allegory or parable. Arun Joshi's interests in these have shifted from the narration of the personal crisis to that of the public. Yet as individuals make up the public, the questions of the crisis of individual identity are not far-off. This is amply illustrated from the reference to "the strange sorry tale"[23] which is about that of the destruction of the city. The great Yogeshwar points out to his disciple—the Nameless-One—the importance of the recurring problems in the cycle of regeneration and decay, concerning a matter of "allegiance to God or to man."[24] This statement makes the novel hinge upon the problems of both religion (God) and politics (man). *Prologue* and *Epilogue* have certain deeper associations as well. These are associated with certain mythical archetypes. G.S. Amur associates the escape of the Nameless-One from the deluge with "Shishumara of the Indian myths."[25] There are, moreover, many other archetypal patterns in these episodes. Usha Bande has drawn our attention to it.[26] The great Yogeshwar is "Purana Purusha" and the Nameless-One is symbolic of the Manu on the raft on the day of the *pralaya* saving the Vedas. The great Yogeshwar is also like Lord Krishna, telling his disciple the gospel of duty and making him feel as vast as the sky and as tall as the mountains. The Nameless-One is also a Christ-figure. He is an illegal child but a chosen one.

II

With this background of *Prologue* and *Epilogue* we move forward to an analysis of the different episodes of the novel before we analyse the problems of crisis of identity in which some of the characters have got themselves enmeshed.

There is some anonymity about the characters of the novel, *The City and the River*. The majority of the characters are not known by their personal names but by the positions they hold in the hierarchy of the rule. There is no name assigned either to the city or the river. But the very opening paragraph of the novel depicts a photographic topography of the city:

> The city over the years has grown. It has spread along the bank of the river and in the north it touches the very margins of the pyramids. As always, it is best seen from the river at sunrise. First comes the narrow brown band of the mud huts, running from end to end, dotted with the green of many mangroves. Next, offset a little to the right, on a higher ground, lies the neat rosy pink oval of the brick colonies and their special schools, clubs, shopping arcades. Beyond the brick colonies stand the famous Seven Hills ranged in their picturesque formation. The hills vary in altitude and are now seat of the Grand Master's government. On the tallest stands the palace: it is easily recognized by the delicacy of its dome which is said to be a marvel of modern architecture. The next tallest hill, for some reason, has been left vacant. On the remaining hills stand tall structures of steel and glass. From the river one cannot make out of the offices that these buildings house, but one is impressed none the less by their immaculate white that on moonlit nights gleams like a goddess's limbs and stays wonderfully unstained during the rains when the mud huts turn black and even the rose of the brick mansions is blotched.
>
> Beyond the palace, on still higher ground, lost in the haze, stand the pyramids and beyond everything else, in the far distance, high up in the blue sky looms the mountain, its snow-covered peaks for ever brooding over this panorama of brown and pink and white. No one has yet climbed the mountain even though for hundreds of years, men have launched expeditions against it and two hundred men have died in the attempt.[27]

The city is governed by the anonymous Grand Master who is "the son and grandson of Grand Masters."[28] The palace is situated on the tallest of the seven hills. The different administrative departments have been housed in the remaining of the hills except the next tallest hill which has been left vacant.

There is a kind of a hierarchy of importance of the hills depending upon their respective heights. The higher the hill is, the more important it is politically; and conversely the lower it is, the lower is its importance. The height of the hills is also a governing factor of the social structure of the administrative set-up. It has been very aptly referred to in the following:

> The social stratification of the city is signified by the altitude at which the different classes live. The Grand Master, the Ministers (who also act as his Councillors), whose social superiority is matched by the geographical height, live and administer the city from the Seven Hills (which are the highest in the city) varying in height according to the status of the Ministers, with the Grand Master living on the highest hill. The middle class people live on a comparatively lower ground in pink brick buildings. The lowly people, including the boatmen, inhabit the area along the river bank which is the lowest in altitude. The level of authenticity varies in inverse proportion to the social position of the different categories of inhabitants.[29]

The Grand Master's ancestors have lived in this palace for seventy years and he is fond of his people, but it is not always so. His sympathies are more with the haves than with the have-nots, who are the mud-people known as "the Nameless-One because outside their home habitations no one knows their name."[30] The Grand Master loves the city as also have his ancestors done. He has set up a Council of the Friends of the People on the Advisory Council which has five members on it, such as the Palace Astrologer, the Minister for Trade, the Education Advisor, the Police Commissioner and the Master of Rallies. The two, the Palace Astrologer and the Master of Rallies, are rather unusual figures in an administrative set-up. But Arun Joshi has done so in his design as a fantasist to expose the hollowness of rulers and administrators. The Grand Master also likes his people but at times he is not sure of it. Of the mud-people, especially the boatmen, turn mutinous. This is a matter of great concern for the Grand Master who sits in conference with his advisors to quell it. Even the young son of the Grand Master comes out with his suggestion, "everyone has his price, father,"[31] meaning thereby that there are steps to settle and decide every problem.

Being perplexed by the affairs of the State, the Grand Master once dreams that he has become a king. All around his throne there is the flood of the river and even the gods are playing one-string which is the musical instrument used by the boatmen. But the sight of naked men emerging from the river disturbs him and he orders them to leave his throne. Their nakedness tightens around the king's throne "like a noose."[32] The disturbed Grand Master wakes up and in the morning asks his Astrologer to give an interpretation of it. The Astrologer finds the dream in conformity with the prophecy that speaks of the coming of a king. The interpretation of the prophecy has been a topic of debate even by the disciples of the great Yogeshwar. This prophecy recorded in ten-verse lines not only forms an epigraph of the novel but has also been repeated in the body:

> Who knows, who can read the signs,
> The workings of immortal time?
> A King I see upon a throne,
> In astronomer's grove the boatmen mourn,
> A thing of darkness growing dark,
> On City walls the shadow's mark.
> The River, I see, from a teacher rise.
> The hermit, the parrot, the teacher die.
> Under a rain the waters burn,
> To his kingdom at last the king returns.[33]

The Grand Master has his eyes fixed upon becoming king and all his actions are directed toward the achievement of this goal. He devises schemes through his advisors to bring people on his side and suppress rebellion of the boatmen. The Astrologer is the arch designer to convince boatmen to accept the Grand

Master as their benevolent servant sent by the gods themselves. The boatmen are poor but their numerical strength goes on increasing. So does their discontent at the Grand Master's indifference towards them. The Grand Master enforces family planning and passes a regulation that to reduce population there should "be only one child to a mother or to a home."[34] The boatmen rebel against it. Much though the Astrologer wants them to act according to the Grand Master's benevolent rule, the boatmen do not get reconciled to it.

On the suggestion of the Astrologer, the declaration is made regarding the triple way or the way of the Three Beatitudes. All these are aimed at the supposed welfare of the State. The first rule is that the people should offer their allegiance to the Grand Master because he is "the father and the mother of city."[35] The second declaration is regarding the public property as the collective property of all; and this can be preserved only when the population is checked. The third regulation is by way of caution which warns the rebellious people of being "received without mercy and be treated according to the Grand Master's law of compassionate righteousness."[36] The boatmen led by their head boatman, who was a woman, pay no attention to these. They fail to convince the head boatman to express their allegiance to the Grand Master and to submit to the three ways of his rule. The Astrologer fails to bring her round to his side. The head boatman argues that restricting the population is not required in a State which has no dearth of anything. Moreover, the mud-people produce much more than what they consume:

> And is it not a fact that out of the mud-people the city shall always extract work equal to what it feeds them, even as it is done to the animals, even though that cannot be said of the brick-people or of their children?[37]

She is also not convinced with the possible threat of the enemies within and without the land. The head boatman recollects a popular belief among the boatmen regarding the prophecy about the coming of a king. Yet she is not in a mood to change her mind to submit herself to the Grand Master's allegiance. Boatmen are not ready to accept anything other than the river as their object of allegiance.

Considering all these belligerent and rebellious attitudes of the boatmen led by their leader, the Grand Master clamps upon the city state a new "Era of Ultimate Greatness"[38] which is aimed at disciplining the city and raising the standards of boatmen's lives. It is inaugurated with the arrest of a boatman and a clown. The offence of the boatman is that his wife has given birth to an illegal child and that of the clown being that he has laughed at the arrest of the boatman because of the homorous situation involved in it.

The Era of Ultimate Greatness makes a travesty of the promulgation of the Emergency in 1975 and to laugh at the State-organized rallies. Joshi has created the character of the Master of Rallies whose function is to organise processions and rallies in favour of the Grand Master and his decisions.

Joshi goes on to tell us about certain important persons not only in the administration but also in people belonging both to brick-colony and the mud-colony. Dharmavira is a Police Officer working under the Commissioner. It is he who has arrested the boatman and the clown. His father is also an official of the Grand Master's government while his father's younger brother is an astronomer of great repute, known simply as the Professor. Bhumiputra or Master Bhoma is a boatman who has received training as a mathematician at the feet of the Professor. He is arrested for his alleged crime of telling people too many jokes about the Grand Master and his Era of Ultimate Greatness. But before his arrest, in his absence one night a very old man by the name of Patanjali, his next door neighbour, is arrested for the absence of Master Bhoma; and he is asked to confess his guilt if he wants to get released. But as he is not guilty, he does not do so and instead dies in the prison known as the Gold Mines. When Master Bhoma is himself arrested, the jeep taking him to the Gold Mines, dashes against a post. Master Bhoma meanwhile walks away and disappears only to return shortly before the great flood when he is shot dead along with many others in Grand Father's Rose Garden where he had been given shelter. Bhoma's sister makes a search for her brother during his absence and it is in it that she is also assisted by the Professor whose favourite student Master Bhoma had been.

It is in his search for Master Bhoma that he goes to see the Staff Secretary at the Education Advisor's office. What he sees in the building housing the office amazes him. The Education Advisor's son exhibits his physical prowess during which he even kills his adversaries. The Education Advisor belongs by caste to the "High of the high"[39] that "wear the sacred thread."[40] But the Education Advisor does not wear it because he had promised not to take it until he had settled things aright which he soon does. He commands a shock brigade of musclemen. The Grand Master on the advice of the Astrologer during the New-Era appoints the Education Advisor to the Council as a sop that he should not join hands with the boatmen. The Professor is almost speechless at the Education Advisor's office which presents to him scenes of wrestling matches and karate practices—all under the leadership of the Education Advisor's son. The Professor is so much absorbed in his laboratory that he has no idea of the Grand Master's city:

> "A city of wonders," said the Professor. "And all these years I never knew. The palace lawns however, leave much to be desired. All brown and yellow. No trees. No flowers. Not a patch of green."[41]

The city thus lacks vegetation, though by the bank of the river there are exotic varieties of roses blooming in Grand Father's Rose Garden. The Professor has not been given any specific information regarding the whereabouts of Master Bhoma but he is told that he had been arrested for telling too many jokes in the classroom. The Education Advisor is, however, sympathetic to the Professor, because he belongs to his constituency and because his students could be useful as "human dynamite"[42] for his own end.

Arun Joshi goes on to tell us about the Council and the Councilors appointed during the Era of Ultimate Greatness. The Grand Master feels uneasy with the dangers from the boatmen whom he tries to subjugate. In the great festival of the river they do not show any allegiance to the Grand Master. To them the river is the be-all and the end-all; and it is to her that they owe their allegiance. They even ignore the Three Beatitudes, and the Astrologer fails to persuade them to accept the new regime as a thing for their betterment to make them disciplined.

Many of the boatmen are rendered homeless when the Grand Master's wife wants the avenues leading from the palace to the river straightened to provide a scenic view of it. When the boatmen protest they are advised to think as if their hearths and homes were still in the same place. Vasu, the editor of an underground journal, calls the avenue "Asthough Avenue"[43] for "the asthough attitude"[44] of the government.

To bring the boatmen round to the official line, the Grand Master leads the reconnaissance of the mud-quarters in half a dozen helicopters at night. The aircraft are all equipped with latest scientific gadgets which cannot only locate rebellious spots below but also record any adverse criticism of the Grand Master. The rebellious boatmen are searched with laser beams. Yet they are in no mood to yield to the Grand Master. The Grand Master does not like music and even the national anthem has been cut to the bare bones, though his own voice is very sweet and hypnotic. The laser beams break even their music instruments into pieces.

It is during one of his reconnaissances that the Grand Master comes down to visit the Grand Father's Rose Garden by the river. He is presented with rare varieties of the roses which he keeps in his flower vase.

In *The City and the River* Arun Joshi also portrays the discrepancies arising out of the caste hierarchy. The Grand

Master himself belongs to the high caste people who wear the sacred thread. It is also proposed that only a person from the class wearing sacred thread qualifies to become the king of the city. The Education Advisor, who is a Brahmin, looks down upon the Police Commissioner, who is from a low caste. The Education Advisor calls the Police Commissioner "low-caste, good-for-nothing swine."[45] Even Bhumiputra or Master Bhoma belongs to the mud-hut. There is a kind of hatred lurking not only between the haves and have-nots but also between the high and the low castes.

Varieties of political malpractices have been mentioned in the novel. These include the official control over the media, the suppression of dissent, black-marketing and profiteering, raising of the prices of essential commodities during festivals and even smuggling in which the Grand Trader operates with the connivance of the Minister for Trade, a cousin of the Grand Master.

The Grand Master takes recourse to two kinds of malpractices and the common people also have two varying attitudes to them: "The malpractices resorted to in order to gain and retain power and the malpractices resorted to in order to eliminate dissent. The responses of the victims range from total surrender to uncompromising resistance."[46] The Grand Master is a great manipulator. He appoints a Rallies Master to organise rallies in his support so as to give an impression that he is a darling of the masses. The Minister for Trade proposes in the Supreme Council that the Grand Master deserves to be crowned king because he meets several requirements to become king:

> First... he must be a wearer of the sacred thread. Second, he must come from a family which has already demonstrated its willingness to make scarifies for this city. Third, he must command the affection of our masses and the trust of the armed forces and the Business class. Fourth, he should be above the petty squabbles of the bazaar.[47]

The Grand Master as a master planner schemes that his son also should succeed him. The Astrologer in his speech to the people says that "the Grand Master must immediately request his son to maintain Dharma Rajya that he has established."[48] He praises the family of the Grand Master because it "has for a hundred years sacrificed its men, its women, its children, its wealth and its very all for the sake of this city."[49] This is, perhaps, an ironical reference to the opinion of some of the Congressmen in favour of the continuation of the Nehru dynasty. The Grand Master also identifies himself with the nation. It is perhaps an ironical reference to the slogan during the Emergency—"Indira is India." He is even identified with the river: "He and the great river are one."[50]

The city state in the novel runs with the help of the police and the military atrocities committed upon the innocent poor. To subjugate the poor rebellious boatmen, the Grand Master requires more guns. The Police Commissioner makes it clear to the Professor who goes to him in connection with the Master Bhoma case and tells him: "This might sound absurd but the fact is that the poorer the city is, the more guns its government needs."[51] The strike at the river front is suppressed with the spraying of bullets out of machine-guns:

> For the next two minutes the machine-guns sprayed the pitch dark hall with bullets. Pandemonium broke loose. To begin with, the workers shouted only for lights as though the darkness troubled them more than the bullets.[52]

The attack on the Rose Garden owned by the Grand Father is undertaken to eliminate the people sheltering here. Master Bhoma and Dharma, an ex-police officer, now living in a boatman's loin-cloths on the Rose Garden, are butchered.

References to political malpractices are scattered throughout the novel. The people living in the city state tolerate the totalitarian regime without any resistance. It is only the boatmen who offer not only active resistance but also armed-rebellion and Master Bhoma on his reappearance after the period of his hiding drafts a charter of demands which he sends to the Grand Master:

> One, immediate withdrawal of the Astrologer's oath. Two, return of all the vanished ones. Three, the public trial of all those responsible for Professor's death and the headman's blinding. Four, the legalising of the illegal children as well as the restoration of the future children.[53]

The third point in the charter refers to the persecution of the prisoners in the Gold Mines, which is the name given to the official prison where the persons opposing the Grand Master are locked up. The woman headman is blinded in the Gold Mines and the Professor in his fast unto death, taken as a means of *Satyagraha*, dies in the process as he declines to take any food or drink. But none of the charter of demands is conceded to; on the contrary, the administration adopts a very tough attitude with the Grand Father, Bhumiputra and Dharma who all live in the Rose Garden. The attack on the Rose Garden is taken up with great military splendour. Much is made up of the fortification regarding the Rose Garden. Several attempts are made to subjugate the people living in it. Several regiments are kept in position to prevent any untoward incident. Even General Starch has to come out to meet the challenge. The result of all this is the butchering of Grand Father, Bhumiputra and Dharma.

III

Arun Joshi exploits in it a medley of traditions such as those of fantasy, science fiction, parable. political extravaganza and so on. It is the political situation that is paramount in the novel. Arun Joshi seems to laugh at the excesses of the period of Emergency. All the major operations during it have been indirectly referred to in the satirical design of the novel.

The City and the River has a parable within a parable which is there in the narrative pattern. The parable is one coined by Master Bhoma and after his disappearance it is retold by Shani to people gathered at the lottery stalls where the listeners get one rose free of cost. The parable relates to the alleged nakedness of the king. It does not particularly refer to the Grand Master but to some anonymous king who was obsessed with designing and wearing new clothes. Once his astrologer comes out with a plan that he can weave a fabric of rainbow colours, but it would be invisible to people not loyal to the king. The astrologer himself weaves the fabric and is supposedly busy all the time with it. Actually, he does not weave any fabric but only imitates the act of weaving on a loom. When the make-believe fabric is supposedly ready, the king is clothed in it. Even when no clothes drape the body of the king, the people gathered wonder at the beauty of the fabric that the king has put on. Only a little child exclaims that the king is naked. This parable is a scathing satire on the yes-men of the person in power. For inventing this parable and narrating it to his students, Master Bhoma is found guilty. This is the parable recited at the lottery stalls.

One of the final episodes in the novel is the meeting of the Council of Ministers in which they unanimously appoint "the Grand Master as the king of the city."[54] The king constitutes a Supreme Council which includes besides the four members of the old Advisory Council, General Starch as one of its members. In the first meeting of the Supreme Council, several points regarding monarchy are discussed. The election of the monarch is ruled out because elections are but "horse-trading."[55] As such the king of the city should not be made an object of horse-trading. It is, therefore, decided that it should be on the basis of the supremacy of heredity. The Grand Master as the king also sees to it that his son succeeds him. The people close to the Grand Master as king are happy to note that the prophecy regarding the coming of a king to the city has come true. But all this is very short-lived. The Grand Master's persecutions as monarch have a natural retribution. The river rises to an unprecedented level and everything that the city has is destroyed. No one had ever realised that "one day the river herself would become the enemy":[56]

> For seven days and seven nights it rained without stop. On the eighth day the sun rose and from a clear sky stared down at a vast sea of water. The sea was calm and gave no hint of agitation that had gone into its making. Of the Grand Master and his city nothing remained.[57]

The city has thus its natural nemesis. But on the ashes of the old city, a new one is bound to grow up. The hermit of the mountain tells the Nameless-One of the circular movements of history.[58]

What is said is an elaboration of the principle of the continuity of life and changing of the old order by giving place to the new. When the Nameless-One wants to know whether he would pass through it all, the Hermit of the Mountain asserts it:

> I did. Another New Era of Ultimate Greatness is about to begin. The Grand Master's army is equipped as never before. The tanks, the lasers sharper, the planes fly faster than the speed of sound. The conflict that shall come will also be the same: a matter of allegiance to God or to man.[59]

When the Nameless-One wants to know when this time comes, the Hermit replies, "That you will know when the time of action arrives. The main thing is to prevent this endless repetition, this periodic disintegration. But to achieve that we need purity."[60] We have to shed off "egoism, selfishness and stupidity."[61] All that mankind has to endeavour is not one of result but of trying. Sacrifice is needed to achieve purity. The Grand Master's city disintegrated because he did not set his ego aside. But it is not that the Grand Master is not beyond redemption:

> God resides as much in a Grand Master as in you or in me. Is not, therefore, always room for hope? We never know when the soul of a Grand Master is touched and in that hour his life is transformed.[62]

The hermit wants the Nameless-One to remember,

> It is what you are inside that governs how to read outside. Man is simply an instrument of the Great God in the highest heaven who is the master of the universe.[63]

In all these lines Arun Joshi has touched upon the subtle problems of metaphysics, which he has done in almost all his novels.

IV

The City and the River follows the technique of fantasy which E.M. Forster treats to be one of the aspects of the novel. But in the *Aspects of the Novel* Forster has not defined fantasy in very clear and definite terms. He goes on to describe fantasy in a rather metaphorical way. It has along with prophecy the "sense of mythology."[64] But it is not that the mythologies adopted by fantasy and prophecy are the same. Forster tells us, moreover, "by their mythologies we shall distinguish these two sorts of novel."[65] Fantasy, says Forster, "implies the supernatural, but need not express it."[66] Referring to Sterne's *Tristram Shandy*, a work of fantasy, Forster says that the name of the God hidden in it is "Muddle."[67] While commenting on *Flecker's Magic*, Forster calls its author, Norman Matson, "a true fantasist"[68] who "merges the kingdoms of magic and common sense by using words that apply to both."[69] Herein Forster comes to a kind of definition of fantasy. But much more appropriate than these definitions is the description of fantasy in an essay on *Erewhon* as *A Book That Influenced Me*:

> I like that idea of fantasy, of muddling up the actual and the impossible until the reader isn't sure which is which, and I have sometimes tried to do it when writing myself.[70]

This technique of muddling up the actual and the impossible is a dominant one in Arun Joshi's *The City and the River*. To understand its mechanism it will be useful if we quote in full Forster's cataloguing of devices:

> which writers of a fantastic turn have used—such as the introduction of a god, ghost, angel, monkey, monster, midget, witch into ordinary life; or the introduction of ordinary men into no-man's-land, the future, the past, the interior of the earth, the fourth dimension; or divings into

and dividings of personality; or finally the device of parody or adaptation.[71]

The City and the River is a work of fantasy on the model of the above description. There are in it the descriptions of the supernatural that provide it with the atmosphere of make-believe. There is a deliberate mixture in *The City and the River* of the real and the imaginary. Arun Joshi takes his characters into no-man's-land, the past as well as the future. The device of parody or adaptations of life and literature are also definitely here in it. Arun Joshi also studies his characters in which he is concerned with the divings into and dividings of personality. In the life of the Professor even the stars have their say. One of his little disciples that materialises from sky is called the Little Star who had once been called Patanjali. The Little Star quotes that he is "thousands of years old."[72] The raft sailing on the river has also an element of fantasy. It has no oars and no boatmen but it sails on with the tune of music. Master Bhoma's disappearance is held up to be a mystery because "this man simply disappeared between his house and the first lock-up."[73] This incident generates lots of fuss. The truth was that Master Bhoma had simply walked away when the jeep carrying him struck against a pole.

There are several other fantastic references in *The City and the River*. It is said about the Police Commissioner that he has "developed a machine for examining people's ears and determining the extent of contamination."[74] This makes a travesty of Draconian regulations which banned even the listening to criticism against the government. Bhoma's parable of the weaving of the invisible clothing for the king and the king's putting it on in a special festival are also effective constituents of fantasy. Everyone sees that the astrologer wove no fabric and that the king put on no robes, yet nobody, except a child, dare comment that the king is naked. In this Arun Joshi makes a travesty of the Era of Ultimate Greatness which admits of no dissent.

Dharma's father, standing before a mirror, sees that his "insides are rotting."[75] Even the doctor advises him to "exercise your soul. Take it for walks."[76] The scroll containing the city's horoscope has also muddling up of the actual and the impossible. There is much debate regarding the interpretation of the illogicality of "the river, I see, from a teacher rise":

> A hundred years ago as young students, the Astrologer and the Hermit had long debated this particular parallelogram. Their dispute had centred on a single line. Where the Hermit read "The river, I see, from a teacher rise," the Astrologer maintained "A teacher, I see, from the river rise."
>
> They had disputed that line endlessly. They had sought their teacher's interpretation, but the great Yogeshwar had merely smiled. Finally, one day, he had said, "Cities, my children, even as men, make their own horoscopes." They had pressed him for more but that was all that he would say.[77]

The mode of fantasy is not very new to Arun Joshi in *The City and the River*. The elements of fantasy are also there in *The Strange Case of Billy Biswas*, but *The City and the River* develops this mode rather consistently from the beginning to the end of the novel.

Arun Joshi is not a solitary example of an author using the technique of fantasy in his novel to write a kind of political parable or satire. A contrast between the real and the unreal, the natural and the supernatural makes the satire effective.

There has been a growing "trend towards fantasy in post-war writing."[78] John Holloway goes on to explain:

> One can of course identify fantasy-writing earlier in the century. But its prominence and importance over the present period is new, and in an allegedly great age of technological advance and materialist preoccupation this is a remarkable fact.[79]

V

The fantasy in Arun Joshi's *The City and the River* does not lead him astray from the world of realism. R.S. Pathak hints at the right perspective of the novel in the following:

> Joshi's latest novel called *The City and the River* (1990) continues to treat, in its own ironical manner, the predicament of his characters in a hostile world. The crisis of the individual, however, has been replaced by the socio-political crisis of the city, which is a conglomerate of individuals and can be said to represent the whole humanity. In this novel also, Joshi poses significant questions about identity, commitment and faith. But these questions are approached from the standpoint of politics. The novel also throws significant sidelights on the relevance of meaning in life.[80]

It is significant that the characters in *The City and the River* have a sort of anonymity about them. The characters are mostly known by their positions and a very few of them have their first names. Even the city and the river are anonymous. The city in which the action of the novel takes place is "a nowhere city."[81] The river, the symbol of the continuity of life, is also nameless. The ageless Yogeshwar has a disciple known as the Nameless-One. The Grand Master, the Astrologer, the Police Commissioner, the Minister of Trade, the Professor and the boatmen have no personal tags attached to them. Even those who are known by their personal tags have rather connotative names typical to the "humorous characters." Bhumiputra, a symbol of rebellion, means the son of the soil. The General of the Army is called General Starch for his stiff attitude. Nevertheless, the characters represent not only the types but also individuals. The element of caricature is not far off in many of the characterizations.

Arun Joshi's novels, as Madhusudan Prasad says, "are characterized by certain existential problems and the resultant anger, agony, psychic quest and the like."[82] *The City and the River* forms a link in Arun Joshi's existential concerns. The cover page blurb of the novel considers *The City and the River* at one level to be "a parable of the times; at another it deals with how men, in essence, entirely free to choose, create by their choice, the circumstances in which they must live." It is in this context that we find in the novel a philosophical focus from the aspect of authenticity that gets unfolded in the context of the political drama; and as the novel progresses, it makes "the question of authenticity acquire significance in the lives of both the people and the city."[83] Among the existential tenets such as absurdity, anarchy, meaninglessness, emptiness, alienation and despair, "the most important element which stresses the sanctity of the subjective individuality is the authenticity of the self."[84] The characters in *The City and the River* either lack in the authenticity of the self or possess it to a great degree. The Grand Master and the galaxy of his ministers and officials lack in the authenticity of the self. Most of them have bartered away their soul to propagate the official version of the Three Beatitudes during the Era of Ultimate Greatness. The boatmen are the people who are aware of the authenticity of existence, and it is for this that they never succumb to the Grand Master's tricks. In between these two groups is a group of people such as Dharma's father and Dharma himself who realise that they have lost their authenticity and therefore suffer from nervous breakdown. The Professor as a representative of the brick people, sacrifices himself to preserve the authenticity of his self.

The quest for authenticity in the seedy surroundings of the modern life has been one of the recurrent motifs of post-modernism. The novelists of the school, The Angry Youngmen in England and those belonging to Black Humour and Absurd Movement in America, "underline the need to protect the authenticity of the self against the determining categories symbolised by the power of State, the military bureaucracy, and constricting social institutions."[85] *The City and the River* also belongs to the same type of the fantasy novel. In it Arun Joshi deals with "the universal predicament of the modern man, besieged as he is by debilitating forces."[86]

The nowhere city of the novel is a kind of a wasteland. Its "tall structures of steel and glass"[87] are "falling apart."[88] It seems that under the Era of Ultimate Greatness it is "preparing to immolate itself."[89] It is "all brown and yellow. No trees. No flowers. Not a patch of green."[90] The river flowing by the city has no vital importance for the Grand Master and his administration. But the boatmen, who owe their allegiance to her, consider her to be their begetter.

In this atmosphere of chaos, the people are also in a state of crisis. The Grand Master, the ruler of the city, is the supreme master to whom most of the people, except boatmen, owe their allegiance. He is an expert political designer, who with the help of a few of his faithful ministers and advisers has so planned that not only should he be crowned king but also his son should succeed him. The Grand Master is "courteous"[91] and "a man of destiny."[92] He has also in him "the froth of overweening ambition."[93] The Grand Master has in his palace a chamber for meditation, full of antique idols of bronze, ivory, stone and wood before which he bows at night, repeating "words from the tongue that he did not understand."[94] The Grand Master tries to fulfil all the wishes of his wife. It is on her desire that he orders the town-planner to straighten the road leading to the river front from his palace for the sake of the scenic view of the river from the palace itself. Yet the Grand Master suffers from a crisis of identity and very occasionally he falls into the mood of meditation which leads him to a consideration of the futility of all things. But he is goaded on by the prophecy contained in the city's horoscope to become its unchallenged master. It is highly suggestive that the Grand Master loves darkness: "The darkness soothed the Grand Master's nerves and also helped him think."[95] He works only after sunset and with the coming of the dawn he feels "a distinct discomfort at the back of his neck."[96] His palace-rooms were, therefore, so designed that "the first rays of the sun were never allowed to reach."[97] The Grand Master has himself a very sonorous voice, yet he doesn't like music and doesn't listen to it:

> It is well known that the Grand Master disliked music. He is never to be seen at concerts, nor is there a single piece of music in the vast halls of the palace. Even the national anthem that he has to sit through during ceremonies, has been cut to the bare bones.
>
> The Grand Master's antipathy to music is considered surprising in a man who possesses the sweetest and most hypnotic voice in the city.[98]

The Grand Master is above all "a master of ambiguity."[99] Even the Astrologer is struck by the "catechism of ambiguity that was the Grand Master's style."[100] Despite all these "he was not without humour."[101] Once during an aerial reconnaissance of the city, he comes down to appreciate the roses in the Grand Father's Garden. The fading and dying of a nameless rose there fills him with strange sadness:

> The sight of all those roses had filled the Grand Master with a sweet sadness. Nor had he forgotten the dead rose bush, so unexpectedly felled in the prime of youth. Man was mortal. Death came suddenly and without a notice. And when a man was dead, what use were his doings.[102]

The Grand Master's dreams of becoming a king get sometimes disturbing. Once in a dream, the sight of boatmen rising against him disturbs him:

> And like a noose, the circle of their nakedness tightened around the king's throne until he could feel their breath, which was like the breath of a volcano, out of the depths of the surrounding sea.[103]

Even in his waking life he concurs with the Astrologer that "things are indeed in a bad way."[104] Even the Grand Master's attitude to his people is ambiguous: "The Grand Master likes his people but, at times, he is not certain."[105] This attitude to his subjects points to his psychological crisis.

The Grand Master is not the lone figure suffering from this kind of crisis of identity and authenticity. Many other persons associated with him experience the same kind of feeling. Even the Rallies Master in his mood of futility questions, "What is the use?"[106] The Rallies Master is a child of the boatmen. He has been given an important portfolio of organising rallies in favour of the Grand Master and his policies. He is a good listener and people confide in him and out of his sixth sense he can read out secrets. Being a child of the boatmen "he had an unhappy life himself and harboured a genuine sympathy for the boat-workers."[107] The Rallies Master has his reporters and informers everywhere and is acquainted with lots of facts. Despite all this, "the Master of Rallies is known to be an unhappy man"[108]:

> His misfortune lay in the fact that instead of teaching him how to row a boat, his parents had wanted him to join the ranks of the brick-people. For fifteen years they spent all their earnings on him. The Master of Rallies was good at studies but after fifteen years when he completed them, like the Education Adviser, he too discovered that no one wanted his services. The boatmen did not have the money to hire him, the brick-people considered him an upstart.[109]

The Rallies Master feels that a great city is preparing to immolate itself, yet he decides to work in favour of the Grand Master and states as his final conclusion, "It is better that the city is destroyed than the Grand Master lose faith."[110] In his depression and ennui he says:

> Peace has fled my heart and only God can restore it. In truth, journalist, when I believed in God I had peace. And, in truth, I felt His presence on the river when I was a child. But where is God now?[111]

He also poses a very pertinent question to Vasu, "What is man that he should be afraid of other men?"[112] Yet he is also aware of the animality of man that makes him "angry and strike back."[113]

The Professor is a star-watcher and a teacher of Master Bhoma. In gazing at the stars, he feels that they have brought him "complete freedom."[114] Yet sometimes with all his wisdom he says to Little Star, "I am tired of being fearful.... I am weary."[115] The Professor's search for his disciple Master Bhoma becomes not only a search for the lost one but also himself. The Grand Father tells Master Bhoma on his reappearance about the Professor's quest:

> No doubt, he has started by looking for you but of late the search has turned into a search for a lost bit of himself. For his lost faith in the city, his civilization.[116]

In his quest for his disciple and his freedom, the Professor is imprisoned in the Gold Mines where he dies. Yet to his last date he never submits his spirit to the age of tyranny which has also produced in him "a wave of nausea."[117] Once in the Gold Mines the Professor feels that the great galaxies of the sky had never given him any hint of the existence of a place like the Gold Mines, in which all freedom was buried. He expresses in disgust, "My life has been a joke, even as the lives of brick-people are a joke. God gave me life that I might serve this earth. I have squandered it on bubbles."[118] In extreme sorrow he expresses, "I am lost."[119] Notwithstanding all these nauseating feelings, the Professor remains a spirit of man's unconquerable mind.

Bhumiputra, as his name suggests, is a representative of the son of the soil. He is also a boatman who has received education and become a teacher. He does not reconcile himself to the Grand Master's Draconian rules. He advises other boatmen to be fearless because the Grand Master's guns are not capable of killing people's spirit which is unconquerable. The administration took him to be an arch-criminal; and with the proclamation of the Era of Ultimate Greatness, he and a clown are the first two to be arrested.

Dharmavir is a Police Officer who in the beginning of the promulgation of the Era of Ultimate Greatness works very enthusiastically for the police force and the Grand Master. The first arrests after it are made by him. He is not only faithful to the Grand Master and the Police Commissioner but he also expresses his disagreement with the Police Commissioner whenever his orders are not very logical. He does not agree with the Police Commissioner on the point of the handcuff. For it he is even reprimanded and warned not to question why. When he goes to search the Grand Trader's premises and to arrest him, he finds nothing incriminating. The Grand Trader offers him a silver chair to sit on which he finds "surprisingly uncomfortable."[120] Dharma feels offended when the Grand Trader desires if the former "could do something for him."[121] The Grand Trader is thrown off-balance by Dharma's "youth and innocence."[122] The Grand Trader is a friend of Dharma's father-in-law and says that Dharma's wife Shailaja used to play on his knees and he being a son-in-law deserves to be treated well with gifts. Dharma wonders how a Grand Trader is in league with powerful persons with whom he shares his profits. Dharma fails to reconcile himself to the situation: "For many weeks now he had been having trouble deciding whether he was living in a city that he used to know or had he been transported to the far-off mysterious demesne of a dark king. At other times he had trouble deciding if he was awake or whether what was happening before his eyes was actually happening and was not part of some children's charade."[123] In these we find Dharmavir an anguished personality.

Dharma is made in-charge of arresting the culprits who disobey the Era of Ultimate Greatness. The boatmen get disgusted with him and "told him time and again that nothing but doom awaited the city where men of his station and authority so totally forgot their *dharma* that instead of protecting the helpless they chose only to crush them further under their heels."[124] In his arrests made at night out of the hastily compiled lists provided to him, "names, addresses and sexes are frequently garbled."[125] Even the Police Commissioner has no answer for it. In this kind of situation, Dharma feels wearier than ever before.

Later on, Dharma gets so depressed with the affairs of the State and the organised State-terrorism that he collapses in his illness and is treated at the Rose Garden. He cannot be treated with any medicine and when after a period of prolonged delirium he gets up, "he claimed he was a boatman"[126] and "took to dressing in a loin-cloth."[127] Dharma along with the other inmates of the Grand Father's Rose Garden is tortured to death in the organised attack on the Rose Garden.

The Minister for Trade is the Grand Master's cousin. He is one of the disciples of Yogeshwar. Talking to the Hermit of the Mountain about the Grand Master's letting loose state-terrorism, the Minister for Trade says, "I get sick."[128] In his visit to a chamber inside the first Pyramid along with the Grand Master, the Minister is reminded of his ancestors whose embalmed bodies have been kept in the chamber. The Grand Master is disturbed by a strange kind of music. The Minister for Trade tells him, "You are tired. In your weariness you let dark thoughts assail you. Your stars are in the ascendant. Nothing can stop you."[129] In the Supreme Council the Minister for Trade is the first one to raise the constitutional problem which raises the status of the Grand Master to the status of a king and makes his son his descendant. Everybody accepts his proposal. The Minister for Trade has a kind of lurking fear in his heart which makes him obey the Grand Master and offer his allegiance to him. It has been hinted how the Minister's father was dead: "The Minister never talked about his father, because he could not forget the day when his father, bullet in his head, was found floating in a great river."[130] In the reign of terror, the Minister for Trade prefers remaining subdued.

The Grand Master is a character to represent the collusion of the businessmen with politicians for their sharing of profits. Even the Minister for Trade is also in league with him through a man called Pinstripe, a descriptive name because of the pattern on his suit. The Grand Trader is unscrupulous and he has his evil links everywhere. The only reality for him in the world is "the reality of money."[131]

The Education Adviser is a high-caste man and a wearer of sacred thread. But he has discarded it and formed a Shock

Brigade which is controlled by his son who organises students as human dynamite. He is also a veteran conspirator and wants the Grand Master to keep him in good humour because of his influential clientele. He is not happy with the Police Commissioner whom he calls "that low-caste, good-for-nothing swine."[132]

The Police Commissioner, like the Master of Rallies, belongs to the class of boatmen. In his heart of hearts he has sympathy with the boatmen. When the Professor goes to him to enquire about the disappearance of Master Bhoma, the Police Commissioner expresses his displeasure with the high-caste Education Adviser who begins the politics of caste-antagonism. He says:

> The way this high and low business is tearing this city apart, Professor, is truly sad. Sad and, in any case unfair. These people do not realize that there are thousands of the low whom I too look down upon. I am not a cobbler or a boatman or a pimp or a thousand other things. But these people don't realize this. Just because the Educational Adviser is the high of the high he refuses to note that there are hundreds with whom I, too, do not eat, with whom I do not drink, who dare not look at my wife and daughters. But this little understanding is beyond his high brains. To him you are either high of the high or dirt. He does not even bother to hide what he thinks. And it hurts. It is all very sad, very unfair. Thank God, the Grand Master is above such pettiness. He understands.[133]

The Police Commissioner justifies strict law and order on the ground that "the poorer the city is, the more guns its government needs."[134] To Dharma he once says, "Don't think I have no pity. I too am of the mud-people after all. But the boatmen have asked for it."[135] Like so many of the others, the Police Commissioner has also been caught in the net of dittoing what the Grand Master demands. In the barricade of the river by the agitating Shock Brigade, one of his Colonels says the following against the Police Commissioner's orders:

> Comrades: The ultimatum of the Police Commissioner is nothing but the dying yelp of the jackal. It is the same animal whom you have thrashed and skinned at a hundred barricades. What has not happened that this jackal has turned into a lion? or, is it that it has learnt to imitate the lion's roar? Let the jackal remember, a lion's roar does not make a lion.[136]

Dharma's father, a profiteer, suffers from a strange kind of disease. He feels like crying, yet cannot cry. He stands before a mirror and raves. A hole appears in his image reflected in the mirror and he begins to think, "My insides are rotting. I too am just vanishing."[137] In his panic he gives up seeing his face in any mirror and when after several days he happens to pass by his mother's dressing table he finds "that the whole of insides was gone,"[138] and only a sketch of the body remained as "the mirror took no other note of his existence."[139] His existence became one of zero. Even his physician advises him some spiritual medicine besides the physical: "These pills may do good or they may not. You should also do exercises. You should exercise your soul. Take it for walks. Let it speak when it wants to speak. Let it rip."[140] Father, moreover, has all his joints made stiff. This becomes a general disease. Those who agree with the official line become "the more spastic."[141] It takes the form of an epidemic and the disease is known as "The Three Truths Syndrome. Stasis of the soul. Atrophy of the brain and locomotor functions."[142]

The City and the River, being a fantasy novel, has some hazy characterization. Anup Beniwal affirms that "the characters do not develop spontaneously and lack psychological depth."[143] This is to say that most of the characters in it are flat ones and lack in the rotundity of the great fictional characters which we find in some of the heroes of Arun Joshi's earlier novels. *The City and the River*, as Beniwal affirms, "is both a continuation and departure from his earlier fictional endeavours."[144] *The City and the River*, however, adds certain fresh aspects to his fictional preoccupations in that in it

> his canvas has widened and the crisis of individual has been replaced by socio-political and existential crisis of the "city" and by implication of the whole humanity. In his novel Arun Joshi still raises his favourite questions about faith, commitment and identity. But these questions are now being analysed from the standpoint of politics—an area hitherto untouched by him.[145]

The merging of fact with fantasy and coalescing of time past, present and future into one mighty sweep transforms the sad, sorry tale of the novel "to a level of politico-allegorical satire."[146]

The questions posed in the novel are metaphysical in nature. The great Yogeshwar advises the Nameless-One to know "Who you are."[147] He also wants him to remember, "What you are inside governs what you read outside."[148] The great Yogeshwar impresses upon the Nameless-One of purifying himself of egoism, selfishness and stupidity. The success of achievement should not be the concern but a trying. All these points of teaching reflect the perennial metaphysical problems which perhaps no character in *The City and the River* except the great Yogeshwar and the Hermit of the Mountain had been able to delve deep into.

The spirit of the novel is fatalistic. The city's horoscope may be a point of debate but the prophecies in it do actually take place and as a result of divine retribution, the whole city and its inhabitants are washed away by the turbulent river. Yet this is a temporary phase because, as the great Yogeshwar tells the Nameless-One, "On the ruins of that city, as always happens, a new city has arisen."[149] In the city of the future as well, the character types also remain unchanged: "The men have other names but the forces they embody remain unchanged."[150] The point of conflict will also be the same: "A matter of allegiance to God or to man."[151] It is to obviate this and "this endless repetition, this periodic disintegration,"[152] as the great Yogeshwar says, "We need purity."[153] Men are simply instruments "of the great God in the highest heaven who is the master of the universe."[154] All these are nothing other than notes of fatalism to which the narrative of the story also leads us.

R.S. Pathak considers *The City and the River* "far more optimistic than (Joshi's) earlier novels."[155] There are instances to support this view as well. But this is rather hypothetical. The great Yogeshwar teaches the Nameless-One:

> God resides as much in the Grand Master as in you or me. Is not, therefore, always room for hope? We never know when the soul of a Grand Master is touched and in that hour his life is transformed.[156]

Besides striking an optimistic note, the above statement may also be a point to support the inscrutability of the human mind. There is always a hope of redemption but we never know when this materializes in the process of the endless repetition and the periodic disintegration. Destruction and creation go side by side. In this cycle the human nature also remains unchanged. Despite all, the existential message of *The City and the River* is deeply religious. Human beings are free to choose and it is this choice of theirs that makes them lead their existence in the world beset with paradoxical problems. It is here that the relevance of man's allegiance to God as against men in power has its relevance. The Grand Master, despite his allegedly good intentions, paves hell for his subjects who are denied the basic civil rights. His fate is a pointer that with the extreme handling of the problems, Nature takes its own course to set things right.

NOTES

1. The blurb to *The City and the River*, 1990.
2. *The City and the River* 12.
3. *The City and the River* 217.
4. *The City and the River* 10.
5. *Ibid.*
6. *Ibid.*

7. *The City and the River*, 11.
8. *Ibid.*
9. *Ibid.*
10. *The City and the River* 261.
11. *The City and the River* 262.
12. *Ibid.*
13. *The City and the River* 263.
14. *Ibid.*
15. *Ibid.*
16. *The City and the River* 264.
17. *Ibid.*
18. *The City and the River* 262.
19. Usha Bande's "Archytypal Patterns in *The City and the River*" in R.K. Dhawan (ed.) *The Novels of Arun Joshi* (New Delhi, 1992), 259.
20. T.S. Eliot, *The Four Quartets* (London: Faber n.d.), 23.
21. R.S. Pathak, "Quest for Meaning in Arun Joshi's Novels" in R.K. Dhawan (ed.), *The Novels of Arun Joshi* (New Delhi, 1992), 64.
22. Pathak 64.
23. *The City and the River* 10.
24. *The City and the River* 262.
25. G.S. Amur, "New Parable," *Indian Literature*, No. 144, July-August 1991, 144.
26. Usha Bande 259.
27. *The City and the River* 12-13.
28. *The City and the River* 13.
29. *The City and the River* 267.
30. *The City and the River* 13.
31. *The City and the River* 14.
32. *The City and the River* 15.
33. *The City and the River* 216.
34. *The City and the River* 16.
35. *The City and the River* 17.
36. *The City and the River* 18.
37. *The City and the River* 20.
38. *The City and the River* 23.
39. *The City and the River* 34.

40. *The City and the River* 34.
41. *The City and the River* 31.
42. *The City and the River* 35.
43. *The City and the River* 38.
44. *The City and the River* 37.
45. *The City and the River*, 84-85.
46. Brahmadutta Sharma, "*The City and the River* as a Political Novel" in *The Novels of Arun Joshi*, (ed.) R.K. Dhawan (New Delhi, 1992), 241.
47. *The City and the River* 213.
48. *The City and the River* 101.
49. *Ibid.*
50. *The City and the River* 164.
51. *The City and the River* 82
52. *The City and the River* 184-85.
53. *The City and the River* 187.
54. *The City and the River* 209.
55. *The City and the River* 211.
56. *The City and the River* 259.
57. *The City and the River* 260.
58. *The City and the River* vide supra, Ref. No. 18, on 179.
59. *The City and the River* 262.
60. *Ibid.*
61. *The City and the River* 263.
62. *Ibid.*
63. *The City and the River* 264.
64. E.M. Forster, *Aspects of the Novel* (Penguin Books, 1970), 115.
65. Forster 115.
66. Forster 117.
67. *Ibid.*
68. Forster 121.
69. *Ibid.*
70. Forster, *Two Cheers for Democracy* (Penguin Books, 1974), 226.
71. Forster, *Aspects of the Novel* (Penguin Books, 1970), 118.
72. *The City and the River* 42.

73. *The City and the River* 44.
74. *The City and the River* 123.
75. *The City and the River* 133.
76. *The City and the River* 134.
77. *The City and the River* 217.
78. John Holloway, "The Literary Scene" in *A New Pelican Guide to English Literature, Vol. 8, The Present,* (ed.) Boris Ford (Penguin Books, 1986), 99.
79. Holloway 99.
80. Pathak 63.
81. Pathak 63.
82. Madhusudan Prasad, "Arun Joshi," *Indian English Novelists; An Anthology of Critical Essays,* (edited) Madhusudan Prasad (New Delhi, 1992), 51.
83. Subhas Chandra, "Towards Authenticity: A Study of *The City and the River,*" in R.K. Dhawan (ed.) *The Novels of Arun Joshi* (New Delhi, 1992), 266.
84. Chandra 266.
85. Chandra 271.
86. Chandra 271.
87. *The City and the River* 12.
88. *The City and the River* 199.
89. *The City and the River* 75.
90. *The City and the River* 31.
91. *The City and the River* 56.
92. *The City and the River* 57.
93. *Ibid.*
94. *The City and the River* 56.
95. *The City and the River* 55.
96. *The City and the River* 56.
97. *The City and the River* 55.
98. *The City and the River* 48.
99. *The City and the River* 197.
100. *The City and the River* 59.
101. *The City and the River* 147.
102. *The City and the River* 55.

103. *The City and the River* 15.
104. *Ibid.*
105. *The City and the River* 13.
106. *The City and the River* 76.
107. *The City and the River* 72.
108. *The City and the River* 71.
109. *Ibid.*
110. *The City and the River* 75.
111. *The City and the River* 76.
112. *The City and the River* 75.
113. *Ibid.*
114. *The City and the River* 28.
115. *The City and the River* 87.
116. *The City and the River* 159.
117. *The City and the River* 80.
118. *The City and the River* 163.
119. *Ibid.*
120. *The City and the River* 91.
121. *Ibid.*
122. *Ibid.*
123. *The City and the River* 93.
124. *The City and the River* 139.
125. *The City and the River* 140.
126. *The City and the River* 197.
127. *The City and the River* 197.
128. *The City and the River* 115.
129. *The City and the River* 203.
130. *The City and the River* 201.
131. *The City and the River* 90.
132. *The City and the River* 84-85.
133. *The City and the River* 81.
134. *The City and the River* 82.
135. *The City and the River* 141.
136. *The City and the River* 206.
137. *The City and the River* 135.

138. *The City and the River* 134.
139. *Ibid.*
140. *Ibid.*
141. *The City and the River* 135.
142. *Ibid.*
143. *The City and the River: A Critical Review* in R.K. Dhawan (edited) *The Novels of Arun Joshi,* 276.
144. *Ibid.*
145. *Ibid.*
146. *Ibid.*
147. *The City and the River* 11.
148. *The City and the River* 263.
149. *The City and the River* 262.
150. *Ibid.*
151. *Ibid.*
152. *Ibid.*
153. *Ibid.*
154. *The City and the River* 264.
155. Pathak 78.
156. *The City and the River* 263.

PART-III
Conclusion

7

Fictional Technique of Arun Joshi

I

Arun Joshi may have been a writer by avocation but he was professionally associated with industrial engineering and management. The fictional technique of Arun Joshi is guided by several factors. It is not that he read theoretical books on the art of fictional technique adopted by the writers who influenced him. It cannot, however, be denied that he acquired the fictional technique from the study of his favourite authors. Among the novelists in English Henry James had a deep interest in the art of fictional technique. The omniscient narrator in *The Strange Case of Billy Biswas* is Romesh Sahai, Billy's friend in America and now an I.A.S. officer. The narrator says that "His little cottage offered the most exhaustive, if not the most interesting, collection of English literature in the north of the Vindhyas."[1] Even as the Collector of Jhansi he is in the habit of reading "the works of Henry James with his urbane, dispassionate tales."[2] The reference to Henry James and his urbane, dispassionate tales points to Joshi's interest in his works. It is because of his interest in Henry James that Romesh Sahai makes a pointed reference to the urbanity of James.

Henry James is often quoted for his interest in the point-of-view aspect of fiction. It is to his book that Percy Lubbock harks back in his book *The Craft of Fiction.* Percy Lubbock is an advocate of a consistent fictional point of view modelled upon the works of Henry James as a champion of the well-made novel. He disapproves of the first-person narrative technique which Joshi has employed. As Percy Lubbock, a Jamesian theorist, says:

> It is very useful for enhancing the value of a picture, where none but the pictorial method is available, where we are bound to rely upon an intervening story-teller in some guise or other; it is much more satisfactory to know who the story-teller is, and to see him as a part of the story, than to be deflected away from the book by the author, an arbitrary, unmeasurable, unappraisable factor. But when the man in the book is expected to make a picture of himself, a searching and elaborate portrait, *then the limit of his capacity is touched and passed*; or rather there is a better method, one of finer capacity, then ready to the author's hand, and *there is no reason to be content* with the hero's mere report.[3]

Joshi adopts the first person narrative technique, which in *The Foreigner, The Apprentice* and *The Last Labyrinth* is that of the omniscient narrative technique adopted by the hero himself. In *The Strange Case of Billy Biswas* the narrative technique is that of the omniscient point of view of Billy's friend, Romesh Sahai, who knew about his strange case as an investigating officer of his past as a friend. In *The City and the River* it is the omniscient author who narrates the tale in the third person. In his stories different points of view of telling the story have been used. Whatever may be the case, Joshi has not adopted any shifting point of view and he has adopted one consistent point of view in one novel.

The point of view of narration is one of the two devices used by a novelist to tell what happens to people and what they do. The first device, as Forster says, "is the use of different kinds of characters."[4] It is in this connection that he divides characters into flat and round.

Plot, characterization and the narrative point of view are the three important aspects to which Joshi has paid great attention.

Joshi is of the opinion that the nature of the theme and subject matter determines whether the work attempted would be a novel or a short story. In a reply to Purabi Bannerji he states:

> Each has its own place. In my case it is the theme which determines whether it would be a short story or a novel. For example, I wrote a short story called "The Gherao" which was about students gheraoing a principal. Thematically I would not like to handle a novel about the academic world which I don't know about; so a short story. The world which I know well is the industrial world which has not so far been handled in a novel.[5]

Arun Joshi refers here to the story "The Gherao" which has a narrow scope, and being not much acquainted with the academic world he would not like to handle a novel about it. So, he had to be content with writing a short story on the topic. Joshi also states that the industrial world is the theme in which he has been involved. Yet he is sorry to say that none of his novels handles this theme. Joshi is not exactly right in this statement. The world of *The Foreigner* deals with the industrial world. The exploitation of the labourers by Khemka, the miserable condition of the workers and Sindi's decision to stay back in Delhi are situations to point out that Joshi has dealt with the industrial problem in it. Sindi, like Joshi himself, is something like an industrial manager. He has grown out of Joshi's own experience. The problem in *The Last Labyrinth* also verges upon the industrial world. Both Som Bhaskar and Aftab Rai are industrialists associated with the plastics industry. The academic world also crops up in some of Joshi' s novels such as *The Strange Case of Billy Biswas* and *The City and the River*. There are several characters in his fiction to reveal to us that Joshi is interested in the academic world. There are several teachers as characters in all his novels except perhaps *The Apprentice.* In *The Foreigner* Oberoi's Professor at Boston on his visit to New Delhi delivers an address which many of his ex-students attend. Even Sindi Oberoi leaves his academic career in the U.S. to come back to the land of his forefathers though on the decision of the flip of a coin which signals to him New Delhi. Billy Biswas (*The Strange Case of Billy Biswas*) is appointed faculty member in the Department of Anthropology of Delhi University. His escape into the *saal* forests of Maikala hills is for his academic mission to study the tribal world along with his students. Leila Sabnis in *The Last Labyrinth* is an academician interested professionally in philosophy and as a pastime in foreign languages. In *The City and the River* the academic world plays a dominant role. The Hermit of the Mountain, the great Yogeshwar, the Professor and his disciple Master Bhoma, are all associated with the academic world. In the background of the above facts we may say that the academic world in its fictional aspect is no less important than the industrial world with which Joshi remained associated.

A significant fact about the fictional world of Arun Joshi is that both in his novels and short stories he is concerned with the decaying upper crust of the Indian society. Even when he refers to the poor life, it is depicted from the viewpoint of the upper class. M.G. Hegde has rightly pointed out that "like his novels Arun Joshi's short stories too satirize the glittering flimsiness of the Indian affluent society."[6]

Influences upon Arun Joshi's fictional technique are those of the authors who influenced him for themes and philosophical outlook. Dr. R.K. Dhawan is of the opinion that Joseph Conrad is a major influence upon Arun Joshi's fictional technique. It is to illustrate this that he quotes Joseph Conrad:

> In truth every novelist must begin by creating for himself a world, great or little, in which he can honestly believe. The world cannot be made otherwise than in his own image; it is fated to remain individual and a little

> mysterious, and yet it must resemble something already familiar to the experience, the thoughts and the sensations of his readers.[7]

Conrad, a great technician of the novel, is of the view that the craft of writing novel has its genesis in the artist's initial perception. But a true artist cannot afford to restrict himself to his own imagination in violating the human experience. To Conrad there is a reality beyond the phenomenal world. According to him, an artist can capture the reality by giving a consistent form to the shapeless facts of actual human existence. Joshi, too, finds the validity of the facts lying beyond the phenomenal world. His novels begin with actual experiences. Along with it he finds a need to discover the reality which lies hidden in the actuality of his own life. Joshi has written, "My novels are essentially attempts towards a better understanding of the world and towards myself.... If I didn't write, I imagine, I would use some other medium to carry on my exploration."[8]

II

The Foreigner tells the story of Sindi Oberoi in a series of flash-backs. The past and the present, the real and the remembered, the world of fantasy and reality have been juxtaposed to add to the suspense. The narrative takes us to various countries like Kenya, England, Scotland and India. Sindi Oberoi studies Mechanical Engineering in a University at Boston where he comes in contact with another Indian student, Baburao Khemka, and also with June Blyth who becomes the focal point of triangular love. Sindi Oberoi narrates the story in an autobiographical manner which is the point of view of the narrative. Sindi Oberoi, the narrator-protagonist enters the novel as an "I" character.

The Foreigner is a novel rich in the story element which has been woven together of two plots—the main plot of Sindi, June and Babu and the subplot of Khemka, his daughter Sheila and Sindi. It is in the course of development of the story element that Joshi sketches the characters involved in the plot.

The Foreigner delineates character in cross-cultural contexts. Sindi Oberoi is a globe-trotter who changes over from Kenya to England and Scotland and from there to America and finally comes down to settle in Delhi, the land of his forefathers.

The Foreigner, in its fictional technique has certain influences of Eliot's poetical technique used in *The Love Song of J. Alfred Prufrock* which he also quotes from in the novel. Sindi's use of phrases from Eliot such as the "irredeemable time,"[9] "the eternal joker snickered within me"[10] convey the sense of his futility which is also patterned with images of muddle. Sindi "stood in the graveyard of cars."[11] For him the only reality of his parents is "a couple of wrinkled and cracked photographs."[12] The character of Sindi as a foreigner has been depicted through plot, dialogue and the use of imagery and style. Joy Abraham has rightly pointed out:

> *The Foreigner* gains a symbolic value in the larger context of human existence. The idea of foreignness is kept before the reader throughout the novel. It again portrays the protagonist's sense of metaphysical anguish at the meaninglessness of human condition. The unreality, insecurity and transitoriness associated with the word "foreigner" form the entire edifice of the novel providing the necessary texture and structure to it. From this point of view, *The Foreigner* has a remarkable degree of maturity and technical competence well suited to its theme.[13]

Sindi Oberoi in his autobiographical narrative assumes subterfuge when he says about himself, "I am not good at remembering events, but for some reason I always remember the beginning and end of an affair."[14] But despite this disclaimer he narrates everything in detail. The narrative begins with the recounting of Baburao Khemka's dead body in a morgue: "They uncovered his face and I turned in spite of myself."[15] A chapter later, the scene shifts to New Delhi:

> Many months later, I was apprehensive as the Sikh taxi driver whizzed me through the dust-laden streets of Delhi.

> Now and then he turned completely around in the seat, his face shining with sweat, and asked me for directions. I kept telling him I didn't know the place myself. I had never been to Mr. Khemka' s house.[16]

The narrative of *The Foreigner* oscillates between past and present and vice versa. It is in this that Sindi Oberoi uses language which is full not only of sentimentality but also sometimes of sensationalism. Sindi is uninhibited and even uses taboo expressions such a "What they needed were cheap prophylactics."[17] The narrative of *The Foreigner* conveys to us a feeling not only of the narrator's sense of loss but also his ultimate grappling with the truth of life which gives meaning to his lost life.

The narrative technique of the novel is oblique, not straightforward. Along with pages of short dialogues written in colloquial prose modelled upon the combination of British, American and Indian English, there are also straightforward third person reportings and also alternations between first person narrative along with free, indirect narration. The protagonist is involved in the several phases of his remembrance of things past. Sometimes he narrates the story in the mood of introspection and sometimes he takes recourse to telling the story in retrospect and again changing over to reporting the story in extro-version.

III

The Strange Case of Billy Biswas unfolds the story from witness-narrator's point of view. The narrative point of view of this novel differs from that of *The Foreigner* where the protagonist himself is the narrator. We can say that while *The Foreigner* is a sort of autobiography of Sindi Oberoi, *The Strange Case of Billy Biswas* is a sort of biography of Billy Biswas told from the point of view of his friend Romesh Sahai. The narrator is an officer of the I.A.S. cadre posted at Jhansi. The *saal* forests of Maikala hills fall within his administrative jurisdiction. He had been Bimal Biswas's room-mate in America. He knew him from a close distance and yet could not know the secretive and the mysterious in the mind of his friend. The story has been unfolded in the flash-back technique. The narrative begins with the recounting of Billy's life in America much before the time of his disappearance into the *saal* forests of the Satpura hills. The narrator makes it clear: "I first met Billy (Bimal Biswas) in New York where for one brief summer we roomed together."[18] Romesh Sahai recounts everything about Billy Biswas and his love for the primitive life and his marriage and other affairs. As the Collector of Jhansi he has also to supervise the search party ordered to salvage Billy from the tribal world. Till the end of the narrative we are not told of the name of the narrator: "I am Romesh Sahai, I said."[19] The Chief Secretary wants him to supervise the search party "from the point of view of administration, of humanity and of friendship."[20]

The narrator Romesh Sahai is acquainted with Bimal Biswas, yet does not understand him completely, though the narrator has a sympathetic outlook for him. He is sure that Billy's disappearing into the woods is not "a stereotype childish escapade,"[21] but a thing of greater significance beyond the ken of people of humdrum life. Romesh Sahai considers the end of the story of Billy Biswas "the most difficult part of this narrative."[22] In a sort he justifies the title in the penultimate paragraph of the novel:

> The strange case of Billy Biswas had at last been disposed of. It had been disposed of in the only manner that a humdrum society knows of disposing its rebels, its seers, its true lovers. Sitting there, watching the shades of evening settle slowly on the drab little town, it seemed to me that nothing but blind blundering vengeance, howsoever camouflaged, awaits all those who dare to step out of its stifling confines. It is a confrontation whose outcome is as certain as the end of solitary boats beating against a maelstrom.[23]

Conrad's narrative technique in *Lord Jim* is one great influence upon the witness-narrator's point of view in *The Strange Case of Billy Biswas*. Like Marlow in *Lord Jim*, as R.K. Dhawan says:

> Romi performs the task as an involved friend and as a detached narrator. Both become more and more involved as the novel progresses. Both follow the tale to the end. And they have another feature in common. Throughout the narrative Marlow repeatedly asserts that "he was not able to comprehend Jim fully."[24]

This is like Romi's disclaimer that he does not understand the enigmatic Billy. Romi, the narrator also says:

> I had neither the imagination nor the obsessive predilections of Billy Biswas.[25]

The statement, as Dhawan says, reminds one of Conrad's narrator in *Under Western Eyes*:

The case of Billy Biswas is strange from the administrative point of view. But administrator-turned-narrator disapproves of such an attitude and suggests the viewpoint of a psychoanalyst and a psychiatrist. The uneasiness in the heart of Billy Biswas leading to the crisis of his character has been brought about in episodes juxtaposing each other. The narrator reproduces the dialogues in their crisp and carefully wrought forms and it has also magnificent use of humour and irony. The dialogues involving the tribals, especially Dhunia, are full of the sense of myth and folklore. Meenakshi Mukherjee has very aptly described it as "a compelling novel about a strange quest drawing upon myth and folklore to reiterate its elementary concerns."[26] Billy in his quest for finding an answer to the crisis of a character in a civilized world escapes into the primitive life to find the ultimate reality, in a concept "something like that"[27] of God.

IV

The Apprentice follows a novel narrative technique, which, however, has been a very favourite device with poets using dramatic monologue. Among the English poets Robert Browning has written several of his poems as dramatic monologues. Joshi's influence here is Camus, who has used it in *The Fall.* Jean-Baptiste Clamence, the narrator in it, discloses the secret of his clandestine existence and reasons for his fall. Ratan Rathor, the protagonist in *The Apprentice* in his dramatic monologue narrates everything in his service career: "He must tell all. All or nothing. What use is a confession if not total."[28] An N.C.C. cadet who has come to Delhi to parade in the Republic Day festival is the non-participant listener to whom Ratan Rathor narrates the story of his life. The speaker in Browning's dramatic monologues anticipates the silent listener's questions which the narrator answers. Like Coleridge's the Ancient Mariner, who wants the wedding guest to listen to the whole of the story, Ratan Rathor also insists his silent listener on listening him out. Besides the influence of Camus' *The Fall,* Joseph Conrad's *Youth* is also one of the influences on Arun Joshi's narrative technique in it. Ratan is modelled upon the character of Marlow, the first person narrator in Conrad's *Youth.* He tells the story of his youth in retrospect to a group of listeners. As in *The Strange Case of Billy Biswas,* here also there are occasional flash-backs in the sustained dramatic monologue of *The Apprentice.* In this it has some similarity with James Joyce's technique used in *A Portrait of the Artist as a Young Man.* Ratan is all praise for the listener whom he addresses as "My friend"[29] and praises him: "You are a patient listener. What better confessor there is than youth that has patience and that is willing to hold judgment."[30]

The narrative of *The Apprentice* has a wide span. It covers the period from the Quit-India Movement to the Chinese debacle in the NEFA in 1962. During this span of about two decades Ratan grows from a boy to a kingpin in the corrupt official hierarchy clearing war purchases. The son of a freedom fighter who sacrificed his all at the call of Gandhi, the man of suffering, Ratan Rathor after his graduation comes to Delhi in search of a job which he gets after a lot of trials and tribulations. His narrative is full of the account of his struggle and meteoric rise to power. "In between he experiences the pangs of the so-called civilization with its inevitable traits, lying, hypocrisy, bribery, graft, drunkenness, womanizing and worse."[31] It has also been said that "Ratan Rathor's style is intriguing, bordering on madness."[32] But it has been questioned. The narrative of *The Apprentice* has an ironical intention. The mock-heroic intention of the narrative is very explicit as the message in it is a bitter commentary on post-Independence India. The hymn to corruption reveals the crisis of character upon which Ratan Rathor once writes an article in which he thinks: "It was as though I had hit upon a new law of gravity or discovered a lost *Upanishad* whose proclamation to the world could hardly wait."[33]

The narrative technique of *The Apprentice* is thus "a fictional experiment—a confessional novel which employs psycho-narration."[34] Ratan's exposure resembles that of an existential hero. As Srinath says, *The Apprentice* "is the tale of conscience-torn man with a curious mixture of idealism and docility, a vague sense of values, a helpless self-deceptive effort to flout them for the sake of a career—in short, with a deep awareness of a conflict between life and living."[35] The mock-heroic tone of the narrative of *The Apprentice* comes "out of an acute sense of an alienation and a quest to understand the meaning of life."[36] To expiate his sins Ratan in his apprenticeship begins with the meanest of the jobs of brushing the shoes of devotees gathered at a temple. This is his existential choice upon which the apprenticeship of Ratan is tested. In the words of V.V.N. Rajendra Prasad: "*The Apprentice* elaborates the theme of corruption of the self in a society which is itself corrupt."[37] This theme has been very well elaborated through the fictional technique of psycho-narration through the device of the dramatic monologue which has here a mock-heroic edge. Joy Abraham unscrambles the chronological sequence of events:

> ... each represented by the symbol G, A, B, C, A, G, D, G, D, A, E, G, F and G:

A Ratan's childhood, the details about his parents, his search for a job,

B Ratan on the job,

C Ratan takes bribe for clearing defective war materials during the Chinese invasion,

D his Brigadier-friend deserts battlefield because of defective war materials; he comes home all depressed, a court-martial is pending against him; Ratan sees a number of soldiers being hospitalized, all wounded; he refuses to confess,

E Brigadier kills himself; Ratan goes to the morgue; is shaken out of his moral inertia,

F Ratan wants to avenge his friend's death; goes to kill Himmat Singh who bribes: realises the absurdity of all things as a mere primitive solution and

G the present moment, *i.e.*, the things he does and talks to the student companion standing on the steps of the temple in Delhi.[38]

V

The narrative strategy of *The Last Labyrinth* goes back to *The Foreigner* in which Joshi has used the protagonist-narrator's point of view. Som Bhaskar, the protagonist of the plot, tells the story of his life in a flash-back. The very first sentence of the novel expresses the motto of his life: "Above all, I have a score to settle. I forget nothing, forgive no one."[39] The narrator Som Bhaskar tells the story of his life to Dr. Kashyap whom he calls simply Dr. K. who is not only a silent listener but also interacts with him. Some of the portions of the narrative have also been narrated by Dr. Kashyap, such as that of Som's surviving heart attack because of the miracle performed by Anuradha and Gargi. The narrative of *The Last Labyrinth* refers to a vast sweep of the problems of life of Bombay and Benares and those of life and death, materialism and spiritualism. The philosophical problems dealt with touch upon the labyrinths of life and death.

Som Bhaskar is a man obsessed with certain possessions. In his hunger for buying Aftab's shares in the plastics industries he comes in contact with Anuradha who lives with the former without being formally married to him. He is also plagued by his love and lust for her.

The Last Labyrinth has an intriguing juxtaposition of not only themes but also locales. Som Bhaskar through his narrative leads us to various spheres of time and space. The narrative has been woven with the descriptive details of the labyrinths of not only Lal Haveli but also of Benares with its labyrinthine streets. Along with it we are also taken into the haunting world of life, love, God and death which is the last labyrinth.

The fixations of Som Bhaskar come alive in his complex narrative as he shuttles between past and present, Bombay and Benares, life and death. He also shuttles from his inside to outside and vice versa. He gets philosophical and cynical at once and also reveals not only the boredom of life but also its reflected glory. Like the heroes of his other novels except *The Apprentice* and *The City and the River* he is an intellectual who keeps on referring to the various schools of thinking in the various fields of life. To contain all this he has taken recourse to using the complex form of the narrative strategy in *The Last Labyrinth.*

VI

The City and the River differs from Joshi's previous works as regards the point of view of fiction. In the four preceding novels Joshi has adopted the first person singular narrative point of view. The three of them, *The Foreigner, The Apprentice* and *The Last Labyrinth,* develop the plot through the confessional mode of narrative in which the protagonist himself relates the story of his life. Besides this autobiographical method of the first person singular, *The Strange Case of Billy Biswas* has been written from the point of view of the witness-narrator, who, however, also adopts the first person singular narrative point of view and not the third person one. *The City and the River* is different from all the preceding novels not only in its theme but also in its structure. There is, however, one common point in all of them. R.K. Dhawan is very justified in his statement that "The clash between the primitive and the modern civilization is a recurrent theme in Arun Joshi."[40] The very title words of the novel joined by *and* indicate the clash of two different opposing symbols indicated by them.

The fictional modes incorporated in *The City and the River* cut across many forms of prose fiction, such as fable or parable, fantasy, science fiction, political novel. While it is true that Joshi did not attempt the form of the pure moral fable or fantasy in his earlier novels, we are, nevertheless, aware of the symbolic themes in them, such as those of "guilt and alienation in *The Foreigner* (1968), the pull of the primitive in *The Strange Case of Billy Biswas* (1971), the failure of the modern civilization in *The Apprentice* (1974), and destruction and death in *The Last Labyrinth* (1981)."[41] The clash in *The City and the River* is between the two ways of life: those represented by brick-people and mud-people. This itself speaks of the political reverberations of the theme. But the narrative pattern of the novel affords it many other layers as well.

Infixed between *Prologue* and *Epilogue* there are nine chapters. In *Prologue* the great Yogeshwar educates his disciple, the Nameless-One, on the last day of his abode with the great teacher. On this very day falls his pupil's thirtieth birthday which his preceptor celebrates and then he teaches his pupil who he is. The subsequent nine chapters follow "the mythical narrative pattern of story within a story told by an old wise teacher, *Guru*, to his keen disciple, preparing him for a quest and a mission. Within this thematic and structural framework, the apparently simple tale of a city and a river unfolds itself, gaining multidimensional meanings."[42]

After giving an account of the fate of the city and its destruction with the devastating flood of the river, the great Yogeshwar sends his disciple, the Nameless-One, on his quest and mission to the city to prevent "the endless repetition, this periodic disintegration."[43]

In *The City and the River*, as R.K. Dhawan writes: "The streak of autobiography"[44] has been left aside. "Nor is it a story of personal private lives. The novel is an ample evidence of Joshi's 'road not taken,' for in this work it turns his focus from the private to the public."[45]

In the nine chapters between *Prologue* and *Epilogue*, the omniscient narrator recounts the Grand Master's dream of becoming king and its confirmation on the basis of an old prophecy by the Palace Astrologer. But there are points of difference in the interpretation of minor details by the Astrologer and the Hermit of the Mountain. The narrative goes on to relate the Grand Master's Council and the Councillors which are all his Yes-men, and confirm every proposal of the Grand Master and in the festival of the river want the boatmen to owe their allegiance to the king. A few of the educated people such as Bhumiputra and Professor rebel against the regime. Master Bhoma relates a parable about the naked king at a lottery stall. Much has been made by the administration of the disappearance of Master Bhoma and his subsequent return. In the new regime, the administration is tough on dissenters who are all jailed in the Gold Mines and persecuted. Dharma's grandfather who gives shelter to Master Bhoma on his return is also persecuted as his Rose Garden is besieged and devastated with all the inmates on it. When all these things reach their height of persecution, Nature had its revenge with the unprecedented flooding of the river which devours the entire city including the seven hills.

This pattern of relating story within a story is one of Puranic tradition which Joshi has exploited for his need. He has also made it dramatic with his befitting use of dialogue and descriptive patches. The narrative of *The City and the River* has in it streaks of "humour and a gentle irony."[46] We laugh at how the Councillors debase themselves at the dictates of the Grand

Master. There are also ironical references to the gagging of the press and organising rallies, managed by the State and physical persecution practised during the Emergency.

The City and the River has a vaster span in its action than in the earlier novels but the predilection of Arun Joshi's protagonist in an apparently indifferent and hostile world runs as an undercurrent of the socio-political and existential crisis of the city by the river. But the crisis of the individual still persists and even the Grand Master is not free from it.

VII

Joshi's use of fictional technique as illustrated in his novels and short stories differs in the scope that these forms allow. Except for the scope, there are common points as regards technique in his novels and stories. Thematically the three of his novels, *The Foreigner, The Strange Case of Billy Biswas* and *The Last Labyrinth* deal with the decaying crust of the Indian society. Ratan Rathor of *The Apprentice* rises to this status while in *The City and the River* there is a clash between the two. His short stories as well deal with the life of the upper crust of the Indian society and even when the subject matter is out of the lower class such as that of the servant in the story, "The Servant" or the peasant boy in "Harmik" or a poor young widow in "The Frontier Mail is Gone," the narrative point of view is that of an aristocratic narrator. There are certain common problems between the novels and the short stories. *The Apprentice*, as Joy Abraham points out, "seems to be the continuation of a short story 'The Survivor' where the hero instead of involving himself practically is complacent of being a survivor of so many things."[47] The key motive in it is corruption. Kewal Kapoor, the protagonist of the story, suffers from a problem similar to Billy's. Kewal Kapoor sums up his life as follows:

> In brief, gentlemen, I am a survivor of that fantastic racket that passes for the MODERN INDIAN SOCIETY. I am a survivor of mendacious mothers and relentless fathers, of two-penny politicians, of lawyers and doctors. Above all

> I am the survivor of that greatest disaster of them all: THE MODERN INDIAN WOMAN.[48]

The survivor theme is also present in "The Frontier Mail is Gone." Leila, a widow of sixteen, boards into the Frontier Mail at a level crossing of Faridabad and goes to Bombay where she becomes the resident of a red-light area. M.G. Hegde calls her "a survivor of traditional morality which pays no heed to human emotions."[49]

His short stories, too, have been narrated from different points of view. The first person narrative point of view has been used in "The Gherao," "The Frontier Mail is Gone" and "The Survivor." The remaining of the stories included in the selection entitled *The Survivor* have been narrated from the third person omniscient point of view and these have also multiple perspective narrative and objective reportage which are also there in his novels. There are thematic similarities between Joshi's novels and stories except *The City and the River*. In both of them, the tone is satirical as the author satirizes the crisis of identity of the affluent society. The story entitled "The Homecoming" is a representative story to support it. On his homecoming from the Eastern front, a young Army officer finds the disparity of life that he had led and the life the city people lead. He is disturbed that "he did not know how to fit it all together or whether it could fit together. Ever."[50] He even wonders as to "the meaning of one man's marriage; one man's life."[51] In his anguish he questions "What life was all about who... could possibly be running the world?"[52]

The portrait gallery of characters in his short stories "includes rich industrialists, travelling salesman, westernized intellectuals, poor peasant boys, young eve-teasers—the survivors as well as the victims of modern Indian society."[53] Some of these re-emerge in his novels. To quote M.G. Hegde again, "As the germ of all his novels could be traced back to one or other of these stories it could be argued that Arun Joshi experiments with various narrative strategies on smaller scale which eventually lead him to the finished triumph of his matured novels."[54]

Arun Joshi has taken recourse to the various devices in forging the technique of his fiction. He has borrowed the technique of writing of the novel from the American and continental writers and has fused these with the Indian concept of the story mixed not only with myth and folklore but also with the device of a story within a story coming down to us from the Puranic traditions. The plots in the novels are related mostly to the upper-class life; and even when the subject matter is drawn from the life of the poor, it has been narrated from the viewpoint of the upper-class narrator. This aspect is applicable much more to his short stories than to the novels. The characters in Joshi's novels belong mostly to the upper-class society, except for the mud-people in *The City and the River*. Joshi's novelistic characters are all complex figures and as such they are seldom at ease with themselves. They go on developing and suffering the different schisms of modern life.

Posing melancholy was high fashion in the seventeenth century English literature. So has been the case with the problems of characters in Arun Joshi's novels among many others, because all of the protagonists find themselves hounded and baited upon by the crisis of identity and alienation in a supposedly mad, bad and absurd world.

NOTES

1. *The Strange Case of Billy Biswas* 58.
2. *Ibid.*
3. Percy Lubbock, *The Craft of Fiction* (1921; rpt. London: Jonathan Cape, 1965), 140.
4. E.M. Forster, *Aspects of the Novel* (Penguin Edn., 1970), 75.
5. Quoted R.K. Dhawan, *The Fictional World of Arun Joshi* (New Delhi, 1986), 20.
6. M.G. Hegde, "Short Stories of Arun Joshi," *The Novels of Arun Joshi,* (ed.) R.K. Dhawan (New Delhi, 1992), 202.

7. Quoted R.K. Dhawan, *The Fictional World of Arun Joshi* (New Delhi, 1986), 17.
8. Reply to M.R. Dua, dated September 3, 1971, quoted in *The Fictional World of Arun Joshi,* (ed.) R.K. Dhawan 18.
9. Joy Abraham, "*The Foreigner*: A Study in Technique," *The Novels of Arun Joshi,* (ed.) R.K. Dhawan (New Delhi, 1992), 159.
10. Abraham 159.
11. Abraham 159.
12. *The Foreigner* 12.
13. Abraham 159.
14. *The Foreigner* 33.
15. *The Foreigner* 5.
16. *The Foreigner* 9.
17. *The Foreigner* 45.
18. *The Strange Case of Billy Biswas* 8.
19. *The Strange Case of Billy Biswas* 226.
20. *The Strange Case of Billy Biswas* 209.
21. *The Strange Case of Billy Biswas* 8.
22. *The Strange Case of Billy Biswas* 225.
23. *The Strange Case of Billy Biswas* 240.
24. R.K. Dhawan, *The Fictional World of Arun Joshi* (New Delhi, 1986), 29.
25. *The Strange Case of Billy Biswas* 152.
26. Meenakshi Mukherjee, *The Twice Born Fiction* (New Delhi, 1971), 203.
27. *The Strange Case of Billy Biswas* 189.
28. *The Apprentice* 118.
29. *The Apprentice* 51.
30. *The Apprentice* 100.
31. The blurb to *The Apprentice.*
32. The blurb to *The Apprentice.*
33. *The Apprentice* 57.
34. V.V.N. Rajendra Prasad, "*The Apprentice*: Self as Labyrinth," *The Novels of Arun Joshi,* (ed.) R.K. Dhawan, 1992), 211.
35. C.N. Srinath, "The Fiction of Arun Joshi," *The Literary Criterion,* XII, 2-3 (1976), 127.

36. V. Gopal Reddy, "The Apprentice: An Existential Study," *The Novels of Arun Joshi,* (ed.) R.K. Dhawan (New Delhi, 1992), 222.
37. Prasad 211.
38. Abraham 210.
39. *The Last Labyrinth* 9.
40. R.K. Dhawan, "Introduction: The Fictional World of Arun Joshi," *The Novels of Arun Joshi,* (ed.) by himself (New Delhi, 1992), 39.
41. G.S. Amur, "A New Parable," *Indian Literature,* No. 144, July-August 1991, 153.
42. Usha Bande, "Archetypal Patterns in *The City and the River*" in R.K. Dhawan (ed.) *The Novels of Arun Joshi* (New Delhi, 1992), 257.
43. *The City and the River* 262.
44. R.K. Dhawan (ed.) *The Novels of Arun Joshi* (New Delhi, 1992), 34.
45. Dhawan 34.
46. The blurb to *The City and the River.*
47. Abraham 220.
48. Arun Joshi, *The Survivor* (New Delhi, 1975), 96.
49. M.G. Hegde, "The Short Stories of Arun Joshi: A Study," *The Novels of Arun Joshi,* (ed.) R.K. Dhawan (New Delhi, 1992), 206.
50. Joshi 104.
51. Joshi 99.
52. Joshi 99.
53. Hegde 208.
54. Hegde 208.

8

Summing-up

I

In the foregoing chapters, an attempt has been made to study first the concept of alienation and crisis of identity *vis-a-vis* the major Indian English novelists and Arun Joshi. The advent of English language in India was a sort of a by-product of British colonialism. Yet with the striking of roots, the alien tongue has been acclimatized and Indianized with the Indian Republic to such an extent that it is now one of the Indian languages. C. Rajagopalachari loved English to the point of characterizing it as the "gift of the Goddess Saraswati to India."[1]

As this language struck its roots, literature in it began to be written. The nineteenth century fictional prose literature is very meagre and it would be futile to research the traces of crisis of identity in the characters present in those works. Even the big three of the Indian English novelists, such as Mulk Raj Anand, R.K. Narayan and Raja Rao, created no major characters suffering from the crisis of identity of some sort or the other. Sometimes these points emerge in R.K. Narayan when he deals with the discrepancies arising out of the cultural chasm and the generation gap. Manohar Malgaonkar, Kamla Markandeya, Balachandra Rajan, Chaman Nahal, Ruth Prawer Jhabwala, Anita Desai, Nayantara Sahgal, Salman Rushdie are prominent of the novelists creating characters faced with the problem of alienation and the crisis of identity. The works of these novelists have been referred to in a sort of sweeping survey after which an attempt has been made to concentrate upon Arun Joshi's fictional creations.

Indian English literature is dressed in English clothes containing within the Indian body and soul. But even this creates sometimes a kind of ludicrous situation, because in the western pomp and show we forget ourselves in aping the West. This is the result of the colonial hangover which has made us what K.R.S. Iyengar has called "a confused wanderer between the two worlds."[2] Some think that the use of English for writing fiction in the Indian setting is an act of artificiality. It is at best an act of translation because few of the Indians think, feel, talk and dream in English. But this plea can be ignored from the point of view of the artistic representation of verisimilitude.

Indian English writers have to portray factors concerning the individual, social and national identity. The literature written in the language imposed upon by certain historical necessities has to be national first. If it is national, it will also reflect automatically the social and individual identity. But more often than not it has been flouted. It has been accelerated by certain sociological and psychological factors. It has almost become a commonplace to aver that the past periods were golden, while the present is leaden. Because of this attitude people in every age have regarded their times to be a wasteland. The spirit of wasteland is the basic paradigm of the twentieth century technological civilization. Innovations in science and technology, the material comforts made available the shrinking of space and time, the utter loss of traditional moral values and the dissemination of scepticism with regard to the spiritual values and many more such factors have rendered man a plagued creature. The dissatisfaction with the present material civilization began from places where there is no dearth of any physical wants. But even though wallowing in the outward abundance and mirth, they have been spiritually bankrupt. The growing cult of the hippie phenomenon and the popularity of the spiritual revival under the guidance of many Indian gurus of sorts in the West have been responsible for the cancerous growth of the concept of corrosive alienation. It is to stress this point that we need re-quoting a summary statement by R.S. Pathak:

> Alienation is one of the greatest problems confronting modern man. Its corrosive impact can be seen in the form of generation gap, the anti-war movement, the hippie phenomenon, the credibility gap the compartmentalization of our lives, the stunting of personal development, the conspicuous absence of a sense of meaningfulness of life and so on.[3]

All these factors taken together have made this age not only an age of anxiety but also one of alienation. In the Indian context the rootlessness has emerged out of cosmopolitanism, urbanism at the cost of urbanity, belittling of rural heritage, commonly supposed to be rusticity, and the growth of the concept of the nuclear family which has rendered the aged redundant. Hence there has been a rise in the concept of absurdity and it is highly meaningful that in some of the absurd plays the old parents are thrown to the dustbins. Again in the Indian background there has been a renaissance of racial consciousness bordering upon the question of Indianization, which has surfaced after the Partition holocaust. Many of our Indian English novelists either knew of it or had a first-hand knowledge of it; and therefore, could not resist themselves from describing the crisis of identity born out of truncated lands, bereaved families and relatives split up beyond the borders. Novelists like Chaman Nahal, Khushwant Singh and Salman Rushdie write their novels on the theme of Partition from this very point of view of the isolation of the battered soul leading to the crisis of the protagonist.

Arun Joshi does not belong to this group. Though born before the Partition of the country, he did not experience this kind of holocaust; and as such he is mostly silent on it. But the crisis faced by his fictional characters lies at the deeper layers of the sociology and the psychology of mankind.

II

Arun Joshi's thematic concern in his novels has perhaps grown out of the positive and negative influence upon him of many of the American novelists and continental existentialist philosophers. It has also developed out of the philosophical idealisms preached in the perennial schools of Indian philosophy and their decadence in the context of our modern consumer culture of the enmasse and the prevalence of the anarchic forces. There are instances of the awareness regarding literary identity as well.

The Hindu psyche of Arun Joshi is always active; and despite all his western acquisitions, he never loses ground and comes back to the nest of the Hindu heritage. Sindi Oberoi in *The Foreigner* seems to be an alter ego of Joshi himself. Conversely, it can also be taken for granted that Sindi's angst and ennui are also Joshi's. On the return from the U.S.A. both the fictional character and his author take up a job in an industrial concern. Sindi marries the daughter of the factory owner, as did his creator Joshi too, after joining the D.C.M. Sindi is restless in his search for roots. Because of his mixed parentage he belongs to neither India nor Kenya, neither to the U.K. nor to the U.S.A. where he was educated. He at last adopts India, the country of his forefathers. There are several American trained characters in Joshi's fiction including his short stories; but none of them resemble their creator, Arun Joshi, as much as does Sindi Oberoi.

Arun Joshi believes in the Freudian motive of writing. The artist, to him, as for Freud, has an introverted disposition; and he is also something of a neurotic. In his ambition to attain aggrandisement, the creative artist attempts to get a vicarious satisfaction in turning away from the reality to the life of fantasy in his creation. According to this also Joshi's fictional characters are the projections of his libido which loves fantasy.

The literary influences upon Arun Joshi are mostly of those authors who nourish some kind of existentialist approach to life in their writings. The continental novelists and philosophers, such as Kafka, Camus, Sartre and the American novelists, such as Saul Bellow, Elison and Bernard Malamud, have their positive influences upon Joshi's fiction, especially in forging his views of life and the fictional characters caught in the net of existence in which most of them look before and after and pine for what is not.

Joshi admits to being influenced by Camus and Sartre and adds that he "never understood anything except odd statements from Kierkegaard."[4] But he has quoted a statement from Kierkegaard in *The Last Labyrinth*: "Prayer doesn't change God but it changes him who prays."[5] Joshi's *The Foreigner* has clear influences upon it of Camus' *L'Etranger*, which literally means a foreigner or an outsider. Like Camus' hero Meursault in it, Sindi seems to nourish anti-ambitiousness and detachment as virtue. The influence of Camus' novel *The Fall* on Joshi's *The Apprentice* is dominant. The character of Ratan Rathor in *The Apprentice* must tell about his life and like Jean Baptiste Clemance, the protagonist of *The Fall*, sees the falsity of his existence and tries to salvage his fragmented and fractured self. *The Strange Case of Billy Biswas* has similarities with several of the novels such as Conrad's *The Heart of Darkness* and *Lord Jim* and John Updike's *Rabbit, Run*. Billy Biswas forsakes civilized human society to adopt a primitive way of life like Kurtz in Conrad's *The Heart of Darkness*. The witness-narrator's fictional point of view in *The Apprentice* has similarities with Conrad's *Lord Jim* where Marlow narrates the tale from the same point of view. Like Updike's "Rabbit" or Harry Angstrom, Billy, too, is a victim of alienation leading to the crisis of his consciousness.

Most of these novelists have an existentialist attitude to life and its problems. Joshi's philosophical burden also verges upon existentialism. His fondness for the theme of alienation and the crisis of identity is the result of his existentialist outlook. The agonizing experiences of modern man are those of alienation and crisis of identity. It is almost paradoxical that our scientific and industrial civilization has led the contemporary man to the edge of doom. When man cannot know himself, there is little scope of "presume not God to scan/The proper study of mankind is man."[6] But this kind of attitude does not strike root in the crisis of the present. Most of the western existentialist authors might be atheists, but not so Arun Joshi whose philosophical outlook is seasoned with the Indian brand of optimism. G.S. Amur has rightly stressed about Arun Joshi's novels that they:

> take us to the heart of darkness—one of his most favourite metaphors is the labyrinth—but he is not a prophet of despair. All his novels hold out promise of regeneration and redemption.[7]

Among the British poets Joshi seems to be influenced by William Wordsworth whose sonnet "The World is Too Much with Us" is the idea behind *The Strange Case of Billy Biswas* and there are certain instances in the novel to prove that Joshi has borrowed and adapted a few expressions from it which have been quoted in the relevant portion earlier. The epigraph to the same novel is from Matthew Arnold's *Thyrsis*: "It irked him to be here, he could not rest."[8] The idea from Arnold's *Scholar Gipsy* has also been exploited. Among the leading poets of the twentieth century, the impact of T.S. Eliot especially that of *The Waste Land* and *Prufrock* is explicit. Joshi also quotes from *Prufrock* in *The Foreigner*. S. Rangachari[9] disengages "T.S. Eliot's Shadow in *The Foreigner*."

It is not correct to say that Arun Joshi has been mostly influenced by British, American and continental authors and philosophers. Besides them he has also made specific references to Descartes and Locke among the British philosophers and to several philosophical ideas from Indian philosophy and Dharmashastra. In most of the cases he takes recourse to the Indian philosophical systems to arrive at some compromise arising out of alienation and its different manifestations. Sindi Oberoi in *The Foreigner*, who has a wrong idea of detachment, has to realize in the end under Muthu's advice that true detachment comes out of getting involved in the worldly affairs for the benefit of mankind. In *The Strange Case of Billy Biswas* the union of Billy and Bilasia symbolizes that of Purush and Prakriti.

In *The Apprentice* the beacon light comes out of the Gandhian ethics. In *The Last Labyrinth* Som Bhaskar's insatiable thirst gets somewhat diluted with his philosophical probings into the problems of the labyrinths of life and death. In *The City and the River* the message from *the Bhagawad Gita* comes into aid. The great Yogeshwar tells his disciple, the Nameless-One, about the inevitable periodic destruction and regeneration out of which only the purity of heart can take us out. Joshi attaches a great importance to Hinduism which to Joshi "is highly existentialist-oriented philosophy since it attaches so much value to right way to live (to exist)."[10] Even Gandhism has its benign influence, especially upon Ratan Rathor, who in the heart of his heart remembers his father's inspiration from this "Man of suffering." Ratan expiates his sins taking into consideration his inheritance and upbringing and how he had allowed his conscience to be sold to the Devil of corruption raising its head in post-Independence India.

Arun Joshi's characters are also concerned with the crisis of identity arising out of the use of different languages. Sheila in *The Foreigner* did not want her brother, Babu, to marry an American because of the language problem. Sindi Oberoi brushed this away telling her that this was a mere pretext as even they also used English for their conversation. Even Gargi in *The Last Labyrinth* consults a Hindi-English dictionary to dissuade Som Bhaskar from taking any revenge as "man's vanity (*ahankar*) brings him revenge enough."[11] Billy Biswas speaks English with a marked British accent, but his creator Arun Joshi establishes his own identity in the use of language in that he embellishes the British model of English language with American and Indian variations in usage and idioms. Along with code-mixing and code-switching in the use of language, the use of striking imagery in the Indian context goes a long way in the delineation of Joshi's characters along with atmosphere.

Arun Joshi is fond of similes which generally juxtapose the abstract and the concrete. Some of the select examples of his similes are, as in "I grant you that you are not stuffed shirt, but then you are stubborn as a mule;"[12] "In her own house she (Sheila) was like a pet animal which went about where it willed, confident of not being noticed;"[13] "Babu looked up at me (Sindi) with hurt dog-like eyes and I suddenly felt ashamed of myself;"[14] "On the left side of his (Mr. Khemka's) face the little finger switched spasmodically like a lizard's torn tail."[15] In these similes the abstract and the concrete have been contrasted. Sometimes its reverse is also true as in "darkness lay upon the city like a burden of cosmic guilt."[16]

Animal images are also there in *The Apprentice* such as "year after year the concrete crept forward. Like a python;"[17] "glossy little houses cropped up where once the jackals had howled;"[18] "a bulldozer worked at the foot of the hill, its black blade swinging in the sunlight like a cobra's hood."[19] Rathor's Brigadier-friend looked like a "caged demented animal."[20] The animal images dominate *The Foreigner* and *The Apprentice,* though they have also been used in other novels, such as, in *The Last Labyrinth* "I looked at myself in the mirror: lean, crow-footed, graying."[21]

III

With the summing-up of the introductory and the background materials above, attention is now paid to the gist of the subsequent chapters dealing with the individual novels. *The Foreigner* and *The Last Labyrinth,* chronologically the first and the fourth of his novels, deal with the world of business relationships as well as the personal. In both these novels, the crisis of the present and that of identity of the major characters have been depicted. This theme has been dealt with by many of the novelists of the younger generation especially Nayantara Sahgal and Anita Desai.

In *The Foreigner* Joshi deals with several aspects of life on the lonely planet. Most of these relate to the themes of alienation, the absurd, the sordidness and seediness of the human existence. *The Foreigner* is a seminal work of Joshi in the sense that all the problems associated with the crisis of identity have been taken up for consideration in it. The autobiographical narrative of his life is a study in rootlessness. He is always haunted by the fact that he is neither an Indian nor a Hindu. He loses his parents in an air crash when he was just an infant. His uncle settled in Kenya, like Sindi's father, brings him up with all care. Sindi is educated under his uncle's guardianship. Even though his childhood is one of affluence, he is conscious of the loss of his parents. Many of his acquaintances keep on pestering him with their queries regarding his parents whom he knows no more than figures in wrinkled photographs. Khemka in Delhi asks him the same question and Sindi is reminded of the same impression.

The root cause of Sindi's malaise is due to the experience of his lost childhood. The loss of both his parents during infancy makes Sindi lopsided in his character. Despite the best care, his uncle perhaps could not give him any substitute for the parental love and affection.

Sindi continues to be a kind of a rolling stone till he settles in New Delhi. From Kenya he moves on to England and from England to Scotland and from Scotland to Boston in the U.S.A. At all these places Sindi is not only dissatisfied with his lot but also continues flirting with British and American ladies and girls. But this way of life does not alleviate either any sense of boredom or alienation in him. Like Eliot's poetical creation *Prufrock*, Sindi is an archetypal Everyman. His narrative makes visible to us the inner landscape of his wasteland. Sindi's character seems to be influenced by that of Meursault, the protagonist in *The Outsider* by Camus.

The major characters in *The Foreigner* get enmeshed in several facets of the crisis of identity. These may be summed up as those belonging to the fields such as individual, interpersonal, national, international, racial and cultural, industrial and commercial as also educational and linguistic identity.

The Foreigner deals with many other themes, besides the main one. These themes are related to the corruption in free India, tax-evasion, educational system, poverty and hunger, the exploitation by the capitalists of the poor labourers and even family planning. Amidst this criss-crossing of themes *The Foreigner* is mainly "a literary representation of rootlessness."[22] The rootlessness of Sindi in *The Foreigner* is mainly at the socio-psychological level. The racial issues surface in the context of intermingling of the Indian students with the Americans. The International Students' Association arranged foreign students' reception by the native Americans. But despite all the goodwill on the part of the Americans, "all it ever achieved was animosity: everybody ended up hating the Americans all the more."[23] Even Sindi reminisces:

> Born an Indian, I had been spat upon; had I been a European, I would have done the spitting.[24]

The rootlessness of Sindi is not geographical but psychological. The American girl June Blyth is right in her assessment of his character when she says, "I have a feeling you'd be a foreigner anywhere."[25] Even Sheila in Delhi declares, "You are still a foreigner, you don't belong here."[26] Sindi is asthmatic in constitution, yet runs after seeking the pleasures of the flesh. His initial attitude to life is that of "a big mocking zero."[27] The life to him appears to be purposeless. He speaks in the vein of an existentialist hero; "somebody had begotten me without a purpose and so far I lived without a purpose, unless you could call the search for peace a purpose."[28] Unable to resolve the crisis of his identity, he even contemplates suicide and keeps on changing places. He takes up certain odd jobs as a dish-washer and later as a library assistant. Yet he experiences only pain and illusion. It is highly significant for Sindi and his creator, both having engineering degrees, to say about the psychological angst of the former: "It was as if two high voltage electrodes had taken root in my head and each of them kept splitting venom into my brain."[29] Sindi realizes the root cause of his crisis of identity. Being rootless, he has no sense of morality. "The randomness of existence"[30] leads him towards madness. Even his decision to come back to India is with the flip of coin in which the tail stands for New Delhi.

In *The Foreigner* Sindi's is not only the lone case of the crisis of identity. Even June Blyth suffers from a feeling of emptiness all the time. In her hunger she changes partners from Sindi to Babu and back. Baburao Khemka has also the same kind of experience. He is given over to seeking pleasures in Boston because of his life of suppression in Delhi. There is also some element of the lost childhood in his character, because there is no reference in the novel to his getting the affections of mother who had probably died in his infancy. He feared his father, but was rather open with his sister, Sheila, to whom he kept on writing of his American experiences of flirting. Even June Blyth calls Baburao's father to be "an awful bully,"[31] because he used to get worried after receiving letters from him. Babu is driven to the edge of despair and breakdown in the light of his failure to get united with June Blyth whom his father would never accept and also knowing that she had also been in love with Sindi.

Not to speak of the Indian and American characters, even Sindi's Austrian room-mate, Karl, feels the void within and he "seemed to have abandoned his homeland."[32] His is also a case of lost childhood. He had a step-mother, who, after the death of his father, brought lovers home, and once in her drunkenness she even tried to seduce her step-son. This harrowing experience made him leave Austria.

June Blyth talks with an Indian student, Arun, about the freedom of choice and the liberation in suicide. To Arun's Indian mind the freedom to die shows the lack of freedom and that "suicide is the end of a battered old road, not the beginning of a new one."[33] But even he speaks in an existentialist vein:

> Arun said dreamily, Random events happen around you, forcing you to make decisions, propelling you on through

> life. It is only vanity that makes us imagine that we are leading our own destiny."[34]

Sindi Oberoi's life in Delhi also begins with his misplaced opinions but he gains in knowledge under Muthu's influence and he learns that his conception of detachment as meaning inaction was a fallacy. In his position as Manager of Khemka's factory "Sindi develops the right attitude towards life, hatred for the senior Khemka's corrupt practices and sympathy for the company's exploited workers."[35] He learns that "detachment consisted in getting involved with the world."[36] From Surinder he becomes "Surrender,"[37] which signifies the message of his self-surrender to his duty for the benefit of the factory workers. Sindi's initial conception of life as a big mocking zero changes later on to the philosophy of Karmayoga of *the Bhagawad Gita.*

The Last Labyrinth, discussed with *The Foreigner* in the same chapter, is a quest for meaning in life. As a tale of two cities, Benares and Bombay, it deals with Bhaskar's business world and personal hunger. Along with these two themes, there is a strong element of the protagonist's crisis of identity. Som Bhaskar embodies "an uneasy juxtaposition of the sensuous-deluded and the rational-ironical (Som meaning 'the moon' and Bhaskar 'the sun') is caught in the labyrinth of worldly desires."[38] Som Bhaskar inherits a plastics factory from his intellectual father. At the ege of twenty-five he is a master of huge fortune. His wife, Geeta, is a model of a wife. Despite all this, Som Bhaskar is at ease neither with himself nor with the surroundings.

Like his father, Som Bhaskar is also intellectually an accomplished person. He had done a paper on Pascal at Harvard and studied the sermons of the Buddha at Sarnath and the philosophical implications of Krishna's teachings to Arjuna.

Despite all this his life is a muddle; and he becomes almost muddle-headed. He wants to grab failing industries, yet he is cynical about money and property. In his personal life also, the more he indulges in sensual pleasures, the more indulgence does he seek; for an insatiable cry of "I want, I want, I want"[39] keeps on haunting him. Som Bhaskar has affair with Leila Sabnis, who is herself a psychologist and philosopher and a polyglot. Because of her too much interest in books she has been divorced. She in a study of his character hints that the trouble with him "is a problem of identity."[40] However, Som Bhaskar denies it on the ground of his age. Leila Sabnis gives a deeper explanation of the problem of identity and its mistaken concept. It is often mistaken for the identity of possession. But to Leila Sabnis there is the identity derived from caste which is his Brahmin inheritance. There is, according to Leila Sabnis, "the identity of an extended joint family."[41] She goes on to explain that Som Bhaskar may be in want of "a mystical identification, identification with a Godhead, as most Hindus want sooner or later."[42] Som Bhaskar has no stamina for that. He has no faith, "he has always been, and will be, a sceptic."[43] She calls him "a compulsive fornicator."[44]

Som Bhaskar's crisis of identity is at the level of his inner personality. His grandfather was a worldly man interested in all the pleasures of life and having nothing to think of the clumsy questions of God and disapproved of his wife holding *Kirtans*. Som's father, on the other hand, was a scientist interested in the First Cause. Som Bhaskar fails to tie himself up with the links:

> Where did I fit in? I was a womanizer all right, and a boozer, but my womanizing and boozing had not settled anything. I had inherited the afflictions of both of them—for what were they if not afflictions, afflictions that had led me into unbearable entanglements.[45]

This confession makes it amply clear that Som Bhaskar is himself aware of his malaise. But despite his awareness of the problem he gets on involved with his hunger for possession as also sex. This aspect of his personality surfaces in his contact with Aftab and Anuradha at a meeting in New Delhi of the Plastics Manufacturers' Association. The antique beauty of Anuradha so charms him that he keeps on shuttling between Bombay and Benares. Anuradha has had a life of suffering and, therefore, knows what it means to lead a life. She has a strange notion regarding marriage. She believes that when she cannot marry everybody whom she loves, there is no logic behind getting married at all. She is not married to Aftab; yet she lives with him as his wife. Som Bhaskar wants not only Anuradha but also all her shares including Aftab's.

Som's getting well after a massive heart attack is an act of miracle even for his physician. Anuradha is behind this cure. She prays to Gargi to give him life as she had once given eyesight to Aftab. Gargi prays for it on the condition that she breaks all relations with him. Even after it Som is not satisfied with himself. He goes to see Gargi residing upon a mountain resort and desires to know about Anuradha and her shares. Knowing his nature of taking revenge, Gargi advises him against it on the ground that man's vanity brings him revenge enough.

Som Bhaskar's life remains a quest for an undefined thing in the mazes of a dark labyrinth. In his uneasiness Bhaskar apostrophizes to Anuradha in her absence to be kind to him because he is "weary. Of so many fears: so much doubting. Of this dark earth and these empty heavens."[46] He is haunted by "the strange mad thoughts that at times carom about my skull. Are they the harbingers, the pilot-escort of melancholia? Of insanity? Faith?"[47] The dilemma of Som Bhaskar's crisis of identity remains unsolved as Som Bhaskar up to the end never gets out of the crisis of identity at the physical, spiritual and cosmic levels. In the words of Joshi himself, in *The Last Labyrinth* the alienation of his characters does not ultimately lead them "back to community." The novel closes with Som Bhaskar's aborted attempt to end himself as he aims his revolver at his skull. But just as his wife, Geeta, intervenes he feels as though he has come out of a sleep. The last sentence of the novel, "I hope she understands," has also an ambiguity about it. Som Bhaskar's arm facing Geeta, "like a traffic policeman,"[48] perhaps points to no direction.

IV

The very title of the novel *The Strange Case of Billy Biswas* points out to something quaint in it. The problem with the protagonist, Billy Biswas, is that of a quest of identity and the crisis of consciousness. Romesh Sahai, sometime friend and now Collector of Jhansi, lays stress on the point that Billy's character is enigmatic. There is something of scepticism in his observation that "the most futile cry of man is his impossible wish to be understood."[49] It is in this context that he calls Billy "a man of such extraordinary obsessions."[50]

People in general and the members of his family in particular are at a loss to understand the workings of Billy's mind. Yet Tuula Lindgren, a Swedish researcher, understands him perfectly and identifies the root cause of the crisis of his identity.

The life of Billy Biswas is one of strange turns and erratic decisions. Some kind of duality in his character and inner crisis keep on haunting him. His parents send him to the U.S. to study engineering; but without their consultation Billy switches over to the study of Anthropology because from his very childhood he had a very keen interest in the tribal world. The presence of the primitive force in him prompts him to choose for his residence in the U.S. the black ghetto in Harlem. His interest in the primitive life and some of the philosophical problems make him think of a few of the perennial problems of the Upanishads, "Who was I? Where had I come from? Where was I going?"[51] To him the Adivasis had perhaps grasped the spirit of the force that prompted the ancient architects to build the sculptural designs of the Konark. Their dark inscrutable faces, to him, contain the wisdom much beyond the ken of the civilized. Billy, too, possesses this primitive force which, to Tuula, is *urkraft*. It is this which acts as a volcanic force in the character of Billy Biswas.

Not unlike the Buddha, Billy forsakes his wife and family to grasp the spirit of nature while living with the aboriginals. Though Billy is well settled in his teaching profession and blessed in his wife, son and parents, the civilized society seems too much for him and he keeps on a search for release. His extramarital sex relationship with Rima Kaul is also due to the fact that she understands him much better than his wife, Meena, does. The estrangement between husband and wife takes the form of the crisis of Billy's character and with every passing day the relationship deteriorates to an extent that, as Meena confesses, "he doesn't want me any more. He hasn't touched me for six months. Not once."[52]

Billy's hellish experience with the civilized world is responsible for his escape into the primitive world. The epigraph from Matthew Arnold's *Thyrsis,* "It irked him to be here, he could not rest" is a true pointer to the predicament of Billy Biswas. The civilized society is to Billy nothing "more than making and spending of money."[53] This expression seems to be an adaptation of Wordsworth's sonnet "The World is Too Much with us." Billy's ideas regarding civilization and nature are almost on all fours with the present sonnet of Wordsworth:

> The world is too much with us; late and soon,
> Getting and spending, we lay waste our powers:
> Little we see in Nature that is ours;
> ....
> —Great God! I'd rather be
> A Pagan suckled in creed outworn.[54]

As Professor O.P. Mathur points out, the "contrast between superficial and the real informs the whole work."[55] Billy's interest in the primitive in the beginning makes him lose his identity. He belongs neither to the wilderness of the primitive world nor to the dazzling light of the metropolitan. In his quest for the true self and authenticity, he tries to grasp the meaning of life. *The Strange Case of Billy Biswas,* says Professor O.P. Mathur, "may be taken as an allegory of the realization of one's true self."[56] Living with the primitive people he has a glimpse of the divine and to the aboriginals he himself achieves it. Billy understands the higher meaning of life, not dreamt of in the hectic civilized life. Bimal Biswas in the end achieves what his name literally means:

"Incidentally, the name of the hero, Bimal Biswas, also means 'pure faith.'"[57] Billy may have lost his identity and may have become a misguided genius for the civilized society but he achieves the true purpose of life.

Billy Biswas's case is rather different from Sindi Oberoi's in *The Foreigner*. While Sindi's character is a study in rootlessness, Billy's is no such thing. Romesh Sahai, the narrator and Billy's friend during the stay in the U.S., confirms this in his explanation:

> In spite of somewhat longish stay in America, neither of us had lost our roots in India or in the city of Delhi, nor did we suffer much except for passing spells of loneliness, from that alienation that many other Indians seemed to be burdened with.[58]

Both of them offer us consolation in that from their initial crisis, they seek a kind of amelioration in the final solution of the problems involved.

V

The Apprentice is an extended dramatic monologue in which Ratan Rathor confesses his guilt of being an accomplice in the crime with the corrupt administrative machinery. His confession leaves no doubt about his experience of the crisis of identity and consciousness. The confession has been related in several modes in which irony, satire, the mock-heroic and fantasy get mixed up with the stream of consciousness technique. Professor O.P. Mathur finds in this dramatic monologue "'a stream of conscience' running parallel to the stream of recapitulative consciousness."[59] In this very apt statement we find a summing-up of Ratan Rathor's predicament. It is also true that it refers to the positive side of Ratan Rathor after his expiation.

Ratan goes on to confess everything of his life from his childhood to his expiation. He lays bare his heart to an N.C.C. cadet come to New Delhi to participate in the Republic Day function. The cadet also belongs to his own home state. It is just in the fitness of things that Ratan Rathor relates the story of the country's independence under the leadership of Mahatma

Gandhi, the high idealism of Ratan's father who was killed during a procession, shouting slogans of patriotism, post-Independence corruption at the polling booth, the sway of unscrupulous politicians, the primacy of personal cause over the national, the decay and corruption in the administrative machinery which caused the nationalist interest to suffer to such an extent that even the honour of the country suffered a setback in the Indo-China war in the North-East. Ratan in the capacity of the Superintendent of the office clearing the purchases of war materials becomes a cat's-paw of the top bureaucrats and unscrupulous suppliers. He is directly responsible for the death of his school-friend who was the Brigadier responsible for carrying the military operations in the North-East during the Indo-China war. He is court-martialled and found guilty. Out of sheer frustration he commits suicide. In the enquiry Ratan is also interrogated, but as Sheikh Himmat Singh has so masterminded that no documentary evidence supports the allegation. Ratan is penitent and in the police lock-up writes a letter of confession which he, however, does not submit.

It is only at long last that Ratan becomes genuinely penitent and expiates his sins in a novel way. He does not become a devotee of any deity as he finds the priest of the temple no less corrupt than the bureaucrats. Ratan chooses to become an apprentice in the path of righteousness. He shines the shoes of devotees visiting the temple. This humble job clears his soul of guilt.

Ratan feels terrible loneliness within himself even when he basks in the sunshine of affluence. He, however, is not beyond redemption. Sometimes in his despair he finds anarchy all around in which he is "abandoned on the planet"[60] and in this condition he passes "through some dark dungeons of the world."[61]

Ratan's confession lightens the burden of his soul and as such it has a therapeutic value. His confession reveals to us the story of his innocence, guilt and expiation. When innocence fails to secure him any job, he takes recourse to the ways of the world and in doing so he outdoes everybody. But it is an irony of his life that even though he gets everything that money can buy he loses the rest of his mind and soul.

Despite all his acts of corruption and shady deals, Ratan Rathor is not a doomed character. In his capacity as Superintendent of an office, his life might have been reduced to a zero; but it was prevented from deteriorating into negative. Ratan has himself given a definition of life as zero and negative life: "Life might well be a zero, for all I know, but it seems to me that it need not be negative. And it becomes negative when you take out of it your sense of shame, your honour."[62]

As compared to his father's life, Ratan's life is one of zero, no doubt; but his candid confession and heartfelt expiation add a positive quality to his character. Even the Sheikh gets aware of it when he admits that his soul was killed but that Ratan's was pawned. The souls that are pawned can be saved but not those that get killed. This suggests that with the purification of his soul, Ratan could do something that his father advised him during his childhood—"to be good! to be respected! to be of use!"[63] Ratan might have got lost in the labyrinths of corruption but he comes out victorious. In the crisis of his identity, he quests for something meaningful, which he attains.

VI

The City and the River investigates the predicament of its characters in a hostile world. Along with the socio-political crisis of the city, the crisis of the individual has also been explored. The city described in it represents the entire humanity. The thrust of the narrative concerns the need to affirm identity, commitment and faith. All these problems have been examined from the standpoint of politics and, as R.S. Pathak stresses, "the novel also throws significant sidelights on the relevance of meaning in life."[64]

The anonymous city by the river run by the Grand Master has tall structures of steel and glass. But despite its magnificent structure, its atmosphere is very hostile to vegetable growth; and as such it is all a veritable wasteland. In his nowhere city ruled by the Nameless Grand Master even the persons are anonymous and most of them except a few are known by their official position. Those characters who bear certain personal nomenclature tag with them have generally connotative names attached to them as exemplified in the case of Bhumiputra. In the galaxy of characters there is no tension between sons of the soil and outsiders. Nevertheless, there is a tension between haves and have-nots. The haves under the official patronage impinge on the world of the have-nots, who have been deprived of their hearths and homes to allow for a new alignment for the road to the river front so as to present a scenic vista of the river from the palace height itself. Besides being deprived of their homes, they are advised to think as though they were still living on their paternal acres. This 'As-though' attitude shakes even their identity. Boatmen realise that they belong to nowhere. They are forced to adopt an attitude of rebellion against the new regime. They do not offer their allegiance to the Three Beatitudes; rather they preserve all of it to the river. With their identity threatened, they cling to the authenticity of their existence.

It is not that only the boatmen suffer from the crisis of identity. Even the Grand Master and the persons close to him experience a sort of alienation between their existence and something not achieved. It is highly suggestive that "the darkness soothed the Grand Master's nerves and also helped him think."[65] With the daybreak he is ill at ease with himself and suffers from a discomfort at the back of his neck. The first rays of sunshine are not allowed to reach his bedroom. It is highly paradoxical that the Grand Master, who has himself a very sonorous voice, dislikes music. In his style he is a master of ambiguity and appreciates humour and even sympathises with the dying rose. But in his dealings with the rebellious boatmen, he adopts Draconian regulations to suppress them with laser beams emitted from the planes of the air force flying high.

Many others as well are aware of the absurdity of the situation in which they have been put. The mood of futility engulfs the Rallies Master who questions, "What is the use?" He is an expert in the art of collecting people shouting slogans in favour of the Grand Master and his moves. Yet he is unhappy with his lot in that his parents, instead of teaching how to row a boat, had sent him to school to study so as to join the ranks of the boat people. He is held in respect neither by his own boat-people nor by the brick-people who consider him an upstart. Nevertheless, he confesses that the loss of peace in him can only be restored by his belief in God whom he found in the past immanent in the river. In his saner moments he poses a question—Why a man should be afraid of other men and finds that it is the animality of humankind that makes him angry and strike back.

The Professor of Astronomy, who is a star-watcher, also feels weary and gets tired of being fearful. The search for Master Bhoma is a search for a lost bit of himself. Yet he has a spirit which compels him not to submit to the Grand Master's nefarious deeds in the prison called the Gold Mines. He prefers death to submission. The Gold Mines symbolise to him the burial of freedom. In his moments of disgust he is compelled to think that his "life has been a joke, even as the lives of brick-people are a joke."[66] Yet despite this feeling of loss and ennui, the Professor's indomitable spirit represents man's unconquerable mind.

Sometime or other even Bhumiputra and Dharmavir as also others are conscious of the futility of the things around them. A few of the characters in *The City and the River* get sick and the sickness is more psychological than physical. Dharma's father, who is a profiteer, suffers from a strange kind of disease. An ordinary mirror seems to give scanning of his insides which are rotting and in this state he comes to be vanishing. The mirror seems to reflect only the skeletal remains of his personality and his existence is reduced to a zero. The profiteer has all his joints made stiff and the persons dittoing the official line become spastic and suffer from an epidemic known as "the Three Truths Syndrome. Stasis of the soul. Atrophy of the brain and locomotor functions."[67]

The great Yogeshwar stresses the main problem in *The City and the River* when he advises the Nameless-One to get aware of his identity: "Who you are?"[68] The sage also points out to the fact that it is the inside of our personality that governs the outside. The purity of the inside is, thus, essential to purge us of egoism, selfishness and stupidity. Humankind should concern itself with trying and not with the achievement. This is an advice on the line of *the Bhagawad Gita.*

Like the other novels of Arun Joshi, except perhaps *The Last Labyrinth, The City and the River* ends with an optimistic note. There is a spark of divinity in everyone of us, may he be a Grand Master or an ordinary boatman. And as such there is always room for hope. Even though human mind is inscrutable, there lurks within it a hope of redemption in the cycle of the endless repetition and the periodic disintegration. Human beings are free to choose their fate, and they choose for the better if they realise the relevance of man's allegiance to God.

VII

The major characters in Arun Joshi's novels, thus, seem to be lost in the crisis of their identity, in which American and continental novelists have their sure stamp not only upon Arun Joshi's choice of themes but also on the treatment of plot and character. Joshi's fascination for dealing with existential themes in which the characters get lost in the mazes of their existence is also in keeping with the favourite image of the maze in post-modern literature. Gabrial Josipovici writes in this context:

> From the cunning passages, contrived corridors and issues of "Gerontion," through the mazes of Kafka, Proust, Borzes and Robbe Grillet, the labyrinth has been the favourite image in modern literature.[69]

While Joshi devotes one full novel to this problem in *The Last Labyrinth,* he uses this image or sometimes the theme in his other novels as well. In *The Foreigner* he uses the image of the labyrinth while talking about his sad affair with Kathy:

> Even after several years, somewhere in the labyrinth of my consciousness the wound still bled. I felt sad and perhaps showed it.[70]

Sindi Oberoi feels himself cut off from his roots and surroundings and tries to get out of the mazes of loneliness and that of the crisis of identity. Coming back to the land of his forefathers he realises that life has a meaning and to achieve it one has to get involved in the world without getting attached to it. The message of *the Bhagawad Gita* comes to his rescue.

The eponymous hero of *The Strange Case of Billy Biswas* also faces the problem of the crisis of identity. Meena Chatterjee, whom Billy marries, talks entirely in English and is never short of words but "the very essence of happening tends to get lost in the maze of verbiage that Meena produced at the time."[71] This points out to the lack of communication between characters. The tribals in this novel are concerned with preserving their ethnic identity and are not happy with the impingement of the civilized world upon the primitive. Billy has in him the instinct of the primitive world, though he is a child of bureaucratic civilization. Even for the narrator Romesh Sahai, the real meaning of life lies not on the surface but in the deeper levels:

> If life's meaning lies not in the glossy surfaces of our pretensions but in those dark mossy labyrinths of the soul that languish forever, hidden from the dazzling light of the sun, then I do not know of any man who sought it more doggedly and, having received a signal, abandoned himself so recklessly to its call.[72]

The crisis of identity has its associations with the inner climate of our consciousness and soul. It is with this that the symbolical image of the labyrinth or the maze is associated in Arun Joshi's novels. *The Apprentice* is the story of a man passing through the phases of innocence, experience, guilt and expiation in "a city of opportunities,"[73] Delhi, in which one can "smell the river."[74] This "unknown city"[75] in which he settles and becomes familiar, becomes "the defeated city"[76] as Ratan Rathor gets conscious of his being lost. The sense of his frustration and alienation is stressed with the use of the images of "a planet turning in the darkness, going heaven knows where,"[77] the omniscient God "going His way, twirling His walking stick"[78] and "dark dungeons of the world."[79] The corrupt world of *The Apprentice* has a nauseating atmosphere which makes even Ratan Rathor vomit several times in the novel, especially when he sees his Brigadier-friend in a hospital morgue.[80] The corridor of the police station where Ratan has to pass one night also "smelled of piss."[81] With the use of such images and several others, referred to at certain appropriate places, Arun Joshi builds up the atmosphere of *The Apprentice,* but even in this atmosphere Ratan Rathor is able to retrieve his pawned soul, while Himmat Singh cannot do so because as he says, "My soul was killed."[82]

The Last Labyrinth has layers of symbols interwoven with the images of labyrinths and mazes. A. Rama Krishna Rao has very rightly drawn our attention to the fact that in it the image of labyrinth is juxtaposed with the image of void. Both these images recur so often in it that it is impossible not to notice them in the study of the text. Som Bhaskar gets lost in the physical and spiritual labyrinths of life and death. As the last labyrinth in the Lal Haveli hidden among the labyrinthine streets of Benares, has death in it, so the last labyrinth in his spiritual quest leads him not to any positive but to a negative solution of the problem of his identity as the novel ends with his aborted attempt to commit suicide.

The labyrinth image has been used as a physical symbol in *The City and the River* as well. The Grand Master's palace has been designed "on the pattern of ancient labyrinths."[83] The different floors of the palace were "the arms of the labyrinth"[84] into which one stepped from swift lifts. *The City and the River* seems to be an extension of the world of *The Apprentice* in that here also Arun Joshi keeps on referring to the different phases of the city situated by a river. *The City and the River* makes the problem of the crisis of identity not only political but also moral and psychological. It would not be out of place to refer to the fact that the Principal in the short story "Gherao" appears "to have got lost somewhere in the labyrinths of his enfeebled brain."[85]

The crises of identity, alienation, rootlessness, those of ethnic, racial, linguistic, national, moral, political and others have become as fashionable today as was the crisis arising out of melancholy in the seventeenth century English literature in which it was a fashion to pose melancholy.

NOTES

1. Quoted M.K. Naik, *A History of Indian English Literature* (Sahitya Akademi, New Delhi, 1982), 126.
2. K.R.S. Iyengar, *Indo-English Literature* (Bombay, 1947), 29.
3. R.S. Pathak, "The Alienated Protagonist in the Indo-English Novel" in O.P. Saxena (ed.) *Glimpses of Indo-English Fiction*, Vol. I (New Delhi, 1985), 68.
4. "Winner's Secrets": An Interview with Purabi Bannerji, *The Sunday Statesman*, 27 February, 1983, iv.
5. *The Last labyrinth* 118.
6. Alexander Pope, *Essay on Man*, Ep. II "Of the Nature and State of Man."
7. G.S. Amur, "A New Parable," *Indian Literature*, No. 144 (July-August, 1991), 154.
8. Matthew Arnold, "Thyrsis" (line no. 41).
9. S. Rangachari, "T.S. Eliot's Shadow on *The Foreigner*," *Arun Joshi: A Study of His Fiction*, (ed.) N. Radhakrishnan (Madurai: Scholar Critic, 1984), 2.
10. R.K. Dhawan, *The Fictional World of Arun Joshi* (New Delhi, 1986), 19.
11. *The Last Labyrinth* 214.
12. *The Foreigner* 141.

13. *Ibid.*
14. *The Foreigner* 153.
15. *The Foreigner* 213.
16. *The Foreigner* 219.
17. *The Apprentice* 121.
18. *Ibid.*
19. *Ibid.*
20. *The Apprentice* 129.
21. *The Last Labyrinth* 21.
22. Dr. Mohan Jha, "*The Foreigner*: A Study in Innocence and Experience" in R.K. Dhawan (ed.) *The Fictional World of Arun Joshi* (New Delhi, 1986), 168.
23. *The Foreigner* 24.
24. *The Foreigner* 30.
25. *The Foreigner* 33.
26. *The Foreigner* 149.
27. *The Foreigner* 114.
28. *The Foreigner* 68.
29. *The Foreigner* 137.
30. *The Foreigner* 195.
31. *The Foreigner* 130.
32. *The Foreigner* 28.
33. *The Foreigner* 81.
34. *Ibid.*
35. O.P. Mathur, "Survival and Affirmation in Arun Joshi's Novels" in *Modern Indian English Fiction* (New Delhi, 1993), 127.
36. *The Foreigner* 239.
37. *The Foreigner* 242.
38. Mathur 127.
39. *The Last Labyrinth* 11.
40. *The Last Labyrinth* 112.
41. *Ibid.*
42. *The Last Labyrinth* 113.
43. *Ibid.*
44. *The Last Labyrinth* 80.
45. *The Last Labyrinth* 156-57.

46. *The Last Labyrinth* 223.
47. *Ibid.*
48. *Ibid.*
49. *The Strange Case of Billy Biswas* 7.
50. *Ibid.*
51. *The Strange Case of Billy Biswas* 122.
52. *The Strange Case of Billy Biswas* 78.
53. *The Strange Case of Billy Biswas* 96.
54. William Wordsworth, "The World is Too Much with Us," in *Fifteen Poets* (The E.L.B.S. and Oxford at the Clarendon Press, 1965), 239-40.
55. Mathur 129.
56. Mathur 129.
57. Mathur 129.
58. *The Strange Case of Billy Biswas* 25.
59. Mathur 130.
60. *The Apprentice* 17.
61. *The Apprentice* 103.
62. *The Apprentice* 148.
63. *The Apprentice* 19.
64. R.S. Pathak, "Quest for Meaning in Arun Joshi's Novels," R.K. Dhawan (ed.) *The Novels of Arun Joshi* (New Delhi, 1992), 63.
65. *The City and the River* 55.
66. *The City and the River* 163.
67. *The City and the River* 135.
68. *The City and the River* 11.
69. Quoted in A Ram Krishna Rao, "The Image of Labyrinth in Borges, Durrell and Joshi" in O.P. Saxena (ed.) *Glimpses of Indo-English Fiction*, Vol. 3 (New Delhi, 1985), 13.
70. *The Foreigner* 72.
71. *The Strange Case of Billy Biswas* 37.
72. *The Strange Case of Billy Biswas* 8.
73. *The Apprentice* 31.
74. *The Apprentice* 13.
75. *The Apprentice* 80.
76. *The Apprentice* 120.

77. *The Apprentice* 44.
78. *The Apprentice* 46.
79. *The Apprentice* 103.
80. "In the corridor in the sand bucket I vomited." *The Apprentice* 128.
81. "In the corridor in the sand bucket I vomited." *The Apprentice* 109.
82. "In the corridor in the sand bucket I vomited." *The Apprentice* 146.
83. *The City and the River* 79.
84. *Ibid.*
85. *The Survivor* 27.

Bibliography

A. PRIMARY SOURCES

Novels

The Foreigner. Bombay: Asia Publishing House, 1968. Delhi: Hind Pocket Books, 1972.

The Strange Case of Billy Biswas. Bombay: Asia Publishing House, 1971. Delhi: Hind Pocket Books, 1973.

The Apprentice. New York: Asia Publishing House, 1974. Delhi: Hind Pocket Books, 1975. Bombay: Asia Publishing House, 1975.

The Last Labyrinth. New Delhi: Vision Books, 1981.

The City and the River. New Delhi: Vision Books, 1990.

Short Stories

The Survivor: A Selection of Stories. New Delhi: Sterling Publishers, 1975.

The only American from Our Village. Contemporary Indian English Stories (ed.) Madhusudan Prasad. 3/e. New Delhi: Sterling Publishers, 1988.

Towards Finding on Expression, The Fictional World of Arun Joshi, (ed.) R.K. Dhawan. New Delhi: Cassical Publishing Company, 1986.

Interviews

Banerjee, Purabi. "A Winner's Secret" An Interview. *Sunday Statesman* (Calcutta) 27 Feb. 1983: IV.

Excerpts from a Talk by Arun Joshi at Dhvanyaloka, Mysore. Sep. 1981. *ACLALS Newsletter* No. 10, Jan. 1982.

Mathai, Sujata. "I'm a stranger to my books." An Interview. *Times of India,* 7 July 1983: 8.

Piciucco, Pier Paolo. An Interview with Arun Joshi. *Journal of Indian Writing in English,* (1997) 87-95.

Ram Atma. "Interview with Arun Joshi." *Interviews with Indian English Writers.* Calcutta: Writers Workshop, 1983.

SECONDARY SOURCES

[A] BOOKS

Arnold, Matthew. *A Selection of His Poems,* (ed.) Kenneth Allott. Harmondsworth: Penguin Books, 1954.

Bhatnagar, M.K. *The Novels of Arun Joshi: A Critical Study,* New Delhi: Atlantic Publishers and Distributors, 2001.

Bhatnagar, O.P. "The Art and Vision of Arun Joshi," *Glimpses of Indo-English Fiction,* Vol. I (ed.) O.P. Saxena. New Delhi: Jainsons Publications, 1985.

Bhattacharya, Bhabani. *A Goddess Named Gold.* New Delhi: Arnold Heinemann, 1984.

Camus, Albert. *The Fall.* Harmondsworth: Penguin Books, 1972.

Chandar, K.M. "The Quest for Faith in Arun Joshi's *The Last Labyrinth,*" *The Indian Novel in English,* (eds.) R. N. Sinha and R.K. Sinha. Ranchi: Ankit Publishers, 1987.

Chandra, Suresh. "The High Culture Fiction of Arun Joshi and Uma Vasudev," *Culture and Criticism.* Delhi: B.R. Publishing Corporation, 1987.

Chatterjee, Margaret. *The Existentialist Outlook.* New Delhi: Orient Longmans, 1974.

Desai, Anita. *Bye Bye Blackbird.* New Delhi: Orient Paperbacks, 1971.

Dhawan, R.K. (ed.) *Explorations in Modern Indo-English Fiction.* New Delhi: Bahri Publications, 1982.

——. *The Fictional World of Arun Joshi.* New Delhi: Classical Publishing Company, 1986.

____. *The Novels of Arun Joshi*. New Delhi: Prestige, 1992.

Dwivedi, A.N. (ed.). "The Novels of Arun Joshi: A Critical Study." *Studies in Contemporary Indian Fiction in English*. Allahabad: Kitab Mahal, 1987.

Eliot, T.S. *Selected Prose*, (ed.) John Hayward. Harmondsworth: Penguin Books, 1958.

____. *The Four Quartets*. London: Faber and Faber, n.d.

Ford, Boris (ed.) *The New Pelican Guide to English Literature*. Harmondsworth: Penguin Books, 1983 (Vol. VIII), The present.

Fuerlicht, Ignace. *Alienation: From the Past to the Future*. Connecticut: Greenwood Press, 1978.

Futehally, Zeenut. *Zohra*. Bombay: Hind Kitabs, 1951.

Forster, E.M. *Two Cheers for Democracy*. Harmondsworth: Penguin Books, 1974.

____. *Aspects of the Novel*. Harmondsworth: Penguin Books, 1970 (f.p. 1927).

Ghosh, Tapan Kemar. *Arun Joshi's Fiction: The Labyrinth of Life*. New Delhi: Prestige Books, 1996.

Gopalkrishnan, M.G. "The Short Stories of Arun Joshi." *Arun Joshi—A Study of his Fiction*, (ed.) N. Radhakrishnan. Madurai: Scholar Critic, 1984: 68-73.

Gupta, G.S. Balarama (ed.) *Studies in Indian Fiction in English*. Gulbarga: JIWE Publications, 1987.

Greene, Graham. *The Heart of the Matter*. Harmondsworth: Penguin Books, 1971.

____. "The Lost Childhood," *The Collected Essays*. London: The Bodley Head, 1969.

Holloway, John. "The Literary Scene," *The New Pelican Guide to English Literature*, Vol. VIII (The present). Harmondsworth: Penguin Books, 1983.

Hurlock, Elizabeth B. *Personality Development*. New Delhi: Tata McGraw Hill, 1976.

Iyengar, K.R.S. *Indo-Anglian Literature.* Bombay: International Book House, 1947.

___. *Indian Writing in English.* New Delhi: Sterling Publishers, 1984.

Kelinnikova, Elena J. Trans. *Indian English Literature: A Perspective.* Ghaziabad: Bimal Prakashan, 1982.

Lubbock, Percy. *The Craft of Fiction.* London: Jonathan Cape, 1965.

Margolis, Joseph. "The Love Song of J. Alfred Prufrock," *Interpretations,* (ed.) John Wain. London: R.K.P., 1965.

Markandaya, Kamala. *The Nowhere Man.* New Delhi: Sangam Books, 1975.

____. *A Handful of Rice.* New Delhi: Hind Pocket Books, 1966.

Mathur, O.P. "Survival and Affirmation in Arun Joshi's Novels," *Modern Indian English Fiction.* New Delhi: Abhinav Publications, 1993.

——. "The Existential Note in Arun Joshi's *The Strange Case of Billy Biswas* and *The Apprentice,*" *Modern Indian English Fiction.* New Delhi, Abhinav Publications, 1993.

Melwani, Murali Das. *Themes in Indo-Anglian Literature.* Bareilly: Prakash Book Depot, 1977.

Mukherjee, Meenakshi. *The Twice Born Fiction: Themes and Techniques of the Indian Novels in English.* New Delhi: Heinemann Educations Books, 1971.

____. *Considerations.* Bombay: Allied, 1977.

Murchland, B. *The Age of Alienation.* New York: Random House, 1971.

Nagarajan, S. "An Indian Novel," *Considerations,* (ed.) Meenakshi Mukherjee. Bombay: Allied, 1977.

Nahal, Chaman. *Azadi.* New Delhi: Orient Paperbacks, 1979.

Naik, M.K. *Dimensions of Indian English Literature.* New Delhi: Sterling Publishers, 1985. F.P. 1984.

Naik, M.K. *A History of Indian English Literature.* New Delhi: Sahitya Akademi, 1982-1987.

Narasimhaiah, C.D. *The Swan and the Eagle.* Shimla: Indian Institute of Advanced Studies, 1969-1981.

Narayan, R.K. *The Bachelor of Arts.* London: T. Nelson, 1937.

Nehru, J.L. *The Discovery of India,* 11th impression. New Delhi: Oxford University Press, 1991.

Pathak, R.S. "The Indo-English Novelists' Quest for Identity," *Explorations in Modern Indo-English Fiction,* (ed.) R.K. Dhawan. New Delhi: Bahri Publications, 1982.

____. "The Alienated Protagonist in the Indo-English Fiction," *Glimpses of Indo-English Fiction,* Vol. I (ed.) O.P. Saxena. New Delhi: Jainsons Publications, 1985.

Pears Encyclopaedia, 1968-69.

Prasad, Hari Mohan. *Arun Joshi.* New Delhi: Arnold-Heinemann, 1985.

——.(ed.) *Response: Recent Revelations of Indian Fiction in English.* Bareilly: Prakash Book Depot, 1983.

Prasad, Madhusudan. *Indian English Novelists.* New Delhi: Sterling, 1982.

____. "Arun Joshi," *Indian English Novelists.* New Delhi: Sterling Publishers, 1982.

Prasad, V.V.N. Rajendra. *The Self, The Family and Society in Five Indian Novelists: B. Rajan, Raja Rao, Narayan, Arun Joshi, Anita Desai.* New Delhi: Prestige, 1990.

——. Ch.A. *The Function of Enigma in Arun Joshi: A Critical Study.* Narasapur (Andhra Pradesh, India): Privately Published, 1996.

Radhakrishnan, N. (ed.) *Arun Joshi—A Study of his Fiction.* Gandhigram, Madurai: Scholar Critic Publication, 1984.

Rangachari, S. "T.S. Eliot's Shadow on *The Foreigner,*" *Arun Joshi; A Study of his Fiction,* (ed.) N. Radhakrishnan. Madurai: Scholar Critic, 1984.

Rajan, B. *Too Long in the West*. New Delhi: Jaico Publication, 1961.

___. *The Dark Dancer*. New Delhi: Arnold-Heinemann, 1976.

Ram, Atma. "Interview with Arun Joshi," *Interviews with Indian English Writers*. Calcutta: Writers Workshop, 1983.

Rao, A. Rama Krishna. "The Image of Labyrinth in Borges, Durrell and Joshi," *Glimpses of Indo-English Fiction*, Vol. III, (ed.) O.P. Saxena. New Delhi: Jainsons Publications, 1985.

Shahane, V.A. "Introduction," *Explorations in Indo-English Fiction*, (ed.) R.K. Dhawan. New Delhi: Bahri Publication, 1982.

Sahgal, Nayantara. *This Time of Morning*. New Delhi: Orient Paperbacks, 1975.

Sarma, G.P. *Nationalism in Indo-Anglian Fiction*, 2/e. New Delhi: Sterling Publishers, 1990.

Saxena, O.P. (ed.) *Glimpses of Indo-English Fiction*, 3 Vols. New Delhi: Jainsons Publications, 1985.

Singh, R.S. *Indian Novel in English*. New Delhi: Arnold-Heinemann, 1977.

Sinha, Ravi Nandan and Sinha, R.K. (eds.) *The Indian Novel in English: Essays in Criticism*. Ranchi: Ankit Publishers, 1987.

Srinath, C.N. "Crisis of Identity: Assertion and Withdrawal in Naipaul and Arun Joshi," *The Literary Landscape: Essays on Indian Fiction and Poetry in English*. Delhi: Mittal Publications, 1986.

Srivastava, Ramesh K. "The Theme of Alienation in Arun Joshi's Novels," *Six Indian Novelists in English*. Amritsar: G.N.D. University, 1987.

U.G.C. Report on Standards of University Education. New Delhi: U.G.C., 1965.

Verghese, C. Paul. *Problems of the Indian Creative Writers in English*. Bombay: Somaiya Publications, 1971.

Williams, H.M. *Studies in Modern Indian Fiction in English*, 2 Vols. Calcutta: Writers Workshop, 1973.

____. *Indo-Anglian Literature 1800-1970: A Survey*. New Delhi: Orient Longman, 1976.

Walsh, William. "India and the Novel," *The New Pelican Guide to English Literature*, Vol. VIII (The present), (ed.) Boris Ford. Harmondsworth: Penguin Books, 1983.

Walter, Inna. "Arun Joshi's Vision of Life, Love, God and Death in *The Last Labyrinth*," *Studies in Indian Fiction in English*, (ed.) G.S. Balaram Gupta. Gulbarga: JIWE Publications, 1987.

Wordsworth, William. "The World is Too Much with Us," *Fifteen Poets*. Oxford: The Clarendon Press and E.L.B.S., 1965.

[B] JOURNALS & CRITICAL ARTICLES

Abraham, Joy. "Vision and Technique in The Apprentice." Dhawan, *The Fictional World of Arun Joshi*, 210-222.

——. "The Foreigner: A Study in Techniques." Dhawan, *The Novels of Arun Joshi*, 143-161.

——. "Narrative Strategy in The Strange Case of Billy Biswas." Dhawan, *The Novels of Arun Joshi*, 191-200.

Abraham, P.A. "Patrick White's Voss and Arun Joshi's The Strange Case of Billy Biswas: A Comparative Note on a Journey into the Interior." *Literary Criterion* 27.4 (1992): 22-30.

Alam, Qaiser Joha. "The Image in Arun Joshi's Fiction." *Language and Literature*, 33-44.

Awasthi, Komal N. and Lalit M. Sharma. "The World of 'Outsiders' in The Foreigner and Voices in the City." Awasthi, 104-114.

Amur, G.S. "New Parable," *Indian Literature*, No. 144, July-August, 1991, 152-157.

Asnani, Shyam M. "A Study of Arun Joshi's Fiction," *The Literary Half-yearly*, XIX, 2 July, 1978.

Bande, Usha. "Anita Desai, Arun Joshi and Anasakti Yoga Language Forum 14.1 (1988): 54-64, Rpt. in Dhawan, *The Fiction of Anita Desai*, 54-65.

——. "Archetypal Patterns in The City and the River." Dhawan, *The Novels of Arun Joshi*, 257-264.

——. "Victor-Victim Syndrome in Arun Joshi's The City and the River." *Victim Consciousness*, 106-113.

——. *Symbolism in Arun Joshi's The Lost Labyrinth.* ed. Srivastava, R.K. Symbolism, 150-162.

Bano Hamide. "The Quest for True Self in Arun Joshi's The Foreigner." *English Studies in India* 3 (1988): 112-122.

Benihal Arup. "A Stylistic Insight into The Last Labyrinth." Dhawan ed. *The Novels of Arun Joshi*, 230-240.

——. "The City and the River: A Critical Review." Dhawan, ed. *The Novels of Arun Joshi*, 274-275.

Bhatnagar, O.P. "Arun Joshi's The Foreigner," *Journal of Indian Writing in English*, 1.2 (1973): 9-14.

——. "The Art and Vision of Arun Joshi." Scholar Critic 4.6 (1984): 30-43 Rpt. in Dhawan, *The Fictional World of Arun Joshi*, 49-68.

——. "Arun Joshi's *The Foreigner*," *The Journal of Indian Writing in English*, I, No. 2, July 1973, 9-14.

——. "Woman characters in the Novels of Arun Joshi." *Commonwealth Review* 6.1 (1994-95): 155-158. Rpt. in Dass, *Feminism and Literature* 155.

——. "Arun Joshi's *The Foreigner:* A Critique of East and West," *The Journal of Indian Writing in English*, 1/2 July, 1973.

Chakravarthy, D.K. *Ratan Rathor's Search for the Last Outpost: An Approach to Arun Joshi's The Apprentice*, Chakravarthy, 35-44.

——. *Waiting for Moonrise: An Approach to Arun Joshi's Novel The Strange Case of Billy Biswas.* Chakravarthy, 45-48.

Chandra, Sudhash. "Towards Authentificity: A Study of The City and the River." Dhawan, *The Novels of Arun Joshi*, 265-273.

Chingre, C.D. "Contrast as Technique in Arun Joshi's *The Strange Case of Billy Biswas,*" *The Indian Journal of English Studies,* Vol. XXX (1991-92).

Damodar, G. "The Outsiderist Tradition in Joshi and Desai." *Kakatiya Journal of English Studies* 13 (1993): 59-66.

Daruwalla, Keki N. "The Last Labyrinth" (Book Review), *Indian Literature,* Vol. XXVI (July-December, 1983).

Das, R.J. "Moral Dilemma in Arun Joshi's *The Apprentice." Journal of Literature and Aesthetics* 1.2 (1981): 39-45.

Devi, P. Janaki. "Search for Identity in the Novels of Arun Joshi." *Journal of English Studies* (Warangal) 10.1 (1978): 620-627.

Dhawan, R.K. "Destiny of a Nation: Arun Joshi's *The Apprentice."* Pandey and Raj Rao 51-60.

Dua, M.R. Joshi's Reply to M.R. Dua, September 3, 1971.

Dutta, Padma. "Problems of Individuation: A Critique on Arun Joshi's Use of Symbols and Archetypes in *The Last Labyrinth." Journal of Indian Writing in English* 18.1 (1990) : 31-40.

Gautam, Hansa. "Tension and Tonicity in Arun Joshi's Novels." *Contour* 1.2-3 (1992): 10-15.

Guruprasad, Thakur. "The Lost Lonely Questers of Arun Joshi's Fiction." Dhawan, *The Fictional World of Arun Joshi.* 155-166.

Hegde, M.G. "Distance and Discovery as Techniques: A Study of the Narrative Strategy of *The Strange Case of Billy Biswas." Osmania Journal of English Studies* 25 (1989): 92-100.

——. "Arun Joshi's Lala Shri Ram: A Study." *Journal of Indian Writing in English* 17.2 (1989): 18-22.

——. "The Short Stories of Arun Joshi: A Study." Dhawan, *The Novels of Arun Joshi* 201-209.

Jain, Jasbir. "Foreigners and Strangers: Arun Joshi's Heroes." *Journal of Indian Writing in English* 5.1 (1977): 52-56.

____. "The Novels of Kamala Markandaya," *Indian Literature,* April-June 1975.

Jamkhandi, Sudhakar R. "Arun Joshi: An Emerging Voice in Indian English Literature." *Literary Endeavour* 4.1-4 (1985) : 36-44.

Jha, Mohan. "*The Foreigner*: A Study in Innocence and Experience." Dhawan, *The Fictional World of Arun Joshi* 168-175.

——. "Chaman Nahal's *Azadi*: A Search For Identity," *Studies in Indian Fiction in English*, (ed.) G. Balram Gupta. Gulbarga: JIWE, 1987.

Jeevan, Parvathy. "Image of Woman in the Novels of Arun Joshi." *Commonwealth Quarterly* 16.41 (1980): 24-34. Rpt. in *Littcrit* 16.1-2 (1992): 85-92.

——. "Arun Joshi: Master of Science and Letters." *Malayalam Literary Survey* 13.3 (1991): 25-29.

Joshi, Surender. "Point of view and Theme in Arun Joshi's *The Strange Case of Billy Biswas.*" Saxena, *Glimpses* Vol. 3. 70-79.

Kalinnikova, Elena J. "In Search of Anti-Hero: Anita Desai and Arun Joshi." Kalinnikova *Indian English Literature : A Perspective* 174-178.

Kher, Inder Nath. "The Archetypes of Love and Death in Arun Joshi's *The Last Labyrinth.*" *Journal of Indian Writing in English* 20.1-2 (1992): 53-66.

Kumar, Sunaina. "A Tribute: Arun Joshi and His Extraordinary Obsessions." *Indian Book Chronicle* June 1993: 20.

Mathur, O.P. "From Existentialism to Karma Yogi: A Study of Arun Joshi's *The Foreigner.*" Srivastava, A.K. *Alien Voice* 107-115. ref.: 524.

——. "Survival and Affirmation in Arun Joshi's Novels." *Worlds Literature Today* 63.3 (1989): 421-425.

——. "Arun Joshi's *The City and The River:* A Leap to eternity." Mathur, *Indian Political Novel* 91-101.

——. "The contemporary and The Cosmic and in Arun Joshi's *The City and the River.*" Yaravintelimath *et al.*, 147-153.

Mathur, O.P. "Arun Joshi and The Gita." Pathak, *Indian English Fiction* 132-145.

——. and G. Rai. "The Existential Note in Arun Joshi's *The Strange Case of Billy Biswas* and *The Apprentice.*" *Commonwealth Quarterly* 5.17 (1980): 30-41.

——. "Arun Joshi and the Labyrinth of Life." Dhawan, *The Fictional World of Arun Joshi* 143-154.

Meitei, M. Mani. *"The Strange Case of Billy Biswas:* Awareness of Worlds Within Worlds." *Quest* (Ranchi) 4.2 (1990): 9-20.

——. "Indian Ethos in Arun Joshi's *The Last Labyrinth."* *Language Forum* 19.1-2 (1992): 160-172.

Mohan, Devinder. "The Image of Fire in Arun Joshi's *The Strange Case of Billy Biswas."* Dhawan, *The Fictional World of Arun Joshi* 194-209.

——. "The Dance of Life and Death: Arun Joshi's Fiction." *Asia Week* 16 Aug. 1987.

——. "The Language of the Splintered Mirror: The Fiction of Arun Joshi." *Ariel* 14.4 (1983): 20-33.

——. "Arun Joshi: *The Foreigner."* Majer Indian Novels and Evaluation, (ed.) N.S. Pradhan. New Delhi: Arnold Heinemann, 1985, 174-191.

——. "Beyond the Litany of Wants: Contexts of Arun Joshi's Fiction Towards *The Last Labyrinth."* Kirpal, *The New Indian Novel in English* 83-90.

Mohanty, Mahendra Kumar. "Filial Relationships in *The Foreigner"* Dhawan, *The Novels of Arun Joshi* 115-121.

Mukherjee, Meenakshi. "Beyond the Village: An Aspect of Mulk Raj Anand," *Critical Essays on Indian Writing in English,* (eds.) M.K. Naik, S.K. Desai, G.S. Amur. New Delhi: Macmillan, 1977.

Narasimhaiah, Sanjay. "Arun Joshi's *The Last Labyrinth."* *Literary Criterion* 15.2 (1981): 81-89.

Padma, T. "Problems of Individuation: A Critique on Arun Joshi's Use of Symbols and Archetypes in *The Last Labyrinth.*" *Journal of Indian Writing in English* 18.1 (1990): 31-40. Rpt. in Prabhakar 285-294.

——. Crypto-myth and Meta-novel: Arun Joshi's *The City and the River.*" Nair *et al.*, 107-115.

Pandey, Lal Udai Bhan. "Anita Desai and Arun Joshi: A Comparative Study." Dhawan, *Recent Commonwealth Literature* Vol. I. 224-226.

Pathak, R.S. "Arun Joshi's Novels: An Indeterminate Search for Meaning in Life." *Scholar Critic* 4.6 (1984): 44-63. Rpt. in Radhakrishnan, *Arun Joshi:* 44-63. Rpt. as "Human Predicament and Meaninglessness in Arun Joshi's Novels (An enlarged and restructured version)." Dhawan, *The Fictional World of Arun Joshi* 104-142.

——. "Quest for Meaning in Arun Joshi's Novels." Dhawan, *The Novels of Arun Joshi* 42-82.

——. *The Indo-English Novelists' Quest for Identity,* Explorations in Modern Indo-English Fiction, (ed.) R.K. Dhawan. New Delhi: Bahri Publications, 1982.

——. "The Alienated Protagonist in the Indo-English Fiction," Glimpses of Indo-English Fiction, vol. I (ed.) O.P. Saxena. New Delhi: Jainsons Publications, 1985.

Pathania, Usha. "Having and Being: A Study of *The Foreigner.*" Dhawan, *The Novels of Arun Joshi:* 133-142.

——. "The Quest for Being: An Analysis of *The Foreigner.*" Kaul & Jaidev 159-166.

Patnaik, B.N. "What is Strange in *The Strange Case of Billy Biswas.*" *Gray Book* 3 (1973): 17-24.

Piciucco, Pier Parlo. "Fictional Technique and Rhetorical Devices in Arun Joshi's *The Apprentice.*" *Literary Criterion* 34.2 (1999): 30-43.

Prabhakaran, M.S. "The Apprentice: An Overview." *Scholar Critic* 4.6(1984): 64-67. Rpt. in Radhakrishnan, *Arun Joshi* 64-67.

Prasad, Hari Mohan. "The Crisis of Consciousness: A Thematic Analysis of *The Last Labyrinth.*" *Scholar Critic* 4.6 (1984): 20-29. Rpt in Dhawan, *The Fictional World of Arun Joshi* 231-240.

——. "Dimensions of Realism in Indo-English Fiction," *The Indian Journal of English Studies,* XXI, (1981-82).

Prasad, Madhusudan. "Arun Joshi: The Novelist." *Indian Literature,* July-Aug. 1981: 103-114. Rpt. in Prasad, Madhusudan, *Indian English Novelists* 50-61.

——. "Cornering Arun Joshi: A Critical Perspective on *The Last Labyrinth.*" *Scholar Critic* 4.6 (1984): 9-19. Rpt. in Radhakrishnan, *Arun Joshi* 9-19.

Prasad, V.V.N. Rajendra. "Arun Joshi: Self as Labyrinth." Prasad, V.V.N 108-129.

——. "*The Apprentice:* Self as Labyrinth." Dhawan, *The Novels of Arun Joshi* 210-216.

Prempati, D. "*The Strange Case of Billy Biswas:* A Serious Response to a Big Challenge." Dhawan, *The Fictional World of Arun Joshi* 176-185. ref.: 4037. Rpt. in Dhawan, *The Novels of Arun Joshi* 174-180.

Radha, K. "From Detachment to Involvement: The Career of the Chief protagonist to Arun Joshi's *The Foreigner.*" Paniker, *Contemporary Indian Fiction in English,* 81-90. Rpt. in Dhawan, *The Fictional World of Arun Joshi* 176-185. Rpt. as "From detachment to Involvement: The Case of Sindi Oberoi in Dhawan, *The Novels of Arun Joshi* 106-114.

——. "Fugitive for Self and the City in Margaret Atwood's *Surfacing* and Some Indian Novels in English." Begum 21-32.

Radhakrishnan, N. "The Women Characters of Arun Joshi." *Scholar Critic* 4.6 (1984); 74-80. Rpt. in Radhakrishnan, *Arun Joshi* 74-80.

Raizada, Harish. "Double Vision of Fantasy and Reality in Arun Joshi's Novels." Dhawan, *The Fictional World of Arun Joshi* 69-103.

Rajan, B. "Indian Virtue," *The Journal of Commonwealth Literature*, September, 1965.

Rajendraprasad, Ch. A. "'After the Fall': A critique on Arun Joshi's *The Apprentice.*" *Revaluations* 2.1(1996): 79-85.

Rama, R.P. "Arun Joshi's *The Foreigner—A Review,*" *Indian Writing Today*, July-September, 1970.

Ranchan, Som P. and Sharma, Sunil K. "Questy for Identity of the Narrator Protagonist in Heat and Dust," *The Indian Journal of English Studies*, Vol. XXIII (1983).

Rangachari, S. "T.S. Eliot's Shadow on The Foreigners." *Scholar Critic* 4.6 (1984): 1-8. Rpt. in Radhakrishnan, *Arun Joshi* 1-8.

Rangan. "The Theme of Alienation and Quest for Identity in Arun Joshi's *The Last Labyrinth.*" Nagarajan *et al.*, 109-116.

Rani, Rekha. "The Language of Dreams in *The Last Labyrinth.*" Dhawan, *The Novels of Arun Joshi* 224-229.

Rao, C. Malathi: "The Foreigner: Arun Joshi," *The Literary Criterion*, XII, 2 and 3, 1976.

Rao, M. Madhusudan. "The Hindu Existential Concern in Arun Joshi's Fiction." Rao, A. Ramakrishna and Sivaramkrishna 149-161.

Rao, Ramakrishna A. "Arun Joshi's Voids and Labyrinths." *Literary Endeavour* 2.4 (1981): 11-17.

——. "The Image of Labyrinth in Borges, Durrell and Joshi." Saxena, *Glimpses* Vol. 3. 3-22.

Ratnakar, Pramesh. "Arun Joshi's Fiction: Cracks in the Mirror." *Occasional Papers in English and Linguistics* 2 (1985).

Reddy, V. Gopal. "The Apprentice: An Existential Study." *Kakatiya Journal of English Study.*" 5 (1983): 9-16. Rpt. in Dhawan, *The Fictional World of Arun Joshi* 223-230.

Reddy, V. Gopal. "From Alienation to Community: A Note on the Novels of Arun Joshi." *Kakatiya Journal of English Studies* 7 (1985-86) : 82-91.

——. (Joshi's) Reply to V. Gopal Reddy, January 8, 1971.

Riemenschneider, Dieter. "The Indo-English Novel," Indian Literature, Vol. XXVI (July-December, 1983).

Ross, Robert. "The Clash of Opposites in Arun Joshi's *The Last Labyrinth." Literary Criterion* 25.2 (1990): 1-9.

Rushdie, Salman. "Reclaiming a City and a History," *Express Magazine* (*The Indian Express*), 11, March 1984.

Satapathy, S.C. "From Passivity to Awareness: A Study of the Narrator-Protagonist in Arun Joshi's *The Apprentice." Journal of Literary Studies* 2.2 (1979): 121-132.

Satyanarayana, E. "Towards Affirmation: A Reading of Arun Joshi's 'A Trip For Mr. Lee.' and 'Survivor'." Narendra Kumar, V.L.V.N. *New Perspectives* 108-112. Rpt. as "Arun Joshi's 'A Trip for Mr. Lele' and 'Survivor'." in *Triveni* 66.1(1997): 30-33.

Sharma, Brahma Dutt. *"The City and the River* as a Political Novel." Dhawan, *The Novels of Arun Joshi* 241-256.

Sharma, D.R. "Arun Joshi and His Reflective Insiders." *Panjab University Research Bulletin (Arts)* 7.2 (1976): 125-134. Rpt. in *Literature East and West* 21.1-4 (1977): 100-111. Also in *Indian P.E.N.* Sept.-Oct. 1977: 1.

——. "The Fictional World of Arun Joshi." *Indian P.E.N.* 43, Sept.-Oct. 1977.1-5.

Sharma, Shyam Sundar. "The Two Worlds in *The Last Labyrinth."* Dhawan, *The Fictional World of Arun Joshi* 240-248.

Sharma, Susheel Kumar. "Philosophical Reverberations in *The Foreigner."* Dhawan, *The Novels of Arun Joshi* 122-132.

——. "*The Strange case of Billy Biswas*: A Psycho-graph of an Alienated Hero." Dhawan, *The Novels of Arun Joshi* 62-116.

Singh, Khushwant. "Arun Joshi." *Hindustan Times*, 24 Jan. 1981: 8-9.

Singh, R.S. "Aloness Alone: Anita Desai and Arun Joshi." Singh R.S., *Indian Novel in English*, Arnold Heinemann, 1977: 164-178.

Srinath, C.N. "The Fiction of Arun Joshi: The Novel of Interior Landscape." *Literary Criterion* 12.2-3 (1976): 115-133. Rpt. in Srinath 40-59.

——. "Crisis of Identity: Assertion and Withdrawal in Naipaul and Arun Joshi." *Literary Criterion* 14.1(1979): 33-41. Rpt. in Srinath, 66-67.

——. "Native Roots and Novel Foliage: An Understanding of the Achievement of Indian Fiction in English." *Literary Criterion* 21.1-2 (1986): 60-85. Rpt. in Srinath 98-116.

——. "Arun Joshi's *The Apprentice:* The Novel of Our Times" Narendra Kumar V.L.V.N., *New Perspectives* 113-117.

Srivastava, Narasingh. "Quest for Identity in Arun Joshi's *The Last Labyrinth.*" *Language Forum* 18.1 (1992): 81-86.

Srivastava K. Ramesh. "The Theme of Alienation in Arun Joshi's Novels." *Ken: A Journal of English Studies* 1(1982): 13-23. Rpt. in Srivastava, *Six Indian Novelists in English* 311-325.

——. "Intricate Alleys in Arun Joshi's *The Last Labyrinth.*" *Indian Journal of English Studies* 28 (1989): 5-12.

Tripathy, J.P. "From Raju to Billy: Changing Aspects of Self-hood." *Language Forum* 18.1-4 (1992): 75-80.

Venkateswara Rao, J. "*The Foreigner:* An Existential Dilemma." *Triveni* 64.1-2 (1995): 73-76.

Venugopal, C.V. and M.G. Hedge. "Soul's Progress from Innocence through Ignorance to Knowledge: A Study of *The Apprentice.*" *Kakatiya Journal of English Studies* (Warangal) 8 (1987-88): 163-169.

Verma, K.D. "The Metaphysics and Meta Structure of Appearance and Reality in Arun Joshi's *The Last Labyrinth.*" *International Fiction Review* 21.1-2 (1994): 44-50.

Verma, K.D. "Alienation, Identity and Structure in Arun Joshi's *The Apprentice." Ariel* 22.1 (1991): 71-90.

Vijaya Kumar, T. "Allegory and the Negation of History: Arun Joshi's *The City and the River."* Kirpal, *Postmodern Indian English Novel* 145-152.

Walter, Inna. "Arun Joshi's Vision of Life, Love, God and Death in *The Last Labyrinth."* Gupta, *Studies* 46-60.

Wandrekar, Kalpana. "The Foreigner: Chaos of Cultural Confusion." Wandrekar 79-91.

Yadav, Kumkum. "The Importance of Being Billy —Victim(s) in Arun Joshi's *The Strange Case of Billy Biswas.*" Bande, *Victim Consciousness* 94-105.

Reviews

Bandopadhyay, Manohar. Rev. of *The Strange Case of Billy Biswas. Patriot* 1 Aug. 1982.

D'Monte, Darryl. "A Hollow Rebel." Rev. of *The Strange Case of Billy Biswas. Times of India* 27 June 1971: 10: 5-7.

Futehally, Laeeq. "Story-Telling." Rev. of *The Apprentice and The Survivor. Quest* 93, Mar.-Apr. 1975: 93-94.

Hariharan, Gita. "A Political Parable." Rev. of *The City and the River. Indian Literature* 144 (1991).

Iyengar, K.R.S. "The Fiction of Arun Joshi." Rev. of *The Last Labyrinth. Humanities Review* 3.2 (1981): 39-40.

Keating, H.R.F. Rev. of *The Last Labyrinth. Times Literary Supplement* 6 Aug. 1982: 863.

Malathi Rao, C. Rev. of *The Foreigner. Literary Criterion* 8.4(1969) : 76-77.

Mathai, Anna Sujatha. "In Search of Meaning." Rev. of *The Last Labyrinth. Indian Book Chronicle* 16 June 1983: 219-220.

Mazumdar, Shubra. Rev. of *The City and The River. Book Review* Jan.-Feb. 1991: 28.

Mukherjee, Meenakshi. Rev. of *The Foreigner. Quest* 60, Sep.-Oct. (1969): 101-103.

Mukherjee, Meenakshi. Rev. of *The Strange Case of Billy Biswas. Quest* 72, Sep.-Oct. 1971: 121-124.

N.B. Rev. of *The Foreigner. Opinion Literary Quarterly* (India) 1 (1974): 50-52, 54.

——. Rev. of *The Strange Case of Billy Biswas. Opinion Literary Quarterly* 1 (1974): 50-52, 54.

Naikar, Basavaraj S. Rev. of *The Last Labyrinth. World Literature Today* 56.4 (1982): 752-53.

R.S. Rev. of *Apprentice. Divine Life* (India) 12 Oct. 1975: 19.

Rao, K.S.N. Rev. of *The Strange Case of Billy Biswas. Books Abroad* 46.4 (1972): 726.

——. Rev. of *The Apprentice. Books Abroad* 49.1 (1975): 185.

Rev. of *The Apprentice. Times of India* 25 June 1976: 10.

Rev. of *The Foreigner. Times of India* 17 Sep. 1972: 9.

Rev. of *The Foreigner. Thought* 24, 15 July 1972: 18-19.

Rev. of *The Foreigner. Indian and Foreign Review* 15 July 1969: 21-22.

Rev. of *The Last Labyrinth. National Herald* (Sunday) 22 Nov. 1981: 4.

Saraiya, Indu. Rev. of *The Apprentice. Indian P.E.N.* 41.8 (1975): 4-16.

Shettigara, Tina. "Entering the Maze." Rev. of *The Last Labyrinth. CRNLE Review Journal* 1 (1982): 53-54.

Tonpe, Vaijayanti Savant. Rev. of *The City and the River. Seminar* 384 Aug. 1991: 48.

Trivedi, Harish. "The Bitch Goddess." Rev. of *The Last Labyrinth. Book Review* Sep.-Oct. 1982: 72-74.

Dissertations

Abraham, Joy. "Themes and Narrative Techniques in the Novels of Arun Joshi." Calicut U, 1991.

Bhuyar, R.S. "Arun Joshi: A Study of His Fiction." Amravati U, 1985.

Dubey, Amitabh. "Thematic Patterns and Structural Design in Arun Joshi's Novels." Dr. H.S. Gour U.

Hegde, Manjunath Gajanan. "Arun Joshi: A Study in Theme and Technique." Karnatak U, 1991.

Joshi, P.S. "Themes and Techniques of Arun Joshi's Novels." Diss. (M.Phil.). South Gujarat U, 1985.

Navaneethan, S. "Thematic Progression in the Novels of Arun Joshi." Bharathisadan U, 1985.

Pradhan, Shanta. "Modern Element in Indian English Fiction with Special Reference to the Novels of Raja Rao, Anita Desai and Arun Joshi." Gauhati U, 1990.

Prasad, V.V.N. Rajendra. "Self, Family and Society in the Novels of Rajan, Raja Rao, R.K. Narayan, Arun Joshi and Anita Desai." U of Krishnadevaraya, 1988. New Delhi: Prestige Books, 1990.

Rajendra Prasad, Chiliki Appala. "The Function of `Enigma' in Arun Joshi's Novels." Andhra U, 1990.

Ranveer, P. Rukmani. "Encaged Sensibility in the Novels of Arun Joshi." Kakatiya U, 1990.

Satyanarayana, N. "New Morality in Indian-English Fiction with Special Reference to Anand, Narayan and Arun Joshi." Kakatiya U, 1987.